CO… …Y

Files

The materials in this book describe and illustrate numerous conspiracy theories that have been advanced by various parties. By definition, conspiracy theories are opinions which may or may not be true. Carlton Books makes no judgement as to the truth or accuracy of any of the conspiracy theories described in this book or as to the truth or accuracy of any of the implied relationships between stated facts. Carlton Books offers as factual only the fact that the theories described in this book really have been proposed and have received media attention.

This is a Carlton Book

This edition published by Carlton Books Limited 1999

ISBN 1 85868 524 9

Printed and bound in Great Britain

CONSPIRACY

Files

DAVID SOUTHWELL
AND
SEAN TWIST

CARLTON

DEDICATIONS:

For Anne-Marie and Cheryl, without whose help this trip to the grassy knolls and smoky back rooms of the world would have been impossible.

For Bill Hicks – a much-missed conspiriologist, comedian and guardian of the truth.

ACKNOWLEDGEMENTS:

The authors would like to offer a tip of the smoking gun to: Lucian Randall at Carlton; Tim Dedopulos for helping us get the gig and deliver the goods; Andrew Collins for inspiring the belief that it could be done; Marc Hodgkinson for coffee-drenched evenings of wrestling conspiracies; Steve Howe for assisting in Guinness consumption and providing research that allowed history to be re-written; Kelly Roberts for eternally optimistic encouragement; Simon Dove and Tracey Richardson, Genevieve Curran, and Sean and Cara York for the strength that comes from friendship; David Brookes and Larry Cornies for research; Kate Phelan for support and for finding us web-crawler Keith Richards; Chris Buse and Jeremy Marsh for photographic evidence; Max Read and Cindy Galloway for enduring epic bouts of writerly self-pity; Andrew Stiles for waiting for the creaking door to open; Storm Constantine for motivation during lean times; Andrew Stephenson at Peter Carter-Ruck for keeping us diligent; Ken MacLeod for Wilde and his Counterconspiracy Theory of History; John Cale, Chris Carter, Fortean Times and Grant Morrison for warping our minds enough to write this book; pioneering conspiracy authors Doug Moench and Robert Anton Wilson and all those conspiriologists researching the Potere Occulto.

CONTENTS

INTRODUCTION

Everything you have been taught to believe is wrong. History is a lie. There is a secret earth that you have been prevented from ever finding out about. Your life has been controlled from the moment of your birth by sinister, hidden forces. You are not paranoid enough and yes, they really are plotting to get you. Everything is a conspiracy and you have been duped.

Conspiracies are everywhere you look. Mel Gibson and Julia Roberts make movies about them. Mulder and Scully have become global cultural icons as the result of a television series in which the heroes try to discover the truth behind a huge range of conspiracies and expose them. Everyone has heard of at least one conspiracy theory and many people believe that the one they know is valid.

Why have conspiracy theories become such a widespread, integral part of our culture?

Maybe they are a reaction to the times we live in. We are saturated with information, but often we are at a loss to comprehend it. The world is full of frightening, inexplicable events that we feel powerless to understand or control. Conspiracy theories provide a narrative – or as some say a plot – to explain what is going on. Possibly, knowing about a conspiracy helps us to feel less powerless; we become insiders to the secret instead of merely being helpless, unknowing victims of dark machinations.

It may also be that we need conspiracy theories. Societies have always found it necessary to devise scapegoats – to explain that the evils of the world are the responsibility of the few. This is possibly one of the most dangerous aspects of some conspiracy theories, which can be little more than clever propaganda designed to provide an excuse for distrusting those who are different to us. It is hard to forget the fact that the Nazis were acknowledged masters of the conspiracy theory.

Of course, another reason why conspiracy theories are everywhere is because they are so damn entertaining! Where else can you find stories with a cast containing extra-terrestrials, film stars, heads of state and age-old secret societies? They even have the added spice of possibly being true, as you can never prove that a really big conspiracy is false. After all, if it is big enough and successful enough, all the usual investigating authorities are destined to be part of it.

When you begin investigating conspiracy theories you find, very quickly, that it is impossible to make one up that is more bizarre and improbable than one already in existence. Often, even the oddest of plots is backed by some facts that could be considered as evidence, and is supported by a considerable number of believers.

That said, it is important to remember that not all conspiracy theories are only believed by the paranoid fantasists that originally dreamed them up. A few years ago it was rumoured that there was a conspiracy to cover up the fact that, since 1932, the US Government had been conducting an experiment on more than 200 poor, unwitting, black men in Tuskegee, Alabama in order to study the effects of syphilis.

It seemed wildly implausible that the respected Center for Disease Control would allow these people to die, and their wives and children to acquire the disease without even telling them. Common-sense suggested it was ridiculous to think that the authorities would plot to do something like this and then conspire to cover it up. Yet the sceptics were proved right. The conspiracy was eventually exposed and President Clinton travelled to Tuskegee to apologize to the survivors of this shameful incident in American history.

So as you read this book and leave behind the safe, secure world of official versions and commonly-accepted views and enter into the scary world of bizarre, mind-boggling and often highly implausible conspiracies, remember Tuskegee. Remember that you may not be paranoid enough. Remember everything you know is wrong.

C

THE ASSASSINATION OF JFK

November 22, 1963, is a day not easily forgotten. Even now, countless millions of people can recall what they were doing on the day President John F Kennedy was shot.

It was a bright, clear and almost summer-like day in Dallas. The sky above the Texas School Book Depository was free from clouds. There could be no better day for a parade to welcome the President and yet, within seconds, several bullets had struck the presidential limousine at Dealey Plaza, and history was changed forever.

Despite the suppression of vast amounts of evidence and the best attempts of the Warren Commission, in the aftermath of the assassination, to promote the idea that JFK was killed by Lee Harvey Oswald acting alone, 73 per cent of Americans believe that their President was the victim of a conspiracy.

It's a view that is backed up by the report of the Select Committee on Assassinations of the House of Representatives, which stated "The Committee believes, on the basis of the evidence available to it, that President John F Kennedy was assassinated as the result of a conspiracy."

A close look at the assassination of JFK produces convincing evidence that Oswald was not acting alone and that a cover-up at the highest levels is still in operation. It becomes more a question of who was behind the conspiracy, rather than if it was a conspiracy at all.

THE STRANGE PART

Despite the official government opinion that the President was killed by a single shot, there were seven wounds found on JFK and on Governor Connally, one of the other passengers in the car. The angles and trajectories of the wounds make a single gunman fairly unfeasible. Lee Harvey Oswald, who was arrested for the murder, was himself assassinated before he could be brought to trial.

THE USUAL SUSPECTS

CIA

Kennedy was about to disband the CIA due to its corruption, its inability to oust Castro from Cuba, and its general hostility to him since the Bay of Pigs debacle. It is alleged that, in self-defence, the CIA plotted with the Mafia and FBI to kill Kennedy and frame a former double-agent, Oswald, as the killer.

Cuban Communists/KGB

Fidel Castro and his KGB allies were still smarting from Kennedy's victory in the Cuban Missile Crisis. As revenge they plotted his murder. Their involvement in his death was discovered by the CIA and FBI who had to cover it up to prevent a public outrage that could have led to a World War III.

Mafia

JFK and his Attorney-General brother, Robert Kennedy, were close to winning their crusade against organized crime. Attempts to blackmail Kennedy over his adultery had failed, so the Mafia decided to have him rubbed out. It is known that Oswald had connections to Mafia members; just why did small-time Dallas mobster Jack Ruby so conveniently shoot Oswald?

Military Industrial Complex

Kennedy had plans to pull out of Vietnam, which obviously angered the Military Industrial Complex which thrives on war. Were connections in the shadowy worlds of the Secret Service and Mafia used to conduct a coup and place Vice President Johnson in the White House? Interestingly, just four days after JFK's assassination, Johnson sent more troops to Vietnam, completely ignoring JFK's recommendations.

Also suspected: The Masons; MJ-12 (Majestic 12, the top secret Defense Committee overseeing America's negotiations with the aliens that do all those abductions); Richard Nixon; and the American oil barons.

THE UNUSUAL SUSPECTS

The Canadian Liberal Party

Over recent years, evidence has emerged linking prominent Mafia captain Lucian Rivard to both Jack Ruby and the Liberal Party of Canada. Rivard is also linked to Oswald's recorded time in Montreal. When the Mafia man was jailed in 1964 to await extradition to the US, officers of the Canadian Justice Department, and members of the ruling Liberal Party, offered bribes to the American lawyers to try and secure his release. Despite the lack of motive, this has been enough for some to suggest that the true answer to the conspiracy to assassinate JFK will be found in Canada.

Jackie Kennedy

The wildest and most discredited conspiracy theory surrounding the assassination is that Jackie Kennedy, sickened by her husband's continuous adultery, arranged for the Mafia to wipe him out and spare her the public humiliation of a divorce.

MOST CONVINCING EVIDENCE

One thing that swings it in the favour of the conspiracy theories is the impossibility of the "single bullet theory" accepted by the Warren Commission. It claimed that the one shot Oswald took from a sixth floor window entered Kennedy's back, yet rose and flew out of his neck, altering its trajectory to cause the seven wounds found in Kennedy and Governor Connally, in the seat ahead of the President's.

MOST MYSTERIOUS FACT

President Kennedy's brain went missing under mysterious circumstances a number of years ago. This is highly suspicious and also very convenient, as modern scientific tests cannot now be carried out to establish the trajectory of the fatal bullets. The tests would have answered once and for all the question of whether there was a second (or even a third) gunman.

SCEPTICALLY SPEAKING

The legendary grassy knoll from where the second gunman was supposed to have shot Kennedy would have been so busy that surely someone would have spotted the 30 or so gunmen that must have been there, to account for all the proposed conspiracy theories.

BRUCE LEE

Sometimes death does not end the web of intrigue that has grown up around a celebrity during his life. In fact, sometimes death is only the start of greater and stranger speculations.

In late July, 1973, when they laid to rest the body of Bruce Lee, dressed in the Chinese costume he wore in the movie *Enter The Dragon*, in Seattle's Lakeview Cemetery, they did not succeed in burying the mystery surrounding his death.

A much-loved, but controversial figure who made many enemies, Lee was 32 and at the height of his career when he suddenly died after falling into a coma. The subsequent coroner's report was inconclusive and the numerous medical experts who looked at the case could only agree on one thing – that death had been brought about by a swelling of his brain.

On the fateful day of his death, Lee met film producer Raymond Chow at his home in the early afternoon and spent a couple of hours working with him on the film *The Game Of Death*. The pair then went over to the home of Taiwanese actress Betty Tingpei who was starring in the movie. Chow left for a meeting and Lee complained of having a headache. Tingpei gave him an Equagesic tablet – a form of powerful aspirin – and he took a nap. Chow rang Tingpei to invite her and Lee out for dinner, but the actress could not wake the sleeping star. By the time Lee arrived at the Queen Elizabeth hospital he was dead.

Dr Lycette of the hospital felt that the death was a result of Lee being hypersensitive to compounds in the Equagesic tablet, but other medical authorities disagreed and rumours of a conspiracy began to spread throughout Hong Kong and the rest of the martial arts world.

THE STRANGE PART

Months before he was officially declared dead, rumours had been circulating around Hong Kong that Lee had died. These grew so strong that journalists on one of Hong Kong's largest newspapers wouldn't believe he was alive until they had spoken personally to Lee and subjected him to some rigorous questioning. This does tend to suggest that his eventual death may not have been as unexpected as the official version of events suggests.

THE USUAL SUSPECTS:

The Triads

In the Seventies Chinese criminal organizations, such as the Triads, often demanded protection money from Hong-Kong-based movie stars. Lee was known to have stood up to their demands and may have been poisoned as a result of this brave move – he was adored by the Hong Kong public so much, that he had to be disposed of in a subtle way.

Secret Martial Art Masters

A popular and plausible conjecture is that Lee was killed on the instructions of a cabal of secret martial art masters who were angered that he had taught too many of their secrets to foreigners. It is true that Lee had already had many problems with the traditional Chinese martial arts establishment. Given the nature of the dim mak known to these masters, this theory is not easily dismissed. (Dim mak is a death touch that can be administered by glancing contact and is impossible for an autopsy to detect.)

Also suspected: a secret group of Hong Kong movie producers; a cabal of Hollywood Masons; Chinese Communists; defeated opponents; and the British Intelligence Service.

THE UNUSUAL SUSPECTS:

Ancient Chinese Demons

It is rumoured that Lee felt his family was suffering from an ancient curse that ensured that the first-born son of any generation would be haunted by demons. The tradition of this curse in his family was so strong that when Bruce was born he was originally given a girl's name to confuse the demonic powers. More than one conspiracy theorist feels that this theory has been strengthened by the strange case of the death of Brandon Lee, Bruce's son, who died after a mysterious handgun accident during the filming of movie blockbuster *The Crow*.

Bruce Lee

An even wilder conspiracy theory proposes that Lee is still alive and that he staged his supposed death in an attempt to escape from either the pressures of fame or the evil intent of various Triad gangs. Those that believe this hypothesis also think that Lee may return at some unspecified point in the future. He certainly is not spotted as much as Elvis.

MOST CONVINCING EVIDENCE

One thing that persuades many that there is a conspiracy behind Bruce Lee's death is the confusion over the medical evidence surrounding his demise. The coroner's report proved inconclusive and the medical authorities put forward no less than five different theories to explain what caused the swelling of the brain that led to his untimely death.

MOST MYSTERIOUS FACT

When interviewed, Lee frequently reflected on the possibility of an early death and at times almost appeared to welcome the prospect. His wife Linda is quoted as saying that Bruce had no wish to live to old age as he found the prospect of losing his physical abilities too horrifying to contemplate. Death as an escape from failing strength and fading prowess as a master of martial art combat may not have been the only reason Lee contemplated dying young. It is known that he took the idea of the firstborn of his family being cursed by demons seriously enough to try and protect his son Brandon by employing traditional magic.

SCEPTICALLY SPEAKING

Much of the speculation of the circumstances surrounding the conspiracy can be explained by the fact that when Raymond Chow announced Lee's death on television he omitted the fact that he had not died at home but in the apartment of Betty Tingpei. The attempt to cover up this possibly embarrassing detail may have led many people to be convinced that there was a lot more going on behind the scenes, especially when there was an unsolved medical puzzle over the exact cause of the fatal swelling of the brain.

THE SHOOTING OF JOHN LENNON

In the "do you remember where you were when you heard the news" stakes, the shooting of John Lennon only comes second to the assassination of JFK.

If you were alive when the murder of John Lennon was announced on the evening of December 8, 1980, you will undoubtedly remember it, wherever you were. As the news broke around the globe everyone was shocked. No one could understand why anyone would want to kill one of the members of the most beloved musical group of all time. Why would anyone want to murder an ex-Beatle? Why would anyone want to deny the world this true musical genius and very influential campaigner for peace?

The explanation offered in the press was that the gunman – Mark David Chapman – was a disturbed loner, obsessed with the Sixties star and convinced that Lennon was in league with the Devil. After a 60-day psychiatric evaluation that turned into a year and 60 days of absolute silence, Chapman pleaded guilty to the murder a matter of hours before his trial was scheduled to start.

It wasn't long before conspiracy theorists were supplementing the media's version of events with their own interpretations of what actually happened on that tragic night which robbed the world of a cultural giant. In their eyes, the shooting was not simply the work of a madman, it was part of a huge political plot.

THE STRANGE PART

One of the usual reasons put forward for why people like Chapman murder celebrities is that they wish to become famous themselves. This obviously is not the case with Chapman. Since he committed the crime he has turned down more than 40 interviews and repeatedly said: "I do not want publicity." His apparent calmness after his arrest is unusual. However, more significant is the fact that he managed to evade metal detectors at two major airports when transporting the murder weapon from Hawaii to

New York – something bound to raise alarm bells with those favouring a conspiracy as an explanation for Lennon's death.

THE USUAL SUSPECTS

FBI

The late FBI Director J Edgar Hoover had a pathological hatred of Lennon and had tried to persuade President Nixon's chief of staff to help him bust the musician and get him thrown out of the country. The FBI kept Lennon under close scrutiny throughout the Seventies and tried to thwart his attempts to gain US citizenship. Many of their files on him are still classified, some because they are linked to British Intelligence information on Lennon. If there was a conspiracy to kill the singer, it is not unreasonable to deduce that the FBI may have played a part in it.

Right-wing Activists/Military Industrial Complex

Reagan had recently been elected President and some felt that opposition to his aggressive foreign policy and plans to spend massive amounts of the budget on expanding the American military was bound to develop around veteran peace campaigner Lennon. In fear of him inspiring the youth to rebel as he had done in the Sixties, right-wing activists and certain sections of the Military Industrial Complex plotted to silence him.

CIA

Chapman had worked for defence companies with close links to the CIA. He also showed some evidence of having been hypnotised. In this light, some have looked in the direction of the CIA's outlawed project to create programmed killers – MK-Ultra – for the real reason Chapman murdered his former hero.

THE UNUSUAL SUSPECTS

Satanic Forces

Lennon was shot outside the Dakota building – an apartment block that had provided the backdrop to Roman Polanski's film about the birth of the Antichrist, *Rosemary's Baby*. Beatles music and lyrics were used as elements in Charles Manson's warped reasoning that eventually led to the ritual killing of Roman Polanski's wife, Sharon Tate. David Mark Chapman believed that Lennon was in fact the Antichrist. These spooky synchronicities have been enough for wild claims that the shooting was the result of machinations carried out by Satanic forces or members of Satanic cult that caused Chapman to be possessed.

CHRISTIAN FUNDAMENTALISTS

Mark David Chapman was not the only one who thought Lennon was the Antichrist. Ever since his "bigger than God" quote, certain American fundamentalists believed the ex-Beatle was a dark force dedicated to corrupting the youth of America by spreading a gospel of love, drugs and rock 'n' roll. With Lennon's return to the spotlight after a self-imposed period as a house-husband, it may be that they decided to silence him once and for all.

MOST CONVINCING EVIDENCE

The strength of the fight put up by the FBI against those using the Freedom of Information Act to try to force the agency to make public its files on the singer is suspicious. As is the fact that even now not all of the material on file has been disclosed. Given that the FBI claim the reason their files cannot be made public is to protect national security, previously paranoid-sounding claims made by conspiracy buffs may have more veracity than it is comfortable to believe.

MOST MYSTERIOUS FACT

Conspiracy theorists who believe that Paul McCartney is dead and has been replaced with a lookalike, examine The Beatles lyrics and album covers in search of clues. In a similar way, fringe researchers into the mystery surrounding Lennon's death have also found significance in certain publicity photos and songs. In the booklet that came with the original *Magical Mystery Tour* album in the States, there is a picture of John and a sign next to him stating: "The best way to go is by MD&C." Given these are the initials of Mark David Chapman, some have seen this as either a strange example of synchronicity or a massive clue signposting an astonishing conspiracy.

SCEPTICALLY SPEAKING

The proposed conspiracy theories all go out of their way to overlook the obvious fact that America's lax attitude to gun control laws and a mentally-disturbed man with an obsession with Lennon are enough of a dangerous combination to provide all the explanation you could ever possibly need.

PAUL McCARTNEY

When you are one of the most famous musicians in the world and your name is known to anyone who has ever listened to pop music, you cannot be too surprised when strange rumours spring up around you – it is the nature of celebrity in the Twentieth Century.

In the latter half of the Sixties a rumour spread through the media, and consequently, the rest of the Beatle-loving world that Paul McCartney was actually dead and that an impostor, named William Campbell, was put in his place.

The alleged conspiracy was first exposed to the public by Detroit disc jockey Russ Gibb. He advised his listeners to seek for clues in the band's music, even if it entailed playing the record backwards. One such "clue" is allegedly featured in the "Number nine, number nine" lyric on The Beatles' *White Album* which apparently becomes "turn me on dead man" when played backwards.

The rumour grew faster than Yoko Ono's hair. Millions of Beatles fans, and those who wanted a new hobby, spent hours of their time looking for new clues which revealed that Paul was dead. People were looking for evidence of a conspiracy in everything remotely related to the Beatles. Every clue confirmed what the many suspected – Paul McCartney was dead and there was a huge conspiracy to conceal this fact.

THE STRANGE PART

On the classic *Sergeant Pepper's Lonely Hearts' Club Band* album, Paul is wearing an arm patch with the initials OPD – commonly recognised as an acronym for Officially Pronounced Dead.

THE USUAL SUSPECTS

The Beatles

Conspiracy theorists of a more sceptical bent have concluded that there are in fact many clues to Paul's death scattered throughout the musical output of The Beatles, but that they have been placed there by The Beatles as a metaphysical hoax. They believe that Paul died spiritually and was re-born in the ways of the Maharishi. This spiritual rebirth and his old self dying became an in-joke among the group and they placed obscure references to it on their album covers and in the lyrics of their songs.

The Record Company

Mass hysteria was created by the rumour that Paul was dead. People fanatically searched for clues and evidence and went to ridiculous lengths to find them. More than one conspiracy theorist has suggested that it was all a hoax cooked up by the record company to help sustain interest in The Beatles. If this is correct, it certainly qualifies as one of the most fascinating publicity stunts of all time. Even those who feel the conspiracy theory is a hoax still love hearing the clues.

CIA

Many people claim that the CIA wanted to bring an end to the Beatles' powerful influence on the world. They may have seen the Beatles and their massive, almost religious, following as a threat to society, which had already witnessed the outrage that John Lennon's comments on The Beatles being "more popular than Jesus Christ" had created. The Beatles were undoubtedly musical and social gods in the Sixties and may have been seen as a threat to the established order by the Agency. Their attempt to destroy The Beatles by murdering Paul was not completely successful as the other three Beatles enrolled the services of William Campbell, the winner of a Paul McCartney lookalike contest.

THE UNUSUAL SUSPECTS

Elvis Presley

A less grounded theory is that Elvis Presley employed the CIA to murder Paul. It has been claimed that Presley had been jealous and threatened by the Beatles' success from the day that the Beatles first set foot in the United States. He was the King of Rock 'n' Roll and no one was going to take that title away from him. So maybe he went to the extreme measure of sanctioning Paul McCartney's assassination. Elvis was popular amongst the highest politicians in the American government, and had extremely powerful contacts. Therefore, if he had been behind McCartney's alleged death, it would be unlikely that he would face any *Jailhouse Rock* for his crime.

The Devil

Another possible explanation was first proposed by the American academic Professor Glazier, who suggested that the Devil killed Paul as repayment for a bargain he had struck with McCartney for the Beatles' immense success in the world. Obviously rock stars were not the only horny beasts running around during the Sixties. Paul is said to have suffered the same fate as Brian Jones of the Rolling Stones, who also paid the price of success.

MOST CONVINCING EVIDENCE

The cover of the *Abbey Road* album was declared as evidence of Paul's death by Fred LaBour in *The Michigan Daily*. He claimed that the Beatles were depicted as a type of funeral group who were leaving the cemetery. John, dressed in white, represented a minister. George, a gravedigger, and Ringo was an undertaker. Paul, of course, was the corpse, who is barefoot and out of step with the others, suggesting an impostor is present.

MOST MYSTERIOUS FACT

Among the many lyrics which could have been related to Paul's death, one in particular stands out. In the song *Glass Onion*, John Lennon sings the words "The Walrus was Paul". It has been claimed that "Walrus" means "Corpse" in Greek.

SCEPTICALLY SPEAKING

The quality of the so-called clues is exceptionally dubious. The *Abbey Road* album cover features the licence plate 28 IF – which some have interpreted as being Paul's age if he had lived – but if Paul was still alive, he would have been 27, not 28. Many of the records that were played backwards sounded so strange and vague that almost any phrase could have fitted with the sound. It is all a case of looking so hard for something that you are guaranteed to find it. No impostor would have been able to duplicate McCartney's exceptional musical talent, though some conspiracy theorists argue that Paul's solo career is the ultimate proof of their claims.

MARILYN MONROE – DEATH OF A GODDESS

On May 19, 1962, President John F Kennedy enjoyed a very public birthday celebration at New York's famous Madison Square Garden. At the celebrity-studded bash, more than 15,000 people saw Marilyn Monroe sing *Happy Birthday* to JFK in breathless, sexual whispers that have entered into pop-culture legend.

Just a few months later on August 4, 1962, the 36-year-old woman, born as Norma Jean Mortenson, was dead – found naked amid her silk sheets, an empty bottle of powerful barbiturates on her dressing table. Marilyn Monroe was a true Hollywood legend and probably the world's first global sex symbol, yet behind the legend is a tragic story of a tortured soul; an alcoholic who had been abused by all of the famous, powerful men in her life. Everything pointed towards the fact that the star had taken her own life.

On the other hand, some have always felt that Marilyn's suicide was just a little too neat and convenient, especially for a range of interested parties such as JFK, Robert F Kennedy, the Mafia, the CIA and the FBI – who all had good reasons for wanting her to be kept permanently silent. The best way for a murder to go undiscovered is for it to look like an accident or a suicide. Conspiracy theorists have never believed Marilyn Monroe deliberately or accidentally took her own life. Remarkably, one thing that almost all those who believe Monroe was murdered agree on, is that if she was killed, it was probably done whilst she was held down with pillows and injected in the foot with barbiturates.

THE STRANGE PART

It became well-known in the years following her death that Marilyn had been the mistress of both John and Bobby Kennedy and that the CIA and FBI were keeping her under surveillance both as a possible threat to national security and as a risk to the President's reputation. Given the level of their involvement in monitoring the star and the clear suggestion that evidence about her last few days of life has been tampered with or covered up, a plot to murder Marilyn is not entirely without credibility.

THE USUAL SUSPECTS

CIA

The CIA was keeping Marilyn under surveillance because her time as JFK's mistress meant that she had knowledge which made her a potential threat to national security. Whether this concerned the CIA's use of the Mafia to try and eliminate Castro and blackmail other heads of state is unknown, but CIA interest in the blonde bombshell is as certain as is its agents' ability to carry out a discrete murder.

MAFIA

Having shared her bed with the President JFK, the Attorney General RFK and various high-powered members of the Mafia – including the mighty Sam Giancana – Monroe knew things that could have destroyed the most powerful people in the US. When her usefulness to the Mafia had run its course with the end of her affair with Robert F Kennedy, they may have felt she was a dangerous loose cannon that needed silencing.

FBI

Marilyn had been attempting to blackmail RFK into continuing their affair and may have been attempting a more audacious blackmail of JFK – threatening to expose the fact that he had only become President with the vote-fixing aid of the Chicago mob. FBI boss J Edgar Hoover was no friend of the Kennedy family, but as a self-styled patriot may have been happy to solve their problem with Monroe, to save the nation from scandal. Once he had arranged for Marilyn's death, he could control the upstart Kennedy brothers, forcing them to allow him to remain as head of the Bureau that had effectively become his own private police force.

THE UNUSUAL SUSPECTS

THE CATHOLIC CHURCH

One organization that the Kennedy clan trusted completely and which had links to the CIA and the mob was the Catholic Church. JFK was the United States' first Catholic President and the Church was keen to ensure that nothing threatened its man in the White House. Some have suggested that the desire to protect him even went as far as arranging for the death of his troublesome former mistress.

MEN IN BLACK

If the prospect of the original men in black – Catholic priests – is not unusual enough, there are some who have suggested that Monroe was eliminated by the actual Men In Black who are charged with keeping the lid on the UFO conspiracy. If JFK knew the truth about extraterrestrial life, he might have told Marilyn and thereby set in chain the series of events that led up to her death when she became uncontrollable and liable to reveal the secrets he had shared with her.

MOST CONVINCING EVIDENCE

In recent years, legal documents dating from 1960 have come to light. These documents seem to prove that the Kennedy family promised to give Marilyn Monroe $600,000 in a trust fund for her mother, Gladys Baker, if Marilyn kept quiet about what she knew of the links between JFK and Mafia boss Sam Giancana. After the star died, it appears as if this pledge was broken and all references to it were covered up. These documents quickly became the subject of a hotly-fought court action in the United States. Debate about their authenticity still rages. However, tests on the paper, ink and signatures have all suggested that the documents are valid. If this is the case, they are the strongest evidence to come to light that the Kennedy clan may have had a hand in the star's death.

MOST MYSTERIOUS FACT

There are a lot of rumours, and more than a dash of good circumstantial evidence, to suggest that among the last visitors Marilyn received at her home were Bobby Kennedy and Hollywood actor Peter Lawford – who was married to Pat Kennedy Lawford and was therefore part of the Kennedy clan. By all accounts, Lawford and Kennedy were accompanied by an enigmatic third man who was dressed in black and carried a medical-style bag. The identity of this mysterious figure could be the vital clue that needs to be solved if anyone is to unravel the truth behind Monroe's death.

SCEPTICALLY SPEAKING

It is easy to connect a lot of disparate dots in a revealing manner when it comes to the death of Marilyn Monroe. Affairs with the highest officials in the land, FBI files and links to the Mafia are all suggestive but do not necessarily mean that there was a conspiracy. By August 1962, Monroe was a psychologically damaged alcoholic: neither an accidental drug overdose nor a deliberate act of suicide would necessarily have been out of character for Marilyn at that stage of her life. The screen goddess always had a legendary quality about her during life and the conspiracy theories may just be an extension of the inevitable Hollywood myth-making process that doesn't stop just because the star concerned does.

JIM MORRISON – DEATH OR DISAPPEARANCE?

Lizard King, Rock God, shamanic spirit of the Sixties. Without doubt one of the biggest personalities of the music scene of his time, Jim Morrison always had a mythical quality about him. This appears to have done nothing but grow since his death in a Paris apartment on July 4, 1971. In fact, many conspiracy theorists feel his death is the greatest myth of Morrison's life; some believe it would take more than heart failure to rob the world of such a larger-than-life character.

After five years of fame, Jim took a break from The Doors after they had fulfilled their contractual obligation to Elektra Records by delivering the seminal album *LA Woman*. They may have been a little disgruntled that he left during the mixing stages of the LP, but this was not the end of the group and they fully expected him to return from Paris.

Morrison was bored with life in LA and sought out Paris as it was a place to inspire him – a romantic city of art and poetry. He mentioned to some people his desire to purchase an old church in the south of France so he could renovate it and use it as a permanent base from which he would only venture back to the hustle of America when business demanded. He took with him his scrap books filled with poetry and ideas, reels from three of the films he was working on and plans to write a play.

He and his long-term girlfriend, Pamela Courson, quickly established a home for themselves in a Parisian apartment. Jim wrote, appeared as an extra in a play, drank vast quantities of alcohol and began to enjoy the freedom of not being recognised every time he stepped outside his door. Jim often expressed opinions during this time that he felt like he needed to change the direction of his life – it was clear that he wanted to get away from things and that he wanted to travel.

While years of drinking, drug-taking and other forms of physical self-abuse had made their mark on Morrison, his unexpected death – recorded as resulting from heart failure – took many by surprise. It also inspired doubts in others that he was actually dead, doubts that intensified when one or two curious facts ended up in the public domain.

THE STRANGE PART

No one who knew Jim really well, other than his girlfriend, actually saw him dead. Even after the official death certificate had been produced, some of his friends and even some members of his family doubted that he had really shuffled off this mortal coil.

THE USUAL SUSPECTS

Jim Morrison

It is rumoured that some people who had contractual arrangements with him in the music business immediately assumed that his death was staged in order to facilitate an easy release from some troublesome, binding contracts that he would have had to fulfil had he lived. Established facts also show that Morrison was enjoying the anonymity of his life in Paris and took great care to ensure that there were no new publicity pictures showing what he looked like after he left LA so he would not be disturbed. He talked of escaping his fame. Faking his death may have been the perfect way to achieve this aim.

Friends of Jim Morrison

Some suspect that the confusion over Morrison's death stems from the fact that they wanted to disguise that he died of a drug overdose. Chief conspirator in this intrigue would have been his partner, the late Pamela Courson, who is purported to have had his body removed from the infamous Parisian junkie joint The Rock 'n' Roll Circus to their apartment in order to avoid a scandal and police questioning. This might explain her actions after she "found" Jim unconscious in the bath – her first few telephone calls were to friends, not to the paramedics.

THE UNUSUAL SUSPECTS

FBI

The FBI had kept Morrison under surveillance when he had been in the US. Files and memoranda to the then Director of the FBI – the infamous J Edgar Hoover – make mention of him trying to "provoke chaos". The Bureau certainly kept tags on those they thought capable of inciting rebellion or drug use among the young, and on people who were in contact with those thought to be subversive – two counts on which Morrison definitely qualified for attention. It should not come as too much of a surprise that some conspiracy theorists have conjectured that the FBI was involved in the strange circumstances surrounding Morrison's (alleged) death because they wished to ensure that Jim did not return to the USA and start provoking that chaos again.

World-wide Witch Cult

Morrison had an intense interest in witchcraft and is said to have been an active participant in at least one witch cult. It is claimed by some conspiracy theorists, with an interesting grasp of the word "fact", that Morrison was abducted as part of a dark plot to obtain the living representation of Dionysus – Greek god of fertility and wine – for ritual sacrifice.

MOST CONVINCING EVIDENCE

Though it is easy to be jaded when hearing conspiracies such as these, there is some convincing evidence to suggest that all is not as it seems with the Morrison case. No autopsy was ever performed, people who knew him well – including band member Ray Manzarek – believed that he was still alive and Morrison's own remarks that he wanted to escape the life of a rock star are all telling. However, the most convincing evidence is that more than a week after he had been "buried", Pamela Courson told a journalist working for United Press that Jim was staying at a special clinic outside Paris to convalesce from illness.

MOST MYSTERIOUS FACT

It is effectively impossible to exhume Morrison's body to prove he is actually dead. Apart from needing the family's approval, you also need the consent from seven French cardinals, who can each demand a right of veto and who are renowned for disagreeing on this type of matter. This is the case will all exhumations from the Père Lachaise cemetery, and Jim had speculated he might be buried there . . .

SCEPTICALLY SPEAKING

Towards the end of his life, Jim Morrison was an overweight, chain-smoking alcoholic who lived very dangerously by keeping up his intake of narcotics while also taking prescription medicines to combat his asthma. The death of someone in those circumstances is hardly surprising – it is pretty much inevitable.

IS THE KING STILL ALIVE?

The official version: Elvis died on August 16, 1977 from an overdose of drugs. He died sitting on the toilet, with his pants around his ankles, a bloated and burnt-out version of his former self and his body is now in residence at Gracelands.

The conspiracy version has it that the death of the King of Rock 'n' Roll was an elaborate hoax on the public and that the original *Hound Dog* is still alive and being spotted by numerous people across the globe.

It has to be agreed that his death did come as a shock – 42 is an early age to die and Elvis did have a history of pulling off some rather bizarre and eccentric stunts. There are certainly some mysterious elements surrounding his alleged death.

THE STRANGE PART

A mere two hours after his death was announced, a man looking remarkably like Elvis bought a ticket for Buenos Aires using the name John Burrows. This was a pseudonym that the King himself had used quite a few times, notably on the occasion he flew to Washington to meet President Nixon. It was on the same visit to DC, that he went to the headquarters of the FBI, announced his desire to inform on fellow showbusiness performers and became an honorary member of the Bureau of Narcotics and Dangerous Drugs. It is alleged that John Burrows flew out of the USA on special State Department papers and this has fuelled speculation that Burrows was none other than Presley making his escape to a new life.

THE USUAL SUSPECTS

Elvis Presley

The hottest contender for the instigator of the conspiracy is none other than Elvis himself. The King definitely felt a prisoner of his own fame and was tired of riding in the trunks of cars to avoid detection and of not being able to get proper medical attention because any hospital he was in would be overwhelmed by fans. At 42, he was going downhill and was too proud to go out with a whimper. Elvis had already once faked his death by setting up deceptive shooting, so it is not impossible he staged a more final fake death.

FBI

Elvis had recently lost a vast amount of money in bad deals with companies that had close links to the Mafia. There is a lot of speculation that the

King decided to collaborate with the Government to help expose gangsters. To ensure his protection, the FBI had to fake his death and provide him with a new life as part of a very unusual witness relocation program.

THE UNUSUAL SUSPECTS

Burger Chain Companies

Could the faked death of Elvis be part of an innovative and radical marketing scam? It has been suggested that the frequent sighting of Elvis cooking fries in numerous backwoods burger joints – which then become very popular, acting as shrines and magnets for Elvis fans – is a joint plan between the King and the burger chain companies. Elvis gets to live a life free from the pressures of fame and is paid in cheeseburgers, while the fast food bosses get to increase business in their more slow establishments.

New World Order

Since Elvis allegedly bought the farm, it has become clear to many cultural observers that he is well on the way to becoming a religious figure. Books comparing him to Christ have hit the US best-seller lists, sightings of Elvis can be seen as similar to spiritual visions, and there is no denying that many fans have shrines to the King and describe visiting Gracelands in terms of making a pilgrimage. If you are of a paranoid bent, you may want to consider the claims that the Elvis conspiracy was instigated by the New World Order as their attempt to lay the groundwork for a future new religion. Has Elvis been cryogenically frozen by the NWO to be revived as the globe's new messiah when it comes to power?

MJ-12

Every Elvis conspiracy is more than a little odd, but the suggested link between the King and Roswell – where in 1947 a UFO was alleged to have crashed and the military recovered alien bodies – is bizarre even by Elvis standards. It has been claimed that the military photographer who captured Elvis on film for US Marine publicity purposes was a man called Barret who just happened to be the US Army photographer brought in to record the dead alien's autopsies. Conspiracy buffs, with a love for the territory of deep weird, have it that the photographer sent Elvis a copy of those alien pictures with the fatal consequence that MJ-12 – the guys behind the UFO cover-up – had to silence the King.

MOST CONVINCING EVIDENCE

Aside from the frequently-quoted fact that Elvis is an anagram for lives, possibly the most convincing evidence surrounds the 900-pound coffin with built in air-chilling unit in which Elvis was buried. How did the Presley family manage to obtain a 900-pound, custom-made coffin ready for a funeral held on the day after his death, and still fail to follow the more basic request from Elvis, such as being buried next to his mother? In the days leading up to his alleged death, the King is said to have made odd nocturnal visits to several funeral homes. Why?

MOST MYSTERIOUS FACT

The King's name is spelt wrong on his headstone. His full name was Elvis Aron Presley, but on his grave his middle name is spelled incorrectly with an additional 'a'. The unique spelling of Aron was an important Presley family tradition. When he was born, Aron was mis-spelled Aaron on his birth certificate and Elvis's father went to great lengths to correct the recording of his son's name. It seems very odd that Elvis's family would have allowed this error to occur on the King's tombstone.

SCEPTICALLY SPEAKING

The King is dead – get over it.

GOODBYE THE ROSE – DEATH OF PRINCESS DI

The death of Princess Diana was an event that affected people across the planet. Britain grieved. The world grieved. Even people who had never devoted any real attention to the British royal family felt deep emotion at the tragic circumstances that robbed the world of someone who qualified as a global cultural icon.

At first it appeared to be nothing more than a simple tragic accident. Diana had enjoyed a romantic meal with her lover, Dodi Al Fayed, at the Ritz Hotel owned by his father Mohammed Al Fayed. A little before midnight they left, accompanied by Diana's bodyguard – Trevor Rees-Jones. They left by the back door to escape 30 paparazzi parked outside. The chauffeur of their bullet-proof Mercedes Benz was Henri Paul, the Ritz Hotel's head of security.

The car sped away and a tourist captured it on video as an innocent looking Citroen followed it and the paparazzi, realizing they had been duped, began to give chase on their motorcycles. After a few minutes pursuit, the Mercedes entered the Pont de l'Alma tunnel at high speed and all we know that Diana, Dodi and Henri failed to emerge from it with their lives. Although the French investigation into the accident has still not produced an official version of events, the instant verdict from the world's media was that it was a woeful auto accident caused by the combination of a drunk driver, pursuing paparazzi and a failure to wear seatbelts.

THE STRANGE PART

The first public suggestion that there was a conspiracy to kill Princess Diana surfaced on the BBC World Service a couple of days after the unfortunate events of August 31, 1996.

In bizarre propagandist tones, the BBC made pains to deride a speech made by Libyan leader Colonel Moamar Qaddafi in which he claimed that the "accident" was a joint French and British conspiracy because they did not want Diana to marry a Muslim man. Conspiracy theories began circulating on the night of her death, most of them speculating on how strange it was that on the day Diana died she had already told one major British national newspaper to prepare for an amazing announcement.

THE USUAL SUSPECTS

MI6

Sworn to protect the British crown, it is alleged that a renegade faction within MI6 took it upon itself to rid the royal family of the one woman that looked capable of destroying the monarchy by exposing the hypocrisy of the Windsors. The fact that she may have been about to convert to Islam and marry the son of establishment bogeyman Mohammed Al Fayed may have been the final factors that made them decide she must die.

Military Industrial Complex

Diana had waged a one-woman war against the evils of landmines, in doing so risking her personal safety and earning strident political criticism in the UK as a "loose cannon". While the Military Industrial Complex makes more money from disposing of landmines than it does selling them, it may have feared the possibility of Diana turning her attention to the arms industry in general. Clearly, it would have been in their best interests to wipe out someone who could have turned into the world's most powerful peace campaigner.

Also suspected: CIA; Mossad; Islamic Fundamentalists; Saddam Hussein; The Freemasons (she died under a bridge – an important Masonic symbol): and the IRA.

THE UNUSUAL SUSPECTS

The Committee of Twenty-Six is allegedly a secret group made up of intelligence agency operatives from the United States and the United Kingdom. Supposedly headquartered in Bristol, England, the Committee is apparently a tool of an even more clandestine group that wants the special relationship between the US and Britain to develop into a union of both powers. Possibly Diana's massive popularity and willingness to tackle the establishment on sensitive issues persuaded them she could be a dangerous opponent to these cryptic schemes.

Princess Diana

Another bizarre hypothesis is that Diana staged her own death so she and Dodi could live a life free from the glare of publicity. Not surprisingly, there's little hard evidence to support this piece of wishful thinking.

MOST CONVINCING EVIDENCE

Claims have been made that Henri Paul was three times over the legal alcohol limit. A second blood test ordered by his disbelieving family showed a level of carbon monoxide in his body that was not only lethal, but that would have to have entered his bloodstream before he got into the car. Security video from the Ritz that night does not show him as a drunk or reeling from carbon monoxide poisoning. The mystery of Henri Paul deepens further with the revelation that he deposited more than 164,000 francs in his bank account shortly before he died.

MOST MYSTERIOUS FACT

The crash happened in the Pont de l'Alma tunnel that was built over a site used in the time of the Merovingian dynasty (between 500-751 AD) as a sacred ritual area. Some secret societies such as the Prieur de Sion and the Templars claim that the Merovingians and all true European royalty – including Diana Spencer's family – are descendants of none other than Jesus Christ. There is historical information that suggests Merove – the founder of the Merovingian dynasty – was connected to the pagan cult of Diana. It is odd that Britain's Queen of Hearts may have died on a former site of worship for the goddess whose name she was given . . .

SCEPTICALLY SPEAKING

Driving at high speed through Paris is dangerous enough without being pursued by a pack of paparazzi on motorcycles. Add a barrage of camera flashes to a chase being conducted at more than 120 miles per hour when the passengers are not wearing seatbelts and you no longer need a conspiracy to explain a fatal crash. When faced by a tragedy such as Diana's death, it is not surprising that some people cannot accept it as a mere random accident. The car crash in Paris may be the perfect example of why some conspiracy theories come into being – if they did not exist we'd have to face the banality and indiscriminate nature of death.

SID VICIOUS

When New York's finest entered Room 100 of the Chelsea Hotel on October 12, 1978, they found a horrific sight. Lying beneath the bathroom sink, clad only in her underwear and covered in blood, was Nancy Spungen. She was dead, killed by a single knife blow to her abdomen. Her boyfriend, himself in a drug-induced muddle, was Sid Vicious, bass player with the then notorious punk band, The Sex Pistols. He was charged with Spungen's murder, and was later released on $50,000 bail.

The romance between Vicious (born John Simon Ritchie) and Nancy Spungen was the thing rock and roll nightmares are made of. After being recruited by Malcolm McLaren to be in a band called The Sex Pistols (named after McLaren's boutique in London called "Sex"), that McLaren had designed specifically to appeal to the disaffected youth of England, Vicious soon found himself at the epicentre of a pop-culture phenomenon. The Pistols, with songs calculated to infuriate all the wrong people (ie anyone over 30) tore through England on the breaking wave of punk rock. With songs like *Anarchy in the UK* and *God Save The Queen*, coupled with outrageous outbursts on television and other media, the Pistols were nothing short of a slow-motion atom bomb shaking the foundations of pop-culture world-wide.

Which wasn't bad for Vicious, considering there was debate about whether he even knew how to play the bass at all. Instead, he relied more on image: cutting himself with razor blades, spitting blood, or even urinating while on stage. He was the anarchy poster boy, beloved by many newborn punk rockers.

He proved irresistible to one fan, an American girl called Nancy Spungen, who came over to England with the express purpose of capturing the heart – or anything else – of a Pistol. She and Vicious met in 1977 and soon became lovers, careening into an affair riddled with drug abuse. Vicious' love of Spungen, coupled with Spungen's abrasive personality, became so intense that it began to tear the band apart. When the Pistols' ill-fated American tour ended abruptly, with lead singer Johnny Rotten returning to England in disgust, Vicious stayed with Spungen, ending up finally in New York's Chelsea Hotel.

After Spungen's death Vicious tried to commit suicide out of despair and carved his entire forearm with a knife. Surviving that, he finally succumbed to a heroin overdose (with heroin which his mother bought for him, fearing that her son might get caught in a police sting) on February 2, 1978. He was only 21.

THE STRANGE PART

Theories have arisen over the possibility of a conspiracy concerning Vicious' death. There are dark hints that there was more at hand than the tragic deaths of two heroin-addicts, and even murmurs that Vicious may not have killed Spungen at all.

THE USUAL SUSPECTS

Unknown residents of the Chelsea Hotel

Keeping in mind the drug-hazed state of mind ofVicious and of Spungen before her death, it's entirely probable that someone other than Vicious may have killed Spungen. In his befuddled state of mind, he may not even have been aware of the murder. The true perpetrators, worried about the truth coming out if Vicious' case went to trial, they ensured his silence by making sure that Vicious' mother bought a lethally-cut dose of heroin for her son.

Former Associates

Some conspiracy theorists feel that former friends and associates ofVicious may have had him supplied with a hit of lethal "hot" heroin. This was meant as an unusual act of mercy to spare him having to face the living hell of a long prison sentence served out in New York's most notorious jail – where he would not have been vicious enough to survive.

THE UNUSUAL SUSPECTS

The CIA and FBI

Just as the murder of John Lennon may be attributed to a mutual desire by the CIA and FBI to remove any pop-culture figure that could possibly lead the population to revolt, Vicious might have been killed because he represented punk anarchy in all its glory. He had the potential to give American youth a role-model that made the young Elvis look the model of respectability. Indeed, some theories suggest that Vicious could have been a simple trial run of a CIA or FBI rub-out program, before attention moved on to the more difficult task of removing Lennon. Both men died, coincidentally, in New York.

MOST CONVINCING EVIDENCE

However tormented and tortuous the relationship was between Spungen and Vicious, it was painfully clear to all those around him that he needed her, perhaps more than anything or anyone else. To kill her would seem completely out of character, regardless of his state of intoxication. In telephone conversations with Spungen's mother after Nancy's death, Vicious never made any comments about it at all. If he was as guilt-ridden over killing her as we would be led to believe, would he be able to hide his pain that well? In all other things, Vicious was not known as a paragon of restraint.

MOST MYSTERIOUS FACT

While returning her son's ashes to England, it's rumoured that Sid's mother dropped the urn in Heathrow, scattering them across the airport floor. A significant proportion of them was sucked into the ventilation system.

SCEPTICALLY SPEAKING

Although it would be romantic to think that all rock stars who die young do so because the "Powers That Be" want them dead, there are times when death is simply a tragic end to a tragic story. Sid Vicious was a young man with next to no musical talent, who was simply in the right place at the right time looking the right way when McLaren created the Sex Pistols. The idea that he could ever be a threat to American society in the way that John Lennon or Jim Morrison were widely perceived to be, is ludicrous. Vicious was the "It Boy" of the punk generation, and nothing more. If his death were to be chalked up to anything, it should be to heroin and the equally dangerous drug of intense media exposure.

OSCAR WILDE

Poet, critic, playwright and dazzling wit, Oscar Wilde was a towering figure in late-Victorian England and its most prominent celebrity. By turns flamboyant, charming, eccentric and outrageous, he electrified polite society. People were in awe of his rapier-like tongue, they roared at his scandalous epigrams and they flocked to see his plays. However, they never quite accepted him. Society wasn't quite comfortable with Wilde, suspecting that he had a darker side. He had – and he made little effort to hide it.

Beneath the facade of civility, the streets of Victorian England swarmed with pimps, prostitutes, drug addicts and debauched behaviour of every description. Many of its most prominent figures indulged in dreadful vices, but provided that they did so behind closed doors they could retain their standing in society. As Wilde himself pointed out, England at the time was the native land of the hypocrite. The only real crime was being found out.

Oscar Wilde was found out. He conducted a tempestuous homosexual affair with Lord Alfred Douglas, the youngest son of the Marquess of Queensbury. The Marquess, a notorious bully who was known to go after leading politicians with a horsewhip, publicly accused Wilde of being a sodomite. Wilde sued for libel. At the trial Queensbury produced evidence that proved Wilde frequented the establishment of Alfred Taylor – a Fagin-like figure who kept a stable of rent boys. Wilde lost his case, was arrested and subsequently convicted of indulging in homosexual practices. His sentence was two years' imprisonment with hard labour. In 1897 he was released and fled to Paris, but died within three years.

Some conspiracy theorists feel that the disgraced playwright's life was ended prematurely to ensure his silence and to save others from being exposed as possessing the same dangerous vice that had been his downfall – hypocrisy. Given the information Wilde had and his impoverished financial state, a career as a blackmailer does not seem impossible. Did he pick on the wrong victim?

THE STRANGE PART

Traditional wisdom has it that he died of natural causes, yet Wilde was only 46. A post-mortem was never carried out and he was buried in a pauper's grave with what seems like undue haste. In his last years, Wilde was desperately strapped for cash. He was not unacquainted with extortion – it was through a case of petty blackmail that he met Lord Douglas – and he may have been attempting to solve his problems by threatening to tell what he knew about the great and the good of Victorian society.

THE USUAL SUSPECTS

Lord Roseberry

A former Prime Minister, Roseberry was a homosexual who had an affair with Lord Douglas's older brother before his young lover mysteriously shot himself. He may have had darker secrets than his sexuality, and Wilde may have known them. If this was true, Roseberry would have had good reason to send Wilde into an early grave.

Agents of the British Crown

There is no way of knowing how much Wilde's knew – or how deeply his potential for blackmail penetrated the ranks of the aristocracy and the politically-powerful. He claimed to have knowledge that would expose at least one Bishop and a Duke. Agents of the Crown could have had felt that murdering Wilde was justifiable if it protected the great and the good of society from scandal.

Marques of Queensbury

Despite ruining Wilde, Queensbury was still consumed by hatred of the man he felt had corrupted his youngest son. Though Queensbury died a few months before Wilde, money and spite can often strike from beyond the grave.

THE UNUSUAL SUSPECTS

The Masons

Wilde was known to have been a Freemason in his early years. With their fearsome reputation for dealing with those who break their secrets or threaten a member of the brotherhood, it is feasible that the Masons may have decided to put an early end to Oscar's acid tongue before he exposed senior figures among them who had also inhabited his twilight world.

Irish Republicans

Roger Casement – Irish Republican revolutionary and former British spy – had a notorious penchant for young men. He, and others like him in the Republican movement, may have been connected to their fellow countryman Wilde. It could be that if Wilde was murdered, a revolutionary order dedicated to freeing Eire from English rule may have been a factor. Republicans may have felt the need to preserve the sexual secrets of their leaders as much as political secrets . . .

MOST MYSTERIOUS FACT

It is well-established that, during his exile, Wilde received more than one visit from an unknown man who provided him with sufficient funds to carry on living in Paris. The identity of this mysterious benefactor has never been revealed. What, to some, may seem like an act of charity could just as easily be explained if the supposed benefactor was in fact a blackmail victim of Wilde's. Perhaps someone who grew tired of paying up, and decided to silence him.

MOST CONVINCING EVIDENCE

The night after Oscar Wilde was arrested, a mass panic seems to have broken out. An unusual amount of odd traffic was reported on the cross-Channel ferries, as more than 600 gentleman hurriedly crossed to France. No doubt many of them slipped back home after the scandal had died down and society went back to looking the other way. However, it is proof that there were names to be named, that Wilde knew them, and that many were scared of being exposed by him.

SCEPTICALLY SPEAKING

The tortures of the trial had broken Wilde's spirit and two years in prison certainly broke him physically. Leaving aside the not inconsiderable matter of his alcohol consumption during his exile, there are more than sufficient reasons to believe that he fell prey to a terminal illness at the relatively young age of 46.

E

ALIEN ABDUCTIONS

One of the most prevalent conspiracy theories disturbing the sleep of millions today is that of alien abductions. All over the world, the lives of innocent men and women are apparently being disrupted by incidents of otherworldly kidnappings. Suddenly, they find themselves forcibly removed from their homes, transported to alien crafts or environments where they are horribly violated by creatures from beyond the stars. What makes these incidents all the more terrifying is the complete helplessness of the victims, who are at the complete mercy of these inscrutable aliens and their disturbing medical procedures.

Researchers into alien abductions have attempted to categorize the kidnappings, searching for common threads of experience among abductees. Among those categories are the basic physical abduction, where abductees talk of feeling tranquillized, then watching placidly as they are moved to an alien ship. They might be moved there by a smaller craft, by some form of tractor beam, or by some kind of inter-dimensional "gate". Some abductees report being moved directly through solid objects, such as the walls of a house.

Another popular form is the bio-energy extraction method, where the abductees' bio-energy, or consciousness, is removed from their bodies by an alien technology that usually takes the form of a white to bluish-white beam of light surrounding and penetrating the abductees' bodies. The consciousness of the victim is often inserted into another body before being returned to its original form.

There are also the telepathic lucid dream versions of abductions, which, while not being as physical in nature as a corporeal abduction, are no less damaging. In this kind of attack, abductees find themselves experiencing a lucid dream created by aliens, in which a normal dream disintegrates and is replaced by telepathic messages or visual images. As in the bio-extraction scenario, a beam of whitish energy emanating from the ceiling above them is sometimes seen by awakening victims.

While abductions have been reported throughout history, there seems to be an increase in frequency of late. It's almost as if the perpetrators – aliens, or whoever is responsible for these heinous crimes against humanity – are growing increasingly desperate.

THE STRANGE PART

While many abduction stories share disturbing similarities, perhaps the most intriguing is the concept of "lost time". Many victims talk of the experience of suddenly losing all sense of time. They check their watches, only to discover that minutes, sometimes hours, have elapsed without their knowledge, leaving unexplained gaps in their lives. They may not even be aware that they have been abducted, but are disturbed to discover that they cannot account for their whereabouts. It is only through hypnosis or the breaking down of externally-constructed mental walls that many can actually remember the horrifying truth.

THE USUAL SUSPECTS

The Greys

The Greys are the most common type of alien experienced in the abduction scenario. Small creatures with melon-shaped heads and huge, black, slanted eyes, they are at the root of many alien conspiracy theories. The current thoughts on their involvement in abductions are varied, from an optimistic hope that they are our descendants coming back in time to save the Earth from destruction, to a darker suspicion that they are extracting sperm and ova from humans in order to save their own race. Under this hypothesis the Greys are a race of clones that has lost the ability to reproduce sexually; the Greys hope to create a hybrid between themselves and humans in order to survive.

The US Government

The Majestic 12 – also known as MJ-12 – is a powerful shadow group within the US Government that may be working with the Greys, allowing them to continue their experiments in exchange for technology. This deal has allegedly helped give rise to weapons such as the B-2 stealth bomber and the F-117 stealth fighter. Many abductees recall seeing military personnel and installations, often without seeing aliens. (This poses the question of whether this arrangement is merely a matter of working in conjunction with the Greys, or whether the US Government has its own agenda – perhaps mind control?) Using masterful disinformation tactics, this group discredits and ridicules any research into UFOs and indeed, anything else that may shed light on the mysterious Greys, thereby ensuring continued abduction work, continued misery for thousands, and continued technological payoffs for the US Government.

THE UNUSUAL SUSPECTS

Dolphins

The Greys may be either future descendants of dolphins or they may be genetic extrapolations of dolphins that travel back to our time for their own nefarious purposes. The similarities between Greys and dolphins, in skin texture and colour, and in their ability to emanate an ultrasonic blast to stun enemies (Greys use the "Stare" to subdue abductees, for example) bear consideration.

MOST CONVINCING EVIDENCE

Following abduction experiences, many victims have found themselves implanted with small metal devices, usually in the nasal cavities, but often found in other areas of the body. When these implants are successfully removed by surgeons, their origins become no less clear. The metal that is used in many of these devices is unknown to today's science, and their purpose remains an unsettling mystery. Are they tracking devices, or something more?

MOST MYSTERIOUS FACT

The commonality of experience among abduction victims, from descriptions of the Greys, procedures and implants, is disquieting. The meteoric rise of books, movies and reports of abductions hints that a greater truth is just lurking beneath the surface, ready to break through at any moment.

SCEPTICALLY SPEAKING

The same phenomenon occurred at the end of the nineteenth century. Though instead of alien abductions, it was fairies. Chalk it up to end-of-the-century madness, coupled with pre-millennial paranoia.

ANCIENT ASTRONAUTS

It has been said that there has never been a time in history where the world has been totally at peace – there has always been some conflict, somewhere. Man seems to be incapable of coexisting with any other person who displays even slight differences in look, thought or belief. History shows us that for the last five thousand years, the world has been riddled with wars, from the ancient Sumerian subjugation of neighbouring tribes for slave labour, to ethnic cleansing in the former Yugoslavia.

Why do we fight each other? It doesn't really help anyone, and there is hardly any occasion where either side wins convincingly. The only answer that comes to mind is that the collective action of humanity is so far from rational as to suggest total insanity, particularly given the astonishing weapons now available to the military in the Twentieth Century. There is only one conclusion: our species is mad.

The real question however is not one of whether we are mad, but rather one of who it was who pushed us over the edge. After all, if we'd been such an insanely self-destructive species to begin with, we would never have made it down out of the trees. Someone, somewhere, is meddling with human history, setting us against each other.

THE STRANGE PART

War goes against the survival trait inherent to mankind. Why have so many peoples chosen to fight when development and co-operation is a far more successful method of prolonging the species, and more in keeping with our instinctive behaviours? Certain scholars, looking closely at the anthropological reasoning behind war, have found that the evidence of motive-based reasoning only fits the accepted facts if we look at humans as puppets, being manipulated by a higher intelligence into fulfilling its desires while still believing we are following our own destiny.

THE USUAL SUSPECTS

THE WATCHERS

Modern Humanity was genetically engineered from our ancestor known as Cro-Magnon man into its current intelligent form around 5,000 BC.

The idea was to create a race that would provide useful labour and other services for its creators, aliens bearing a degree of resemblance to us but arriving from an advanced civilization developed elsewhere. On the Earth, major civilizations first start arising around this time, in the vicinity of the Middle East. The aliens remain among us, watching and guiding humanity, duping us into providing certain industrial and other services they need through their manipulation of politics, religion, television and capitalism. They control many major organizations, and are also behind much of the extremely illegal but still quite healthy slave trade. They consume some of what they need, and ship some off-planet.

THE UNUSUAL SUSPECTS

The World Bank

War is an expensive business and most countries that find themselves engaging in a medium to long-term conflict need financial support from the world banking system both during the war (to fund weaponry) and afterwards (to fund rebuilding). These loans are often repayable at huge interest rates, making war very profitable for the banks.

The Catholic Church

Organized religions have often openly bankrolled wars in many different parts of the world in order to suppress another conflicting belief. It is not too far-fetched to imagine that they have also been behind other wars in a more discreet or under-handed manner, to help ensure that our feelings of mortality are always present, and that we turn to religion for solace.

The Freemasons

As an organization, Freemasonry has members in power in almost every armed force and government in the world. It has often been suggested that the Freemasons have engineered wars across the globe in order to put down enemies to their Brotherhood. It does seem a little extreme, though.

MOST CONVINCING EVIDENCE

Ancient Sumerian texts talk about angelic beings – The Anunnaki – or "Those Who Came From The Sky" who introduced teachings and technologies into the culture which led to the Sumerians becoming the most feared of all the Middle Eastern civilizations at that time. The same beings are discussed in religious texts by Hebrew sources as "The Nephilim" and by Zoroastrians as "The Watchers". They are always considered with a degree of trepidation, are said to have cross-bred with humans, and are usually spoken of as taking a mysterious shadowy role behind human society.

MOST MYSTERIOUS FACT

Several primitive societies surviving to the present day have knowledge that is inexplicable in its antiquity. This is always attributed by those peoples to ancient visitors from outer space. The best – and least explicable – example of this is the Dogon tribe of East Africa. The tribe has long held a legend that one particular star in the night sky is actually a binary star system, with two suns orbiting each other. Astronomers using ultra-high-powered telescopes recently discovered this to be the case – the legend is true. But there is no way a low-technology society such as the Dogon could have discovered the existence of binary star systems, and they are so few and far between that the chance of the Dogon having picked the right star from those visible in the sky by chance is mind-numbingly small.

SCEPTICALLY SPEAKING

If the Watchers were powerful enough to rebuild our genetic code to make us intelligent, and smart enough to remain in control ever since, why didn't they just take over lock, stock and barrel and either put visible overseers in place to keep us in line, or build mental obedience and controls into our mindsets? Manipulating us into constant warfare seems clumsy and inefficient to say the least.

CATTLE MUTILATIONS

For decades, cattle farmers around the world have been plagued by a problem, a problem that is as inexplicable as it is horrifying: the grisly puzzle of cattle mutilations. Representing more than just a simple financial loss associated with missing livestock, this exercise in abject cruelty may have a purpose, but like its perpetrators, that purpose remains cloaked in shadows.

While the majority of cattle mutilation cases occur in the United States, (particularly in New Mexico), the phenomenon has been reported in Puerto Rico, South America, and Canada. Details of the mutilations may vary from case to case, but there are enough commonalities to suggest an orchestrated program of sorts is underway. More often that not, the bodies of mutilated animals are found drained of blood. Missing organs have been removed with surgical precision, with the carcass often appearing to have been cauterized. And the perpetrators show a particular interest in sensory organs such as the eyes, the reproductive and defecatory systems, and the anterior digestive tract.

As many as 10,000 cattle may have died in this manner, and as a result several theories have sprung up surrounding this disturbing trend. If dealing with predators, disease, and rowdy young men in search of cow-tipping weren't enough, cattle ranchers now have to contend with an unknown sadistic force that comes and goes like an eviscerating thief in the night.

THE STRANGE PART

No marks around the bodies of the mutilated cattle are usually found, with the exception of a few tripod marks surrounding the bodies. Clamp marks have been found on some cattle, suggesting that the mutilation takes place somewhere other than the field in which they are found.

THE USUAL SUSPECTS

UFOs

The theory that aliens (such as the Greys) are seeking to find a way to save their race through bonding with our own gene pool, strays into the arena of cattle mutilation. The aliens could somehow be using cow blood and organs in their experiments, possibly because bovine parts are similar in chemistry to their own. More optimistic theories suggest the aliens are using cows to run random radiation tests in their efforts to save us all from nuclear annihilation. This is backed up by the reports of some human abductees, who claim to have seen cows being led onboard UFOs while they themselves were suffering experimentation.. UFOs are often seen in the sky in the nights preceding cattle mutilations, and cattle have been known to become restless and stampede when a UFO is visible. This would seem to indicate that cows in general have had more experience with UFOs then they are letting on.

Black Helicopters

These mysterious craft have also been seen around cattle fields preceding mutilations, startling cattle with white hot searchlights. The prescence of such craft would lend credence to the theory that the animals are airlifted away to be mutilated, with their dead bodies simply being dropped back into the field after the process is completed.The black helicopters are often associated with secret government programs and the rise of the New World Order, and could possibly be using cattle to test powerful chemical weapons without hindrance of government guidelines.

Satanists

First thought to be responsible for the mutilations, Satanists were alleged to be using the cows as part of their profane ceremonies, so much so that they were investigated by law enforcement agencies. Nothing conclusive was ever found.

Also suspected: US Military; major chemical companies.

THE UNUSUAL SUSPECTS

Natural Predators

Despite the precision of the mutilations, despite the lack of any footprints leading up to the bodies, wolves, coyotes or a so-far-undiscovered predator is thought to be responsible.

El Chupracabra

This mythical monster from Central America, referred to as "The Goat Eater", may be responsible for cattle attacks, perhaps in an effort to expand its palate.

UNKNOWN CATTLE DISEASE

An especially virulent, and as yet undiscovered, cattle ailment has also been blamed: a virus so powerful and quick that it can remove the organs and the blood in the space of a single night, and then completely vanish from any forensic detection.

MOST CONVINCING EVIDENCE

The neatness of the organ removal, coupled with the complete exsanguination of the bodies, points towards a high degree of technological sophistication, rather than to tooth and claw. Wounds are found to be cauterized, which could be the work of laser cutters. What is interesting is that such technology was not in use when the first cattle mutilations were reported, back in the early Seventies. The blood is also removed with such attention to detail that not one drop can be found around the bodies. This would seem to indicate either military or extra-terrestrial involvement, with the parties involved slipping up only occasionally by leaving clamp marks on the animals' legs.

MOST MYSTERIOUS FACT

After the bodies are returned to their fields, they are totally shunned by other animals. There is something so fundamentally wrong with the bodies that even carrion specialists, such as crows, vultures and the like, will not touch them.

SCEPTICALLY SPEAKING

Why would aliens need cow blood in their efforts to interbreed with humanity? Wouldn't it make more sense to kidnap gorillas or other members of the ape family? Surely the suspected government collaborators in the Trilateral Commission could get them a few rhesus monkeys from research facilities, no questions asked. Cattle mutilations could be nothing more than a twisted version of the crop circle phenomenon, with well organized pranksters, equipped with medical equipment and vacuum cleaners, killing cattle in the dead of night instead of tramping down wheat in circular designs in some poor unsuspecting farmer's field.

ALIENS IN HOLLYWOOD

Have extra-terrestrial forces taken an active interest in the world's entertainment industry? It would seem reasonable that if the aliens are here, and are planning at some point to come out of the closet, then it might be better to soften us up first by preparing us for the idea. The best way to get the idea of outer-space visitors seeded casually into the public consciousness is through the use of TV and film, in dramas and documentaries, and the best place to do that from is Hollywood, the heart of the world's film industry.

Over recent years, there has been a glut of Sci-Fi films, series and documentaries dealing with certain common themes. There include "Aliens who arrive without warning and try to take over the world", as in *Independence Day* or *Space: Above And Beyond* and *V*. These are the ones who appear out of nowhere all over the world and, sooner or later, start killing people, only to be beaten off. Then there are "Aliens who arrive subtly and do mysterious things", like you'd find in *Fire In The Sky*, or *The X-Files*. It is important to note that while humans often see these aliens as frightening, they rarely do lasting harm; indeed, they're often shown to have been okay after all, just doing science things. Even in *The X-Files*, it has yet to be shown that the aliens are actually harmful. Finally, you get "Aliens who are our friends next door", like in *Men in Black*, *ET*, or *Cocoon*, aliens who arrive in limited numbers and end up proving to be rather friendly in general.

The message this is sending is clear: aliens who appear suddenly in massive numbers are evil, whereas the ones who approach subtly, in small numbers or isolated areas, are actually our friends. This is perfect propaganda for the Greys – the small, large-eyed, noseless aliens – who are here in small numbers, carrying out subtle research on us as part of their technology deal with the US government.

Once the public has been prepared sufficiently to be able to cope with the revelation of extra-terrestrial contact, the news will be broken over a period of years. The process will start with an official sighting of "something unexplainable", and end with a statement along the lines of "We've found them, here they are". In 1998, a panel of previously-sceptical world scientists announced officially that some UFO sightings did provide evidence for aliens on earth, and NASA astronauts made a sighting of something unexplainable, so it could be that the process has already begun – but is it for the good or bad of humanity?

THE STRANGE PART

It could be that the major theme park and movie companies have a significant part to play in progress of this conspiracy. One of them was rumoured to be creating a space exhibit for touring around the US. This exhibit would focus on extra-terrestrial encounters and was to generate enormous publicity for the "fact" that Roswell happened and that there was a conspiracy between the US Government and the Greys. Some feel that it would have been used to prepare the public for an impending announcement by the government on the reality of UFOs.

THE USUAL SUSPECTS

The Greys

These are the little critters so familiar to popular culture, with the roughly triangular heads, big oval eyes, and little slit mouths. They get their name from the colour of their skin. They are here for research purposes, and have been in league with the US Government ever since the Roswell crash. While the government still believes that they are interested in mutual advancement, they may well be after something far more sinister – such as humans for breeding purposes.

The US Government

Aliens may just be a way of diverting attention from the government's own experiments into human biology and psychological manipulation. By implanting the myth of the Greys into the public consciousness, State scientists are able to get up to all sorts of unpleasant research without fear of the repercussions. Their ultimate goal is, of course, a weapon that will allow world domination.

THE UNUSUAL SUSPECTS

The Nordics

Another race of aliens, conforming strangely to the old Nazi vision of the Master Race – tall, muscular, human-like beings with short blond hair – may be behind the manipulation. The Nordics are aware that the Greys are working with the government for sinister purposes, and want to help humanity, so they are trying to portray the Greys as sinister. Hollywood is an ideological battlefield, with pro-Grey and pro-Nordic films slogging it out at the box office.

MOST CONVINCING EVIDENCE

As part of the publicity launch for a proposed venture where visitors to a theme park would have a chance to view a replica alien corpse. a former chairman of a major entertainment company appeared in a documentary that suggested that the US government had an alien craft in a secret research lab (care of Roswell, natch), that this had been covered up, and that soon we would all be meeting the aliens face-to-face. The chairman and his corporation must have been fairly certain of the accuracy of their information to go on record with these startling claims.

MOST MYSTERIOUS FACT

At a private preview screening of *ET* in the White House, President Reagan is reputed to have turned to Stephen Spielberg and said: "Only three people in this entire room know how Goddamn true to life this film is."

SCEPTICALLY SPEAKING

Dr Seth Shostak of SETI, the group searching for evidence of alien civilizations in the universe, was so irritated by major entertainment corporation's allegedly unscientific and one-sided announcement of the "truth" in the promo video for a proposed venture, that he personally complained to the chairman of the company about how the corporation was misleading children. The cynical observer might also point out that while the public flock to sci-fi films and alien exhibits, profit-based organizations are going to do their very best to exploit them.

MARS MONUMENTS

Of all our sister planets in our solar system, Mars has long been thought to be the most capable of sustaining life. The Red Planet has inspired speculative writers from H. G. Wells to Ray Bradbury to weave tales of its fictional inhabitants, encouraged by what appeared to be "canals" on its surface, a sure sign of life at some point in its history. But when the NASA's Mariner Project to Mars (1965–1971) transmitted pictures of an apparently dead planet of rocks and sand, it became clear that there was no life there, and perhaps never had been.

But speculation rose again in 1971 when Mariner 9 beamed back photographs from the Elysium Quadrangle on Mars, showing pyramid-like mountains. This speculation rose to a fever pitch in 1976 when NASA's Viking Mars Mission snapped photographs of what appeared to be a city of pyramids in Mars' Cydonia region. Among those 50,000 photographs taken by the Viking probe, Frame 35A72 carried the biggest surprise: a picture of a giant face in the Martian soil – a face that was 1.2 miles wide, 1.6 miles long and 1,500 feet high. If that wasn't enough, there was also a five-sided pyramid near the face, estimated to be two miles wide.

While the world sat stunned by the image, NASA quickly downplayed any possibility that this face was anything more than just a natural rock formation, the accidental creation of wind and erosion, and most definitely not a deliberate work of art by long-dead Martian hands. As independent researchers continued their investigations, cataloging the constructs as "The City", "The Fort", "The Pyramid" and "The Face", with growing evidence that these were signs of alien life, NASA's constant dismissals began to sound more and more suspicious.

Finally, NASA, perhaps bowing to public pressure, agreed to take closer photographs of the Cydonia Region with the new Mars Observer Probe in 1993. But just as Observer was about to go into orbit around Mars, it mysteriously stopped working.

THE STRANGE PART

The Pyramid was discovered by researchers to have a precise mathematical design, (including a constant logarithmic base) and when viewed from above, strongly resembles Leonardo Da Vinci's "Man In A Squared Circle". Further, the Pyramid, the City and the Face all form the points of a perfect equilateral triangle.

THE USUAL SUSPECTS

NASA

NASA could be lying about its true feelings about the Monuments on Mars, for reasons both sinister and well-intentioned. By lying about the Observer's breakdown, NASA could continue to study the monuments without the interference of a nosy media, hoping to keep any technological discoveries for itself, thus ensuring increased Federal funding. Or it could be hoping to shield the public from knowledge that might bring panic and social discord. The panic that Orson Welles caused with his radio production of "*The War of the Worlds*" makes it easy to imagine what public reaction to Mars discoveries could be. The Associated Press uncovered proof that NASA does indeed try and obfuscate news it views potentially harmful, so the groundwork is there. NASA is also bound by its constitution to work in accordance with the government to withhold any information regarded as a threat to national security. The undeniable proof of alien life on nearby Mars would surely fall into that category.

The Superpowers – Russia and America.

The denial of the Monuments could be an attempt by these governments to stall while they prepare a media blitz to acclimatize humanity to the existence of aliens. This is borne up by Ronald Reagan's obscure references to alien life forms in at least three separate speeches.

THE UNUSUAL SUSPECTS

Martians

Perhaps there is still life on Mars, and they are less than happy with the constant attention by NASA and Russian space probes. By destroying several craft that have come too near their home, the Martians would have sent a sharp message to stay clear. In this scenario, NASA would simply be bullied into denying the Monuments in order to save mankind from more damaging reprisals.

Ancient Egyptians

Judging from the Egyptian motifs in the sphinx-like Face and Martian Pyramids, it has been suggested that ancient Egyptians travelled to Mars through a dimensional gate or with alien assistance. This would explain beliefs in Egyptian mythology about the dead needing to journey to the Land of the Dead (Mars) while being mummified (a crude interpretation of the suspended animation necessary for a long space flight). The ancient Maya are suspected for similar reasons.

MOST CONVINCING EVIDENCE

The similarities between the Face and its surrounding constructs, and the Sphinx and the Pyramids at Giza, are shocking. The shared design on both creations, from a head dress to a similar expression, coupled with the relative physical placement of the pyramids, suggests a shared time of construction. This would predate modern man, and would fit with current archeological theory leaning towards the creation of the Sphinx being long before the rise of the Egyptians. The crude face could be said to resemble Australopithicus, which would have been man's current state of evolution when the Face and Sphinx were constructed.

MOST MYSTERIOUS FACT

Carl Sagan, media celebrity and author of *Contact*, discounted the Monuments while paradoxically professing to believe in extra-terrestrial life. His close connection to NASA bears consideration on this point. Was he picked to speak out because of his reputation?

SCEPTICALLY SPEAKING

Governments lie. It's what they do. If an alien ship landed in the Tower of London, painting the ravens pink and stealing the Crown Jewels before departing for the stars with a rude sound, all it would take to cover it up would be the government telling people it was a movie promotion. And everyone would believe them. It's easier to sleep at night if you do. However, just this once, they actually might be telling the truth – so much of the conspiracy is based on unprovable conjecture given the impossibility of nipping over to Mars to check it out.

MEN IN BLACK (MIB)

If you've seen a UFO and report it the police, you can expect many things: ridicule, questions concerning your alcohol consumption, odd looks from friends, and perhaps a call from the local newspaper looking for a bit of light news for the next day's edition. But even worse than the preceding events, you may receive a visit from the dreaded Men In Black.

The Men In Black have long been associated with UFO sightings and phenomena. They are reported to appear at the homes of some UFO witnesses shortly after they've reported their sighting to the police or media, threatening them to keep quiet. Any materials found related to a UFO sighting are promptly confiscated. In some cases, they have even knocked on the doors of witnesses before they've told anyone else of what they have seen, seemingly knowing everything that has happened before the witnesses had a chance to sort it all out in their heads themselves. The Men In Black deliver their message in a variety of ways, from direct threats to roundabout hints, but their message always carries the same dark undertone: "Keep your mouth shut, or you'll regret it . . ."

The Men In Black are so called because of their sartorial colour of choice – black. Black suits, black hats and black sunglasses . . . this intimidating colour scheme extends to their cars – vintage models of Buicks, Cadillacs or Lincolns. They have been described as having complexions ranging from olive to grey to dark, with slightly slanted eyes, speaking in an almost computer-like monotone. Their age is difficult to determine, since all of them seem to be verging towards middle-aged. They move in a robot-like manner, and are perhaps best summed up in one word: "odd".

Despite their numerous appearances and incredible powers of intimidation, finding conclusive proof of the existence of the Men In Black is as slippery a task as acquiring evidence of the existence of the very UFOs they seek to protect.

THE STRANGE PART

The Men In Black definitely seem to be not of this world. Examples of this can be found in reports of MIBs disintegrating coins in their hands and inexplicably trying to sing to birds in trees. In one incident, a MIB sat down on a chair, which caused his trouser leg to rise up. There, apparently grafted to his leg, was a large green wire. In other cases, MIBs are seen crossing muddy fields, yet arrive without a single spot of mud on them. In the most vicious cold weather, they will show up wearing nothing but a thin coat, oblivious to the deadly chill.

THE USUAL SUSPECTS

Aliens

In an effort to keep their activities on Earth quiet, aliens would employ the Men In Black to suppress any media attention to their activities by intimidating eyewitnesses of UFOs into fearful silence. From their inhuman way of moving and mechanical way of speaking, the MIBs could be androids, programmed by the aliens involved in the sighting they are sent to suppress. Some people think that the Men In Black are aliens themselves, possibly Greys or another race, the Horlocks, (a reptilian race without souls). This would explain their remarkable strangeness around other human beings.

US Government

Working in conjunction with the aliens, the US Government would utilize the MIBs and their attendant oddities to suppress reports of UFOs. The Men In Black would be actors instructed to be as odd and bizarre as possible, thus adding to the already confused and emotional state of eyewitnesses. The MIB would be untraceable agents, not linked to any known governmental institution, thus allowing the "Powers That Be" to keep their hands clean of any violation of human rights.

THE UNUSUAL SUSPECTS

The Planet Sirius

The symbol of the Eye of Horus has been linked with secret societies in allegiance with the planet Sirius. This same symbol has been seen on some MIBs, and some Men In Black have said they work for an organization called "The Nation of The Third Eye". The role they play in the plans of the denizens of Sirius is unclear.

UFO Eyewitnesses

If UFO sightings are nothing more than a complete mental breakdown of the witness involved, then the appearance of the MIB could be just a continuation of the hallucination, perhaps representing the witnesses' need for punishment and correction.

MOST CONVINCING EVIDENCE

The power of the Men In Black cannot be discounted. They have been responsible for the cancellation of *Space Review*, a magazine dedicated to studying flying saucers, and have even gone as far as gassing an eyewitness during a terrifying interrogation. It is possible that incontrovertible proof of alien existence does exist, whether it is photos, videos or actual aliens, but has been suppressed by the ruthless efficiency of the MIBs. Research has discovered that the lineage of the Men In Black may go back as far as the Elizabethan age.

MOST MYSTERIOUS FACT

The vintage automobiles of the MIBs are often illuminated from within by other-worldly greenish glows, and their clothing has a "shiny" alien texture to it that doesn't correspond to any known fabric on Earth.

SCEPTICALLY SPEAKING

If there were truly aliens, with the technology capable of allowing them to travel between the stars and capable of wiping out the memories of abductees, then why would they waste their time by sending loonies in bad suits to knock on doors? Surely a good death ray would do the trick.

SECRET BASES ON THE MOON

The Moon has always held a fascination for humanity – both as a source of romantic inspiration for poets and as an astronomical curiosity for scientists. However, is it also a secret base for the Third Reich? Apparently so.

As early as 1942, the rumours go, the Nazis landed on the Moon with the aid of giant rocket saucers. These Nazi flying saucers are reported to have stood 45 metres high, contained 10 storeys of crew compartments, and had a diameter of 60 metres. Upon landing on the Moon, the Nazis quickly began building underground bases, solidifying their hold on the lunar surface while losing their grip on power in Europe below.

This colonisation continued through the Forties, with the Nazis ferrying up more people, raw materials, and robots in their giant, interplanetary, Nazi saucers. After the end of the Second World War in 1945, the Germans continued their space efforts from their Neu Schwabenland base in Earth's south polar region. This colonisation continues to this day, with the full knowledge and assistance of other world powers.

THE STRANGE PART

Where to begin? What gives this rumour credence is the growing speculation that the atmosphere on the Moon is not arid and airless – that it does contain air, water, and supports vegetation. These theories state that a spacesuit is not needed to walk on the Moon – just a pair of jeans, a pullover, and your choice of sneakers. It is argued that if there was not any moisture on the Moon, how could American astronauts leave such huge footprints on the Moon's surface?

THE USUAL SUSPECTS

The Nazi Party of Germany

Perhaps sensing the inevitability of defeat by the Allies as early as 1940, the Nazis decided to move their base of operations to a more lunar plane, thus ensuring the long-term success of the Third Reich. Knowing Hitler's love of the supernatural and the fantastic, this does not seem implausible – just typically far-fetched.

The Axis Powers of Japan and Italy

Germany kept close ties with its allies during the Second World War, sharing it's advances in weaponry with Italy and Japan. Rocket designs of

German origin were routinely tested in Italy's research facilities, and in July of 1945, at the end of the War, a German U-Boat reportedly delivered a new invention to Japanese research and development units: a spherical, wingless, flying machine. Working under German instructions, the Japanese constructed the device, without knowing how it worked. Once activated, it roared off into the sky in a burst of flame, never to be seen again. Shaken, the Japanese scientists decided to forget about the whole thing. However, in January, 1946, a Japanese-German team, numbering in the hundreds, flew to the Moon in another saucer, surviving a near crash landing.

THE UNUSUAL SUSPECTS

NASA

NASA may be lying about the truth of the Moon's atmosphere, in order to keep other countries from wanting to explore it as well, thus ensuring a monopoly on the Moon. The story goes that when the United States and Russia constructed their own moonbases in the Fifties, they were the guests of the Nazis when they landed.

Vril Society

A major mystical, secret order that was the source of much of the perverse ideology behind the early philosophies of the Nazi Party, the Vril Society claimed high-ranking members of Hitler's regime, major industrialists and powerful occultists among its ranks. It lent its name and money to the development of the mysterious Vril flying craft. It is known that some members believed the Aryan race developed from aliens who that landed in Sumeria around 4,500 BC and were viewed as gods. Could Vril have been the power behind the establishment of Nazi moonbases?

Aliens

Some conspiriologists believe that the Nazis were in league with extra-terrestrials and that the many advances they made in genetics and rocket science can be traced to a helping hand from beyond the stars. Debate rages over exactly which type of alien was assisting Hitler, but the favourites are the Aryan-looking Nordics rather than the Greys. However, given the type of experimentation on humans the Greys seem to love, and the depraved medical research performed by some of the human monsters of the Nazi regime, no one is ruling out an alliance with that particular branch of villainous space scum.

MOST CONVINCING EVIDENCE

Why are there so few photos of the dark side of the Moon? Could it be to hide the gigantic swastika banners blowing in the breeze there? In fact, it is a different sort of photograph that may actually lend some credence to the Moonbase conspiracy theories. In recent years, convincing UFO photographs, taken during World War II, clearly show Nazi-produced flying craft that look remarkably similar to the classic concept of a flying saucer. These craft – going under such fabulous names as the Vril Odin 7 and Haunebu II – were developed at secret bases similar to the famous rocket base Peenemunde. It is well-known that German scientists – many of whom ended up as founder members of NASA after the War – had planned to turn Peenemunde into a space port and springboard for moon colonisation after what they thought would be the inevitable Nazi victory against the Allies.

MOST MYSTERIOUS FACT

There have not been any lunar landings – at least in the public's eyes – in over twenty years. Is this to distract the world's attentions from the colonies – Nazi, Russian and American, with populations estimated at over 40,000 – at work there?

SCEPTICALLY SPEAKING

The drives needed to power such huge saucers – listed by conspiracy theorists as "free energy tachyon drives" – cannot help but raise eyebrows. But with the backwards-engineering associated with the salvaged technology from the Roswell crash and the lack of photos of the Moon's dark side, one can't help but wonder.

ROSWELL

It was July 3, 1947 when W W "Mac" Brazel saddled his horse and rode out to check his sheep on his sprawling New Mexico ranch. There had been a thunderstorm the night before, and Brazel felt concerned for his animals' safety. But as he rode, he came across bits of strange wreckage strewn across the land. He also discovered what appeared to be a wreck of some sort. A huge gouge had been dug into the earth, running for hundreds of feet. Mystified, Brazel retrieved a piece of the strange material that littered the ground, and showed it to a neighbour. Wondering if he was holding something from a government project or possibly a UFO, he drove into nearby Roswell to tell his story to the local sheriff, George Wilcox, and by doing so, launched one of the most enduring nesting grounds for conspiracies in the Twentieth Century.

The truth about the incident at Roswell has remained hidden behind government subterfuge and the unreliability of ageing eyewitnesses. What is undisputed is that Wilcox dutifully reported the wreckage to Intelligence Officer Major Jesse Marcel of the 509th Bomb Squad. For the next few days, the site was closed off as the US Army Air Force removed the wreckage. On July 8, 1947, a press release prepared by the USAAF reported the debris was from a "flying disc". The following day, however, the government quickly retracted the story, stating firmly that the mysterious debris was not from a flying saucer, but merely the wreckage of a crashed weather balloon.

And there the story ended, or so the US government hoped. But strange stories began to grow, gaining strength by the unusual silence from military and government leaders. Among these stories were tales that it was indeed a crashed flying saucer, that the government was covering it up; that there were actual alien bodies aboard the ship, and even that some of the aliens had survived. More than 50 years have passed since the incident at Roswell. Conspiracy theories have flourished, generating much media attention and providing an eternal burr beneath the skin of the government. Eventually the US Air Force to released a report – *The Roswell Report: Case Closed* – on June 24, 1994, in a vain attempt to shut the lid on perhaps the greatest Pandora's Box the conspiracy world has ever known.

Not surprisingly, it failed.

THE STRANGE PART

During the clean up of debris, Glenn Dennis, a mortician working in a Roswell funeral home, answered a few phone calls from the morgue at the local airfield. The Mortuary Officer there was looking for information on how to best preserve bodies that had been outside for a few days without suffering further contamination of the bodies' tissues. He also requested small, hermetically-sealed coffins.

THE USUAL SUSPECTS

The US Government

A crashed UFO would have been a major technological windfall for the US government, and it would have wanted to keep such a find as secret as possible. Some people feel that the Roswell crash led the military into trying to decipher the mystery of the downed craft, reverse-engineering the alien technology to derive new weapons and anti-gravity capabilities. President Truman allegedly visited the crash site, and may even have spoken to surviving aliens. Shortly afterwards, Truman instigated the removal of all of the UFO crash material, including that found at Roswell, into the keeping of an anonymous multinational syndicate that now controls all UFO technology.

The US government has even been accused of torturing the alien survivors of Roswell, if not killing them outright, according to a secret policy of dealing with extra-terrestrials.

Other less fantastic theories place the blame on to the military, testing secret planes built using Albert Einstein's withdrawn work on gravity field theory.

The Greys

There's no shortage of theories that state the Greys are using mankind to perfect genetic manipulations in order to save their own race. Alarmed that mankind had graduated to using nuclear weapons in 1945, (much in the same way we would if we discovered a pet hamster with an Uzi) the Greys reportedly began reconnaissance missions around military bases. This could have been the case at Roswell, where two ships may have collided or the reconnaissance craft could simply have been struck by lightning.

THE UNUSUAL SUSPECTS

The Soviets

During the raging Cold War paranoia, it was suspected that the Soviets might have perfected their offensive missile capability with pilfered Nazi technology. The Roswell debris could have been the remains of a failed missile attack.

Hollow Earth Mole Men

There is a theory that the middle of the Earth is a hollow space containing land masses, a sun and oceans. According to that theory, the race living there might have been alarmed, much like the Greys, at the rise of nuclear testing by the creatures living on the surface of the planet. Flying out of the huge polar holes that lead to the hollow part Earth, these "Mole Men" may have crashed their ship on a reconnaissance mission.

MOST CONVINCING EVIDENCE

The need for the Air Force to release a "final report" implies a guilty conscience. If there was really nothing to Roswell, why go to the trouble, expense and possible ridicule of commissioning and publishing a report? The sudden leaps forward in technology that followed the Roswell crash, especially the invention of transistors, is suspicious.

MOST MYSTERIOUS FACT

After driving out to the airfield hospital, the Roswell mortician Glenn Dennis saw several bits of wreckage carved with strange engravings. Speaking to a nurse there, she explained about the bodies, going so far as to draw him pictures on a prescription pad. A few days later, she was mysteriously assigned to a post in England, and then seemed, apparently, to drop off the face of the Earth.

SCEPTICALLY SPEAKING

The wild variations in the accounts of several "eyewitnesses" and the pure schlock of such gems as the purported Roswell alien autopsy video give this potentially devastating event all the appeal of a trailer park fun fair. It has become the Elvis sightings equivalent of alien conspiracies.

SPACE SABOTAGE

Travelling to the stars has always been a daunting task, but is it being made more difficult than it need be? Is someone – or something – doing its best to keep mankind on Earth, by sabotaging space flight after space flight? The problem has become so widespread that NASA has jokingly referred to this enigmatic and often deadly force as the "Great Galactic Ghoul". But is it the subject for levity, or something far more terrifying?

The high incidence rate of spaceflight accidents, disappearances and technological foul-ups would have crippled any other endeavour that didn't have the benefit of government funding. From simple faults such as wires burning out in satellite systems to the tragedy of the Challenger explosion, the Great Galactic Ghoul shows no national preference – both Russian and American space programs have been plagued by its disruptive hand.

Recent examples include the fiasco surrounding the Hubble telescope. Once in space, the much-vaunted telescopes was found to be far from perfect, thus making its pictures far more blurred than expected. Then an expensive repair mission was needed, but the Hubble pictures are still being discounted as more a triumph of selective filters, designed to hide the telescope's imperfections, than the groundbreaking shots the project's supporters claim them to be.

Another example was the Mars Explorer mission of 1993, which was launched to take closer pictures of the mysterious Cydonia Region of Mars. Just as the craft was entering Martian orbit, it suddenly stopped functioning. Other failures include: the Soviet Koralb 11 (blew up); Sputnik 24 (blew up): NASA's Mariner 3 (missed Mars): Mariner 8 (fell into Atlantic); the Apollo 13 mission; and the fiery deaths of the astronauts in the Space Shuttle. The list goes on and on, and is either a testament to staggering incompetence or evidence of an ongoing act of sabotage, perhaps even on a galactic scale.

THE STRANGE PART

Missions to Mars fare the worst when it comes to sabotage. One of the most disturbing was the fate of the Russian Phobos probes. Launched in

1988, the Russians sent the two probes to investigate Phobos, the smaller of Mars' two moons. The Russians were interested in the irregular orbital patterns, which led many to believe Phobos was either an artificial construction or perhaps hollow. The first probe was somehow lost on the journey from Earth. Phobos 2 made it to Mars and on its way to the small moon took photographs of a cylindrical-shaped shadow on the surface of Phobos. Shortly after that, the probe was destroyed. Its final picture, beamed back to Russia, has been declared too sensitive to release to the public. On the night that final picture was sent, orthodox Russian priests were asked to go to the Phobos 2 Control Centre in Moscow to discuss the pictures received.

THE USUAL SUSPECTS

NASA

As horrible as it sounds, especially with human lives being lost in some accidents, it is possible that a secret contingent within NASA could be sabotaging missions in order to satisfy elements in the US government that do not want the space program to discover the alien presence surrounding Earth. Corresponding dissidents would, of course, exist in the Russian space program.

Competing Contractors

The financial windfall associated with landing a lucrative government contract would prove irresistible to many businessmen. The best way to succeed in the cut-throat tendering process would be to discredit fellow competitors, using whatever means available, including sabotage. The power of the dollar, especially one from a government source, would easily overcome the sanctity of human lives in the eyes of many.

Also suspected: The FBI; MJ-12; sheer human incompetence.

UNUSUAL SUSPECTS

The Greys

For reasons of their own, it would be in the best interests of the Greys to keep Earth isolated from the rest of the Universe. If the Greys are rebellious slaves escaping from their masters and using human genetic material to reproduce and save themselves from the degradation of their cloned bodies, it simply would not do to have mankind drawing the attention of other alien races, particularly those masters.

Martians

The surprising number of incidents involving Mars missions goes beyond pure coincidence. The Monuments on Mars indicate that there was – or may still be – life on Mars, life that may wish to be left alone or that will make its presence known in its own good time. The breakdowns, disappearances and erratic behaviour of craft around the Red Planet has led some NASA employees to joke about a Great Galactic Ghoul living in between the asteroid belt and Mars. Perhaps this Ghoul is nothing more than a disgruntled Martian.

MOST CONVINCING EVIDENCE

Before the launch of the Mars Observer on September 25, 1992, NASA technicians its outer housing for a routine check. Inside, they were shocked to find the probe filled with garbage. This garbage included metal filings, dirt, paper, fibres, and plaster of Paris. Even though Hurricane Andrew had blown through the area, it was impossible for debris of this kind to have entered the probe driven by the force of the storm alone . . .

MOST MYSTERIOUS FACT

In July, 1998, the Galileo spacecraft was passing Europa, one of Jupiter's moons, when it suddenly stopped transmitting information. It has long been speculated that Europa, along with Mars, may be able to sustain life.

SCEPTICALLY SPEAKING

We are a race that has trouble programming our VCRs. Is it any wonder our spaceships keep blowing up?

REVERSE ENGINEERING

Have you ever felt that the world was moving too fast? Have you ever wondered at the amazing technological leaps mankind seems to have made in such a relatively short amount of time? Have you ever felt a pang of uneasiness when you consider that humanity went from barely being able to fly a crude airplane to walking on the moon in under 70 years?

The unprecedented way humanity's level of technology has increased in the Twentieth Century is simply baffling and may be may be signs of one of the most pervasive conspiracies of all time. While the scientific community pats itself on the back and ascribes such progress to the diligence and ingenuity of its members, a look at the "innovations" of the last few decades seem to owe more to "intervention" than ingenuity.

In fact, many theorists feel that the true force behind the current technological juggernaut is not elbow grease and endless nights burning the midnight oil, but alien assistance. For reasons unknown to the general public, governments worldwide are reverse-engineering alien technology – that is, taking apart alien artifacts to discover what makes them work, then applying that knowledge to their own ends. This knowledge is putting us light years ahead of where we should be technologically and, perhaps, even culturally. Like children playing with fire, we are not mature enough to handle it, and are in serious danger of getting burnt.

THE STRANGE PART

Most of the major leaps in technology occur after 1947 – from more powerful computers to the Apollo missions to the Moon. It was in 1947, coincidentally enough, that the US Government allegedly salvaged a crashed UFO from Roswell, New Mexico.

THE USUAL SUSPECTS

The US Government

It has long been theorized that a UFO (or UFOs) crashed near Roswell and Corona in New Mexico in 1947, and that the US Government quickly made off with the remains. Caught in the Cold War with the USSR, the US was desperate for any military advantage, and so began the slow process of reverse engineering the alien technology found aboard the crashed flying saucers. Much of this reverse engineering is thought to occur at the infamous Area 51, a secret military testing site in New Mexico.

The Greys

In exchange for being allowed to kidnap and experiment on humans with impunity, one theory has the US Government – and possibly other governments – agreeing to look the other way in exchange for alien technology. This would explain why incidents of abduction and UFO sightings are treated with ridicule by government authorities as they try to divert attention from what is truly going on – the sale of humanity for capital gain.

THE UNUSUAL SUSPECTS

Time Travellers

Time travellers could be bringing technology in the hope that leaving their futuristic gadgetry with us could change circumstances in their time, altering it to their advantage. Other theories state that the US Government has experimented with short-range time travel, and is bringing back technology from our own future. Similar theories lay the blame on dimensional travel, with advanced tech coming from more advanced versions of our own present day.

Benevolent Aliens

In preparation for an invasion force coming to Earth, benevolent aliens have provided world powers with the technology to defend themselves, as evidenced in the Star Wars satellites. The advances seen by the everyday populace – cell phones, microwaves, home computers – are merely lucrative spin-offs generated by reverse engineering of this technology and are a bonus for the government contractors that undertake secret defence work.

MOST CONVINCING EVIDENCE

Perhaps the most incriminating bit of technology, that ushered in the current wave of progress, was the transistor. This has been rumoured to be a direct result of reverse engineering work on the crashed ship at Roswell. Other more sinister applications of this alien science could be the US military's weaponry, including the B-2 stealth bomber.

MOST MYSTERIOUS FACT

Curious citizens who have reported seeing strange lights that resemble UFOs around Area 51 – and an NBC News crew that filmed something odd in the sky in 1992 – have had to contend with armed forces harassing them and confiscating cameras and video equipment. Some people have even been chased by black helicopters, which are often seen around areas of suspected alien activity.

SCEPTICALLY SPEAKING

One problem with the reverse engineering theory is that it assumes humans are brilliant. If we went back in time and handed Mr Cro Magnon a Pentium laptop, a remote control garage opener, and a Thigh Master, the reverse engineering theory would have us believe that he'd be founding MagnonSoft in ten years. Sadly, he'd probably grunt at the items and then drop them on to someone's head. Well, maybe he'd keep the Thigh Master.

M

AMELIA EARHART

She was the golden girl of the aviation set, a media celebrity, and an inspiration to women everywhere. Amelia Earhart strode into the male-dominated world of flying, setting new flight records for women, with a noble mix of courage and grace. Beloved by an America torn apart by the ravages of the Depression, Earhart was a national hero. Her sudden disappearance while trying to fly around the world in 1937 shocked the nation.

Amelia Earhart was born July 24, 1897, in Atchison, Kansas. Coming from a wealthy family, Earhart studied to be a nurse's aid in Toronto, and worked as a Voluntary Aid Detachment nurse in a military hospital during t World War I. In 1920, she moved out to California with her family. It was there she attended an aerial meet, and her love of flying was born. Quickly learning to fly, Earhart set a women's altitude record of 14,000 feet two years later, and as the years passed, her reputation as a pilot flourished.

In 1928, New York publisher George Putnam, asked her to become the first woman to cross the Atlantic on the "Friendship" flight between Great Britain and America. She agreed, setting another yet another record. She was tagged with the name "Lady Lindy", after the first pilot to cross the Atlantic, Charles Lindbergh. Earhart disliked this name, because she had merely been a passenger on the "Friendship" flight.

As if to prove herself even more, Earhart continued to set new records. In 1928, she flew across America, travelling from the Atlantic to the Pacific coast. In 1931, she set an altitude record of 14,000 feet in an autogiro. A year later, in 1932, Earhart flew across the Atlantic alone, landing in Ireland. She became the darling of the lecture tours, and was honoured by President Hoover and by Congress, becoming the first woman to receive the Distinguished Flying Cross. But her greatest challenge still lay before her – a flight around the world.

On June 1, 1937, Earhart flew out of Miami, Florida in her Electra aeroplane to circumnavigate the globe. Accompanied only by her navigator, Fred Noonan, she set out first for Puerto Rico. From South America, they flew to Africa, then to the Red Sea. By June 29, they were in New Guinea, ready for the long flight across the Pacific. They were almost home. They left New Guinea at 0:00 GMT, with the US Coast Guard ship Itasca positioned off Howland Island, near Hawaii, to provide radio contact.

She never arrived. Earhart sent a message to the Itasca at 7:42am, saying that they were unable to see the ship, and that their gas was running low. A brief message came through at 8:45am, then silence. The people of America, listening at their radios, was stunned. A shaken President Roosevelt sent out a military search party consisting of 66 aircraft and nine ships, but nothing was found. On July 18, 1937, the search was reluctantly called off. Amelia Earhart and Fred Noonan were gone.

THE STRANGE PART

In an uncharacteristic loss of control, Earhart made an error while trying to lift off from an airfield near Pearl Harbor. The undercarriage collapsed, severely damaging the plane. In what could be construed as an omen, it was the same plane she disappeared in over the Pacific.

THE USUAL SUSPECTS

Amelia Earhart

It was known that Earhart had suffered dysentery during the flight, perhaps impairing her judgement, causing her to crash. It could also have been suicide – Earhart may have been burnt-out by the constant attention and expectations of the media. Or she could have simply chosen to disappear, setting up a new life after away from the public eye. Some theories have her going to an isolated island to live peacefully with native fishermen.

The Nazi Party

It has been suggested that Earhart was on a secret mission for President Roosevelt to monitor Nazi activities around the globe. Shot down or captured by the Germans, this would explain the sizable military force Roosevelt sent out to rescue her in an attempt, perhaps, to retrieve sensitive American information or useful data on the Nazis.

THE UNUSUAL SUSPECTS

Temporal Rift

Earhart may have flown into a temporal rift, which is what the Bermuda Triangle is rumoured to be. This would explain the trouble with radio contact between the plane and Itasca, and her confusion. Perhaps her plane is simply lost in the past or the future.

THE JAPANESE
Along the lines of the Nazi Party theory, this theory sees the Japanese capturing Earhart, coercing her to take to the airwaves as the dreaded "Tokyo Rose", the female propaganda machine that was a deadly scourge to GI morale during World War II.

THE US GOVERNMENT
If Earhart was an American spy, perhaps she discovered something disturbing about her employers. In retaliation, the Air Force would have shot down her plane, then valiantly mounted a search party for public relations purposes, while ensuring that no evidence remained.

Also suspected: UFOs; sea monsters.

MOST CONVINCING EVIDENCE

Despite the largest military search for civilians ever mounted, no wreckage or material from Earhart's plane was ever found, suggesting that either Earhart was off course (with her formidable flying skills, this is doubtful), that the plane never crashed, or that it was wiped off the face of the Earth. Or perhaps the military only said they couldn't find it.

MOST MYSTERIOUS FACT

For a week after Earhart's disappearance, several radio operators on ships and aircraft heard a distress signal coming from the vicinity of Gardner Island. It's possible Earhart may have landed there, but mysteriously nothing was ever found. Sixty years later searchers believed they might have found items of Earhart's clothing, which rather begs the question: why wasn't this noticed before?

SCEPTICALLY SPEAKING

A light plane hitting the ocean at roughly 80 miles an hour would be like a car hitting a cement abutment at the same speed. Add scavengers like sharks and other hungry fish. End of mystery.

JIMMY HOFFA

The disappearance of Jimmy Hoffa has become the stuff of North American urban legend. The unknown whereabouts of the body of the ex-Teamsters union leader is a source of never ending conjecture. What is even more compelling is that while everyone is in agreement that Hoffa is indeed dead, no one has ever been arrested for killing him. The efforts of police, from Detroit detectives to the FBI, have not uncovered the killers. Their identity remains as mysterious as the final resting place of Hoffa himself.

James Riddle Hoffa was born February 14, 1913, in Brazil, Indiana. After getting a job as a warehouseman at Kroger, the grocery store chain, Hoffa joined the International Brotherhood of Teamsters, atrade union. By 1957, Hoffa had climbed the union ladder to become President of the Teamsters, a position he held until 1971.

During his tenure as President of the Teamsters, Hoffa was often linked with the Mafia and with illegal activities. Robert F Kennedy investigated Hoffa in the Fifties and Sixties, which ended up with Hoffa being convicted for jury tampering (during an earlier trial in which Hoffa was accused of receiving illegal payments from a trucking firm). In 1967, Hoffa was sentenced to eight years in a Federal prison. His sentence was commuted in 1970 by President Nixon, with a condition of parole being that Hoffa should refrain from union activities until 1980.

This didn't impress Hoffa, who began to make moves to regain control of the Teamsters. By 1975 he was on the verge of success, but this didn't fit in with the future plans of the Mafia. Having had trouble with Hoffa, La Costra Nostra hoped his successor, Frank Fitzsimmons, would prove more compliant. With the strong possibility that the stipulation barring Hoffa from union activities could be annulled, coupled with his strong loyalty base in the Teamsters, there was a chance that Hoffa could be President again. This was not something the Mafia wanted to see.

On Wednesday, July 30, 1975, Hoffa drove out to the Machus Red Fox Restaurant on Six Mile Road in Detroit, Michigan. It is known that he was due to meet someone there, but exactly who that was has never been revealed. Bearing in mind Hoffa's well-founded paranoia, it must have been someone he trusted. He was last seen alive at around 2:30pm in the restaurant's parking lot. He then disappeared, surfacing again only in public myth and speculation.

THE STRANGE PART

The final resting place of Jimmy Hoffa remains a mystery, with claims ranging from the outrageous to the macabre. One story has him buried in the depths of Lake Michigan, while perhaps the most outrageous was the one put forth by Donald "Tony the Greek" Frankos, who told Playboy magazine that Hoffa was buried beneath the end zone of the New York Giants football stadium. More plausible theories have Hoffa's body placed in the foundations of a shopping mall, while the FBI are partial to Hoffa coming to rest in a vat of bubbling zinc in a Detroit car factory.

THE USUAL SUSPECTS

The Mafia

There was potential for the Mob to make a lot of money from the Teamsters, especially with access to the massive Teamster pension funds. If an uncooperative Hoffa regained control of the Teamsters the loss of this lucrative source of income would mean a sizeable financial setback to the Mafia. There were also rumours that Hoffa had told the government about the Mob's involvement in the Teamsters, as a condition of his restriction on union involvement being lifted. This alone would merit revenge in the eyes of the Mafia.

Tony Provenzano

Hoffa had upset some members of the Mob on a more personal level, among them Tony Provenzano. "Tony Pro", as he was known, held a grudge against Hoffa from their time together in prison, and may have put a contract out on the ex-Teamsters leader. He went to great pains to establish an alibi on the day of Hoffa's disappearance.

Chuckie O'Brien

O'Brien may have been the man Hoffa expected to meet at the Red Fox, an apparently trustworthy decoy set up by the true killers. O'Brien grew up in Hoffa's home, effectively as an unofficial "adopted son", and would not have been seen by Hoffa as a threat. O'Brien, himself, came under investigation when the police heard he was alleged to be in debt to the Mafia.

Union Officials

Not wanting to lose their positions within the union if Hoffa was elected President, some union officials may have put a contract out on him.

Also suspected: Tony Giacalone: Joseph Giacalone

THE UNUSUAL SUSPECTS

The Teamsters Union

Not wanting to experience the corrupt reign of Hoffa again, members of the Teamsters may have concluded that, in the light of his popularity with the membership, there was no other route to removing him than murder.

The FBI

A long-shot theory centres around the FBI. It may not have wanted the combative Hoffa to be in control of one of the most powerful unions in the US, especially with Hoffa's grudge against law enforcement. Involvement in his disappearance would explain the Bureau's "inability" to solve the case.

MOST CONVINCING EVIDENCE

The car Chuckie O'Brien was driving the day of Hoffa's disappearance was seized by the FBI. It was a new Mercury Brougham, belonging to Joseph Giacalone. Police dogs found Hoffa's scent in the back seat, as well as evidence of his blood and skin. O'Brien blamed the blood on a fish he was inexplicably delivering to a friend.

MOST MYSTERIOUS FACT

Knowing full well how the Mafia worked, Hoffa would never have got into a car with people he didn't trust – not without putting up a fight, at least. There's a darker element of betrayal to the story: whoever killed Hoffa, or led him to be killed, were friends he trusted to be loyal.

SCEPTICALLY SPEAKING

If you run with wolves, chances are you'll get bitten. The only thing that separates this from any other Mob hit is the surprising lack of evidence buttressed by the silence of the killers. If Hoffa's body had been found, this would be nothing more than a half-forgotten footnote in the bloody history of Mob business. As Mob conspiracies go, it should be considered small-time – despite the way some conspiracy buffs view the case.

MARTIN LUTHER KING

He was a man of peace, and like most men who try to make the world a better place, his life ended violently. Dr Martin Luther King was an eloquent speaker, making moving speeches for civil rights in the Sixties, from the famous civil rights march of 200,000 people on Washington in 1963 to the more private confines of a church. He fought with dignity for a seemingly impossible goal – equal rights for all men and women, despite the colour of their skin. During the turbulent Sixties, many in America hoped King's dream would never come true.

King fought against the bigotry and ignorance in the US with weapons his enemies didn't expect – intelligence and compassion. He refused to stand down from what he believed in, angering those who felt blacks were nothing more than second-class citizens and should not dream of being anything more. King's quiet persistence raised fears of a changed status quo, from the Ku Klux Klan up to the FBI. He made powerful enemies and, in the end, they defeated him the only way they could, by silencing him forever.

Returning to Memphis in April, 1968, King booked a room at the Motel Lorraine. He had returned to hold another demonstration, disgusted that an earlier protest held in the city in March that year had collapsed into violence. He was determined that this protest would not follow the same route. During his previous stay in Memphis, he had been criticized for staying in a white-owned hotel. To prove a point, King stayed in the Motel Lorraine – owned by blacks, but in a worse area of town.

On April 4, 1968, as evening was setting over Memphis, King was shot as he stood on the second-floor balcony of the Motel Lorraine. The threat to the status quo was eliminated. James Earl Ray, a local criminal, was arrested for the murder, and was accused of shooting King from the bathroom of a nearby boarding house. Doubts, though, began to rise whether or not Ray was the true assassin.

THE STRANGE PART

James Earl Ray, who apparently had little money, somehow managed to become a world traveller following King's assassination. With his newfound wealth, he flew to Canada, England, and then Portugal. When he was arrested in London's Heathrow Airport he was preparing to fly to Belgium.

THE USUAL SUSPECTS

The FBI

It was no secret that head of the FBI, Herbert Hoover, thought King was one of the most dangerous men in America. In its attempts to remove King from his position of power, the FBI secretly taped King's alleged extra-marital activities and used the tapes in the hope of convincing King to avoid public embarrassment by committing suicide. When that failed to work, there was only one alternative . . .

The CIA

Another theory suggests that King's assassins were provided by the CIA, disguised as Memphis police. Ray was framed for the crime; government agents carried out the actual killing. This would seem to substantiated by the fact that when Ray was arrested, he was carrying several pieces of fake ID and more than one passport – documents rumoured to be the work of a CIA identities specialist.

The Ku Klux Klan

King represented everything that the Klan hates. He was a man who refuted their stereotypes of blacks and threatened their narrow view of the world. By killing King, especially in the American South, the Klan would send a message to the black community graphically illustrating what happens to blacks who rise above their Klan-appointed station in life.

THE UNUSUAL SUSPECTS

The Memphis Police

Memphis was not particularly friendly to King, and the violent end to the demonstration in March 1968 did not endear him to the city, let alone to the police force. It has been rumoured that CIA agents posed as policemen and killed King, they may not have had to – the police could have had their own grudge against the civil rights leader, racially-motivated or otherwise. It's interesting to note that the office of the Director of the Memphis Police Force was heavily populated by members of the military shortly before the killing.

Inside Members of King's Party

It has been suggested that the conspiracy to kill King extended into his own camp. Rumours have persisted that more than one of his close followers was a spy for the police or FBI and may have helped throw pursuers off the scent of the true killers by pointing to the boarding house window after King was shot.

The Mob

The Mafia was allegedly approached by the FBI to kill King, and offered a million dollars to do the job. The Mob refused, mysteriously citing the "screw ups" the FBI caused directly after the Kennedy killing, but they may have had second thoughts if the pot was sweetened.

MOST CONVINCING EVIDENCE

Despite the large number of death threats directed at the civil rights leader, the Memphis Police quietly withdrew the expected police protection surrounding King one day before he was assassinated.

MOST MYSTERIOUS FACT

The only witness to claim he actually saw Ray at the boarding house after the shooting was Charles Stephens; other witnesses claimed that Stephens was too drunk to have seen anything. His wife refuted her husband's story, insistently claiming the man she saw in the boarding house was not Ray. The authorities went with her husband's story. For her troubles, Mrs. Stephens was committed to a mental institution.

SCEPTICALLY SPEAKING

Of all the political assassinations in the Sixties, all with disturbingly clear government ties, the murder of Martin Luther King has to vie with RFK's for the title of being the most arrogant. It is staggering that it took the FBI over 15 days to publicly announce that a bundle, thrown by the assassin, belonged to James Earl Ray. Perhaps they should have announced they were giving him a "head start" as well.

DEATH OF A DREAM – ASSASSINATION OF RFK

Around midnight on June 5, 1968 there was magic in the air at the plush Ambassador Hotel in Los Angeles. Glamorous, charismatic and idealistic, Senator Robert F Kennedy had just won the California primary for the Democratic nomination for President. It looked like he was going to fulfil the dreams of many Americans and go all the way to the White House – just like his brother, John F Kennedy, had done before him.

Riding on the applause and congratulations of hotel workers, supporters and watching members of the public, RFK was being escorted by his security team through the hotel's pantry when his charge toward the presidency came to a tragic halt in a hail of gunfire. The hopes of many Americans lay dead on the tiled floor of the pantry.

After a fierce struggle that saw a small man, seemingly possessed of super-human strength, hold his own against several security guards, the apparent gunman – Sirhan Bashira Sirhan – was wrestled to the floor. His eyes were said to be enormously peaceful and the suddenly tranquil assailant was arrested. At the police station Sirhan claimed to have no memory of what had happened and showed all the symptoms of having been hypnotized.

The Los Angeles Police Department investigation into the murder quickly concluded that Sirhan was just another nut – a lone assassin in the mould of Lee Harvey Oswald. The courts agreed, Sirhan was convicted and thrown in jail. As far as officialdom was concerned, the tragic matter was over. As for the conspiracy theorists, the shooting of RFK is case that definitely deserves to be looked at again.

THE STRANGE PART

At first glance the RFK case seems open and shut: there is no denying it, Sirhan was arrested with a gun in his hand at the scene. However, that is where all simplicity in this case ends. Sirhan was in the wrong position and out of range, and could not have shot Robert Kennedy. The Senator was shot from behind, but all witnesses place Sirhan in front of him in a face-to-face position. All witnesses placed Sirhan's gun as being between one and five feet from Senator Kennedy, but the autopsy findings clearly establish that the Senator was shot from a weapon held between less than one inch and no more than three inches away from his body.

THE USUAL SUSPECTS

CIA

If, as many people suspect, the CIA had a hand in the assassination of Robert Kennedy's brother, then they would certainly have a significant reason to fear Robert becoming President. If RFK reached the White House, he would probably launch an investigation into his brother's death – and investigation that could have proved the Warren Commission was nothing more than a cleverly constructed cover-up and that the President John F Kennedy was removed in what amounted to a military coup.

Mafia

When his brother was President, Robert Kennedy had been Attorney General and led a successful war against the Mafia. Their attempts to blackmail him over his affair with Marilyn Monroe may have failed and they could have decided that if RFK gained power there would be no way to prevent him from continuing his war against them even more effectively. In this situation, the traditional Mafia solution involves bullets and hitmen.

Military Industrial Complex

Kennedy had pledged to end the war in Vietnam if he became President. Given the vast amounts of money that the American misadventure in South East Asia was generating for the Military Industrial Complex, it is certain that its members would have done anything in their power to stop his election to the White House.

THE UNUSUAL SUSPECTS

MJ-12

Also known as Majestic 12, this ultra-secret cabal of scientists, senior members of the intelligence community, and of the military is understood by some to be the force behind the conspiracy to suppress the truth about UFOs and aliens. Already suspected of putting an end to JFK, MJ-12 might have killed RFK to prevent him from exposing their dealings with the alien Greys when he became President.

Neo-Nazis

Some conspiracy theorists feel that Robert Kennedy's ability to appeal both to black and to white voters would have allowed him to heal the racial divide in America and forge a nation free of discrimination and hatred. Obviously, this is not the type of place those who cherish the Nazi philosophy want to live in, so it speculated that a cabal of neo-Nazis used their connections inside the US intelligence community to carry out the execution of the enemy they feared most.

MOST CONVINCING EVIDENCE

Bullet holes in a door frame at the crime scene, which are documented in FBI photographs, clearly show that more bullets were fired than could have come from the gun Sirhan is meant to have used to kill Kennedy. The police never disclosed that these bullets existed, even though the removal of the spent bullets by LAPD investigators was witnessed by other police personnel. The door frame in question was then destroyed by order of the court directly after Sirhan's trial concluded.

MOST MYSTERIOUS FACT

According to the psychological evaluation presented in court, Sirhan was definitely under a form of hypnosis at the time of the killing. Officially, this state was described in court as self-hypnosis, but others have doubted this. Claims have been made that the late hypnosis expert, William Bryan, boasted that he had hypnotized Sirhan. This might not amount to much if it was not for the fact that in Sirhan's diaries, which are filled full of strange automatic writing, one name is scratched into the paper over and over – DiSalvo. It might not be a coincidence that Bryan's most famous hypnotic subject was the alleged "Boston Strangler" – Albert DiSalvo.

SCEPTICALLY SPEAKING

The RFK conspiracy is probably one of the hardest to be sceptical over, but it would be dangerous to underestimate what a determined lunatic can achieve when he has easy access to a powerful handgun. Especially when scandalously bad security allows that same armed lunatic to be given a perfect opportunity to shoot someone famous.

ROBERTO CALVI

Few conspiracies can claim a more colourful cast of characters than that involved in the mysterious death of Italian banker Roberto Calvi. By the time he was discovered, in the early hours of the morning of June 18, 1982, hanging from Blackfriars Bridge in London, his story already involved the Vatican, the CIA, the KGB, an American cardinal of dubious moral virtue, a secret order within Freemasonry and mobsters with nicknames such as "The Shark" and "Frankie the Strangler". As well as boasting an incredible array of players, the conspiracy centred around Calvi can also claim to be one of the most labyrinthine plots to be investigated by conspiriologists in recent years.

Among the indisputable facts surrounding the strange affair is that Calvi was a member of P2 – a secret society within Freemasonry that had more than 950 members. Some were in the Italian Government or secret service but members could also be found amongst the ranks of Cardinals and high-powered bankers. P2 was founded by Licio Gelli – who had been a member of both the Gestapo and the Communist underground during World War II. Although originally created as part of the CIA's Gladio conspiracy to fight communist influence in Italy, P2 received funding from the KGB and CIA.

Calvi was the President of Banco Ambrosiano and through his association with fellow P2 member Archbishop "The Gorilla" Marcinkus – head of the Vatican Bank – he created hundreds of fictitious "ghost banks" through which Mafia drug money was laundered. Calvi soon became known as "God's Banker" and the vast profits he made were used to fund an amazing variety of illegal and terrorist actions on behalf of P2.

After an investigation by Italian bank examiners into why Banco Ambrosiano was about to collapse with debts of more than $1.3 billion, Calvi was charged on more than 65 counts of money-laundering, fraud, embezzlement and bribery. He fled to London with the assistance of associates in the Mafia, but within days of arriving in the city he was dead.

His widow managed to force the authorities in London to hold a second inquest into her husband's death. After hearing evidence that Calvi was planning to name those involved in the highest levels of the P2 conspiracy – including those from the Vatican – that inquest overturned the earlier verdict of suicide, declaring "cause of death unknown".

THE STRANGE PART

On the same day that Calvi was found hanging from Blackfriars Bridge, his secretary, Graziella Corrucher, is alleged to have committed suicide by leaping from the window of her office in the Banco Ambrosiano. The coincidence of two "suicides" on the same day in this case is not the only thing that has alerted investigators to the idea that there was a major conspiracy behind Calvi's death.

THE USUAL SUSPECTS

The Masons

Given that P2 was a secret society with Freemasonry, it is, perhaps, not too surprising that numerous conspiracy theorists blame the Masons for Calvi's death. The feeling that they may be involved is greatly strengthened by the Masonic symbolism of death. The threat of being hanged in a place where the tide will cover your corpse forms part of the oath you have to take when becoming a first-degree Mason. The alleged Masonic involvement has led to wild claims that the Masons within Scotland Yard helped cover-up Calvi's murder and persuade the first inquest to return a verdict of suicide.

The Mafia

Calvi was laundering Mafia drug money and members of the mob – including a London-based gangster – had helped him flee to London. If they believed he was about to commit the cardinal sin among gangsters of betraying his comrades to the police, there is little doubt that they would have enforced the Mafia vow of silence in time-honoured fashion.

THE UNUSUAL SUSPECTS

Knights Of Malta

Dating back to at least 1530, the Knights of Malta is an organisation that has counted at least two heads of the CIA among its members during recent years, as well as Licio Gelli, Michele "The Shark" Sindona and Roberto Calvi. Allegedly dedicated to fighting the Knights Templar across the centuries, their links to intelligence agencies suggests that the Knights of Malta would not be strangers to the most permanent ways of disposing of those who betray the order.

The Vatican

Golf-obsessed Paul "The Gorilla" Marcinkus, as head of the Vatican Bank was heavily involved with P2 and the embarrassing Banco Ambrosiano fiasco. Calvi's widow has suggested that if he had lived her husband would have revealed that other high-placed members of the Vatican were involved with P2. It is possible that the Vatican wanted to prevent this scandal from surfacing and therefore employed someone to prevent Calvi making his information public.

MOST CONVINCING EVIDENCE

The high number of mysterious deaths, suicides and disappearances associated with those who knew Calvi and were members of P2 alongside him provides convincing evidence that a conspiracy was at work. Founder of P2, Licio Gelli, mysteriously vanished from the Swiss prison cell he was being held in. Another close associate of Calvi and member of P2 – the Mafia lawyer Michele "The Shark" Sindona – died in his Milan cell. His last words were reported to be: "They have poisoned me."

MOST MYSTERIOUS FACT

Roberto Calvi's favourite novel was Mario Puzo's classic *The Godfather*, which Calvi would recommend to people by saying: "Read this to understand the way the world really works." Calvi's associate, Michele Sidona, was so impressed by the films based on the book that he used Mafia money to purchase a share in Paramount – the company that produced the movies. Some of those who have investigated Calvi's death have concluded that it was linked to the Masonic Grand Lodge Alpina who may have been behind the murder of Pope John Paul I – an incident referred to in *The Godfather III*.

SCEPTICALLY SPEAKING

Calvi's body has been subjected to four autopsies and has twice been exhumed from the Calvi family vault in the tiny Italian hamlet of Drezzo – without ever providing conclusive evidence that he was murdered. If Britain's top pathologists and Scotland Yard Detectives could not find evidence of foul play, is it not fair to suggest that a man facing financial ruin and a lengthy prison sentence may just have committed suicide?

GLENN MILLER

Glenn Miller was one of the biggest stars of the Golden Age of radio, thrilling millions with his orchestra and swinging hit tunes. Chattanooga Choo Choo, Little Brown Jug and his signature tune In The Mood, played across America and made Glenn Miller a household name and a "must-see" on the New York swing scene. But at the height of his popularity, in 1941, Miller apparently vanished from off the face of the Earth. Even now, when swing music exists only as retro fad and soundtrack for Gap commercials, the mystery of Miller's disappearance continues to puzzle music lovers everywhere.

Miller was born March 1, 1904 in Clarinda, Iowa. His love of music was evident very early on – he bought a trombone using money he earned from milking cows. In 1927, Miller joined up with Ben Pollack's orchestra, working alongside other musical greats such as Benny Goodman and Dick Morgan. He stayed with this band until 1935 when he formed the Glenn Miller Band. By 1939 the Glenn Miller Orchestra began smashing attendance records at its shows, and was soon the darling of the nightclub set. At their peak, Miller and his orchestra were recording four albums a week

Miller landed a residency on CBS Radio, playing three times each week, competing with the Andrews Sisters for top spot on the hit parade. By 1941, the Glenn Miller Orchestra appeared on the silver screen in the film Sun Valley Serenade which was followed by Orchestra Wives in 1942.

Miller was a patriot. Despite the success he was enjoying, he disbanded his orchestra and signed on with the US Army Air Force in 1942. Putting his musical talents to use, he formed the "Allied Band of the Expeditionary Forces" to boost the morale of servicemen. As expected, he was extremely popular. But on December 15, 1942, Miller got on a plane in England to fly to Paris for a show. He had planned to go on ahead of his band, who were to follow him the next day. His band arrived safely, but Miller was never seen again.

THE STRANGE PART

Knowing he may not be transferred to Europe during the World War II because of his celebrity, Miller fooled Army officials by applying for his transfer under his full name – Alton G Miller.

THE USUAL SUSPECTS

British Bombers

The day of Miller's ill-fated flight across the Channel, a group of British bombers was returning to England. Their original bombing mission had been called off, and the Lancaster bombers still carried their full complement of explosives. Standard procedure in such a case was to drop the unexploded bombs into the English Channel off the south coast of England, near Eastbourne. Crew members on one of the bombers claim to have seen a small Norseman airplane crash into the water where their bombs were exploding. For unknown reasons, this was never reported to the authorities.

US Intelligence

Miller may have been an American spy, who was either shot down on a secret reconnaissance mission or simply went deep undercover for the duration of the war, choosing not to announce his identity at the war's end. This theory is backed up by Miller's transfer closer to the European theatre, since surely the US Army would have seen through so simple a ruse as the one Miller allegedly employed to leave American shores.

THE UNUSUAL SUSPECTS

Glenn Miller Himself

Tired of the constant touring and lack of privacy, Miller could have followed the path allegedly walked by many pop stars since – he may have faked his own death so that he could escape the spotlight and concentrate on his music.

Paris Prostitute

This theory has Miller dying of a heart attack in a Paris brothel in 1944. Having faked his own death in 42, Miller engaged in a life of debauchery until finally expiring in the arms of a French madame. This was reported extensively in European papers, with proof allegedly coming from US Secret Service files. His death was kept hushed up in order not to demoralize American troops, or perhaps to avoid cutting down business in Paris' more seedy sections.

Also suspected: alien abduction; temporal vortex created by damage to ley lines caused by German bombings; and Nazi abduction for the personal amusement of Hitler and demoralization of America.

MOST CONVINCING EVIDENCE

Even though Miller disappeared on December 15, 1942, he was not reported missing until December 24. That would give Miller enough time to successfully hide or for responsible authorities to cover their tracks.

MOST MYSTERIOUS FACT

The plane on which Miller was a passenger had a crucial war-time mission – it was being sent to France to refill empty champagne bottles.

SCEPTICALLY SPEAKING

It is sad, but if Miller hadn't died so mysteriously, he would have become a half-forgotten name on dusty 78 records, collected only by anally-retentive jazz purists in an effort to make themselves look superior.

DOROTHY KILGALLEN

Of all the mysterious deaths that swirled around the assassination of John F Kennedy in 1963, few are as curious as that of Dorothy Kilgallen. What separates the tragic loss of Kilgallen from the scores of officially unrelated deaths connected to that fateful day in Dallas, is that Kilgallen was a popular member of the media, very much in the public eye long before her involvement in the investigation surrounding the assassination. But as her death may prove, even celebrity may not be enough to protect you if you cross the wrong people.

Kilgallen's media career began in 1931 when she signed on to work for the Hearst newspaper syndicate as a fledgling writer. At first, she was relegated to writing about "woman things", but her ambition and skill soon overrode the chauvinistic limits placed upon her, and she moved on to far meatier stories, including covering the legendary Sam Sheppard trial. (Sheppard's story was the basis for the popular Sixties television series, *The Fugitive*, as well as for the Harrison Ford movie.) Not content with simply being a top notch writer, Kilgallen moved into other media, working as a panellist on the popular television show, *What's My Line?*, as well as hosting her own radio show in New York – a programme so successful that it ran for some 20 years after first hitting the airwaves in 1945. Her popularity, buoyed by her sharp wit and intelligence, endeared her to many fans.

But it was during the trial of Jack Ruby for the murder of alleged Kennedy assassin, Lee Harvey Oswald, that Kilgallen may have taken the first steps that would lead to her death. After attending Ruby's murder trial in Dallas in 1964, Kilgallen became convinced that there was more to the story than was being reported in the press. After voicing her doubts in her daily newspaper column, *The Voice Of Broadway*, Kilgallen returned to Dallas to interview Ruby. Excited by what she learned, she returned to New York and wrote a column that linked Dallas police officer JD Tippet (thought to have been shot dead by Oswald shortly after the assassination as he tried to flee) to Jack Ruby and to Bernard Weissman – a man who was publicly known to dislike Kennedy. In her column, Kilgallen revealed that all three men had met in Ruby's strip club just one week before Kennedy was shot.

After she revealed more ominous material, the FBI launched an investigation into Kilgallen. But still she persevered, undeterred. She travelled to New Orleans, ostensibly to gather further proof of a cover up, then returned home with plans to reveal all in a book. The threat that Kilgallen posed to the forces behind Kennedy's assassination may have caused her demise. Dorothy Kilgallen was found dead in her bed on November 8, 1965. The official explanation of her death was "accidental". An autopsy found an acute mix of ethanol and barbiturates in her system, so suicide could have been the cause of death. But why would Kilgallen commit suicide when the book of her career was set to be published? Was her death truly accidental? Or was she silenced, as were so many, because of her knowledge of the truth surrounding the Kennedy assassination?

THE STRANGE PART

None of the files Kilgallen had compiled, including the transcripts of her interview with Jack Ruby and the information she gleaned in New Orleans, were ever released to the media.

THE USUAL SUSPECTS

The FBI

Herbert Hoover himself ordered the investigation into Kilgallen, determined to discover just how she was uncovering her information, especially her publication of Ruby's testimony to the Warren Commission. Before Kilgallen broadcast that to the world, it had been classified Top Secret. Kilgallen's refusal to be cowed by the FBI combined with her determination to reveal the truth behind Kennedy's death – including suspected FBI involvement – may have sealed her fate.

The Mob

Another suspect in the Kennedy assassination, the Mafia, may have silenced Kilgallen, trying to make her death look like a suicide. The Mob may have been acting on its own, or under orders from the FBI or the CIA.

Also suspected: agents of the military industrial complex; pro-Castro Cubans; and anti-Castro Cubans.

THE UNUSUAL SUSPECTS

Richard Kollmar

Kollmar, Kilgallen's husband, was in the apartment at the time of her death, and reportedly didn't find her body until noon the next day. There are rumours that she was romantically involved with singer Johnny Ray. Allegedly, she called him from a public payphone to say that she had the story of the century, but that she didn't feel comfortable talking about it over the phone. Her husband's jealousy as a result of this affair may have played a role in Kilgallen's demise.

Jealous Rivals

Kilgallen made no secret of the impact she felt her investigations would have. In the cut-throat world of journalism, where a single scoop can make or break a career, someone may have decided to trim the competition.

MOST CONVINCING EVIDENCE

Kilgallen was found in bed, apparently having died while reading a book. Her glasses – which she needed in order to read – were not on her face, nor within her reach. The book was one she had told friends she had already finished reading, and she was still wearing make up, which Kilgallen always removed before retiring.

MOST MYSTERIOUS FACT

Shortly after Kilgallen's death, Mrs Earl T Smith, a close friend of Kilgallen, also died mysteriously.

SCEPTICALLY SPEAKING

It's okay to report the truth – just make sure it's the approved truth.

THE DISAPPEARANCE OF PHILIP TAYLOR KRAMER

Rock stars who vanish or stage their own deaths are as much a part of the staple diet of conspiriologists as aliens, Masons and the CIA. Therefore, it should not come as much of a surprise that when the former bassist of American rock band Iron Butterfly joined the ranks of the missing, conspiracy theories about his disappearance would quickly start to circulate.

However, Philip Taylor Kramer was not your average rock star and his disappearance certainly ranks as a lot more mysterious than your average conspiracy revolving around a musician who decides to "do an Elvis". For starters, as well as being a former rock musician in a successful Seventies act, Kramer was a mathematical and computer genius who had worked for the US Government on projects related to developing nuclear missile technology.

In the days and weeks before his disappearance on the morning of February 12, 1995, Kramer was very excited about the prospect of making a major technological breakthrough. Reliable sources have reported that the innovation was either in the field of fractal data compression or faster-than-light communication – two areas in which a major advance would have radically changed the face of science and commerce.

On the morning he vanished, Kramer set out in his van to pick up an associate from Los Angeles International Airport. The last person to see him was his father-in-law – a cancer patient at a medical centre – with whom, it is alleged, Kramer left a small device. An unpaid airport parking charge proves that he arrived at the airport and spent 45 minutes there, but he did not pick up the person he went to meet. Before driving into oblivion he made a series of odd phone calls to family and friends. His last call was to an emergency operator and finished with the words: "I'm going to kill myself and, I want everyone to know, OJ Simpson is innocent, they did it."

Taylor was carrying credit cards, a bank card and a mobile phone, none of which have been used since February 12, 1995, when he and his van pulled a perfect vanishing act. Unlike Elvis, he has never been spotted flipping burgers or serving shakes – a singular and significant fact in the disappeared-rock-star-conspiracy field.

THE STRANGE PART

Ron Bushy, co-founder of Iron Butterfly and a close friend of Kramer's, was one of the last people to speak to him on the day he vanished. Shortly afterward, he said: "I honestly believe that he has been abducted by our government or an agency that is part of it or maybe a foreign government or a company." The reason for this was that the mathematical breakthrough Kramer was working on could in theory allow for the nearly instantaneous transmission of matter. As Bushy also said: "We are talking "Beam me up Scotty' time!"

THE USUAL SUSPECTS

NSA

The National Security Agency has a keen interest in any development in computing that has the potential to change the nature of communications technology or affect the NSA's ability to crack codes. If Kramer had found a method of perfecting fractal compression it could have meant that even the NSA's most powerful super-computers would not have been able to defeat the likely advance in cryptography the discovery would have offered. Faced by possibility of unbeatable computer security, the NSA may have decided to spirit Kramer away before a foreign government did.

The Computer Corporations

If Kramer had made the breakthrough on Fractal Compression it would have revolutionized the computing industry – making redundant all of the current software, modem and chip development in which the major computer corporations have invested hundreds of billions of dollars. Faced by financial ruin, it is possible that some of the major players in this sector may have felt it necessary to prevent Kramer from revealing the nature of his breakthrough.

THE UNUSUAL SUSPECTS

Philip Taylor Kramer

All rock stars who disappear seem to be suspected of faking their own deaths and Kramer is no exception. Some conspiracy buffs feel he went to ground to avoid financial problems while others think it is more likely that he has gone into hiding to protect his family and to be able to work on his innovative theories without interference from the government or anyone else.

Aliens

Given that Kramer's ideas seem capable of fulfilling many of the prophecies of science-fiction, it is not too surprising to find that there is a section of the conspiracy community that is convinced that Little Grey Men rather than human forces spirited Kramer away. After all, they reason, if Kramer had been able to pass on the secrets of his breakthrough, their superiority in the technology stakes would have been compromized.

MOST CONVINCING EVIDENCE

James A Traficant Jr, the Representative for Ohio, has made two attempts to get the FBI to investigate the case on the grounds that the nuclear technology knowledge that Kramer possessed make his disappearance a matter of national security. Usually it does not take a politician to point out to the FBI and the intelligence services that the disappearance of a major scientist with close ties to the defence industry is worthy of investigation – especially when he designed the guidance systems for the majority of America's nuclear missiles. It is significant that the authorities' interest in Kramer's disappearance has been minimal, verging on the negligent.

MOST MYSTERIOUS FACT

In the last few days before he vanished, Kramer told his wife Jennifer: "Honey, we are going to have to live behind walls. Honey, people are going to want to get at me." His paranoia seems to have been grounded in reality. It is reported by his father Raymond Kramer – a fellow scientist – that their laboratory was broken into more than once and that the intruders unsuccessfully attempted to breach the security of their computer system to gain access to data on Philip's "breakthrough".

SCEPTICALLY SPEAKING

By all accounts, in the weeks before he vanished, Kramer was a man under stress and short on sleep – two elements that may have plunged him into a state in which he could have wandered off without any memory of who he was. One or two black-hearted sceptics have commented that a man who is crazy enough to believe OJ is innocent is, without a doubt, sufficiently mentally troubled to attempt suicide.

LORD LUCAN

One of the most mysterious vanishing acts ever accomplished by a fugitive was the disappearance of Richard Bingham, the Seventh Earl of Lucan. "Lucky" Lucan was a member of the aristocracy and a professional gambler, a man with a well-known taste for the easy life. A popular socialite in well-to-do London circles, Lucan's expensive hobbies had left him heavily in debt. He had become estranged from his wife, and the couple were in the process of fighting a bitter custody struggle over their three children.

On the night of November 7, 1974, the 29-year-old nanny who looked after Lucan's children, Sandra Rivett, was brutally murdered in the family's home with a length of lead piping. When Lady Veronica Lucan went to investigate, she too was attacked and badly injured. The alarm was raised when she staggered into a pub close to the house, covered in blood, declaring that her husband had murdered the nanny.

Penniless and without his passport, Lord Lucan borrowed a friend's car that same night, left a letter saying that he was innocent, and vanished. The bloodstained car was later retrieved at Newhaven Docks. The last sighting of Lucan himself had been some 18 miles away, in the town of Uckfield. Although he has been declared financially dead, Lucan is still legally marked as alive, and the warrant for his arrest is still active. This means that Lucan's son is unable to inherit his father's seat in the House of Lords, and a case has been made to have the missing Peer finally declared dead.

THE STRANGE PART

Much like Elvis, Lucan is regularly sighted around the world. Reports have placed him walking on mountain slopes in Sicily and in permanent residence in Southern Africa. Scotland Yard still investigate supposed sightings of the Earl, and has had as many as 70 different sighting reports under investigation at once. If he is still alive and in hiding, Lucan would be in his sixties, having been penniless and on the run for a quarter of a century.

THE USUAL SUSPECTS

LORD LUCAN – DEAD

The most common theory is that the Earl is dead, having committed suicide in despair and remorse after bungling his attempt to kill his wife. He drove to the English coast, and then swam out into the English Channel to drown.

LORD LUCAN – ALIVE

In this version, Lucan was helped out of the county by a rich friend – possibly the now-deceased Sir James Goldsmith – who flew him from the

South of England to France in a private plane. The benefactor also provided money and clothing. Once within Europe, it would have been relatively simple to move around without a passport – border controls are often lax – and slowly make his way down to Botswana, where he now lives. Funded by people who would rather not see the peerage dragged into disrepute by a trial, he lives in modest comfort.

THE UNUSUAL SUSPECTS

Freemasons

While it is uncertain whether or not Lucan was a Freemason, many members of the nobility are part of the ancient fraternity. Uncertain of Lucan's guilt but desperate to prevent a hugely-embarrassing trial, the Masons helped "Lucky" out of the country, and set him up with a peaceful life somewhere out of the way.

Meonia

Lucan may have been a member of the mysterious organisation dedicated to preserving the bloodline of certain aristocratic British families and ensuring the continuation of Britain through mystic means. If one of their own was in trouble, the secret order would have seen it as their sacred duty to protect him from the threat of prison.

MOST CONVINCING EVIDENCE

Despite the family attempt to get Lucan ruled as legally dead, the English police are not convinced. Scotland Yard has announced a suspicion that Lucan is living in Botswana in Southern Africa, and that the frequent trips made by his children to the area has been observed. Lack of funds made the investigation difficult to carry out. Lucan's children, now in their thirties, dismissed the suggestion as absurd.

MOST MYSTERIOUS FACT

Retired Detective Superintendent Alec Edwards, of Scotland Yard, has been quoted in the national press as saying: "There were influential people who would rather he [Lucan] wasn't found . . . You could imagine the counter-publicity that could generate."

SCEPTICALLY SPEAKING

After all this time, Lucan has become something of a tragic-heroic figure. He could make a fortune by revealing himself and telling his story. In fact, he has everything to gain by revealing himself, and his theoretical backers, if they exist, have little to lose in a time so rife with scandals. If the Earl could be exonerated of the charges, he would become a genuine British hero. There's simply not enough scandal left to make hiding him worthwhile any more.

LEE HARVEY OSWALD

The history books tell us that on November 22, 1963, in Dallas, Texas, Lee Harvey Oswald shot and killed John F Kennedy from a window in the Texas School Book Depository. The history books go on to recount that roughly 45 minutes later, Oswald then shot and killed Officer JD Tippit of the Dallas Police Force, and was later apprehended in a movie theatre. Two days later, Oswald was himself shot by Jack Ruby, apparently outraged at the murder of the President. According to the Warren Commission, which investigated the assassination, there the story ends – the late Oswald was the lone gunman, there was no conspiracy, case closed.

However, conspiracy theories continue to swirl around the incidents of that fateful day in Dallas, suggesting that the least probable theory is that Oswald acted alone. There also remains the mystery of Oswald himself. Even the most cursory of glances at him and his alleged activities around Dallas in the days preceding the assassination, is rife with inconsistencies and bizarre elements worthy of a conspiracy all on their own.

On October 26, 1957, Oswald joined the Marines in San Diego, California. While he was in the Marines he became enamoured of Russia and its politics. After a dishonourable discharge on September 13, 1960, he announced he was going to renounce his American citizenship and move to the USSR. He arrived in Moscow a little more than a month later. Traveling to Minsk, he married Marina, the daughter of a KGB Colonel. The glorious life in Russia apparently soured and Oswald returned to the US with his wife in 1962. Back in the US, Oswald's drifted from one job to another and was suspected of an assassination attempt on Major General Edwin Walker on April 10, 1963 in Dallas.

His political views got him arrested in New Orleans on August 9 that same year when he was involved in a fight with angry Cubans while passing out "Fair Play for Cubans" pamphlets. A friend of his wife – a Russian exile with CIA connections – arranged for him to get an interview back in Dallas at the Texas School Book Depository. Lying about his past, Oswald was hired on October 15, 1963. The rest, as the books tell us, is history. Or is it?

THE STRANGE PART

There are conflicting reports, of Oswald's activities before the Kennedy assassination. A Texas car salesman, Albert Guy Bogard, reported that Oswald took a car for a test-drive before the shooting, remarking about a large amount of money he would be getting soon – yet Oswald never had a driver's license. Another sighting has Oswald showing off at a Dallas area rifle range, expertly shooting the bulls-eyes in other patrons' targets – this, despite Oswald's inferior record as a marksman while in the Marines. Maybe these "Oswalds" were actors hired by the true parties behind the assassination to ensure the real Oswald would pay for the crime.

THE USUAL SUSPECTS

The Mafia

Jack Ruby originally claimed he shot Oswald to spare Jackie Kennedy the pain of a public trial. However, plenty of evidence abounds that Ruby was a member of the Mob. With several of the most believable conspiracy theories surrounding the assassination of JFK involving the Mafia, it probably is not coincidence that Ruby took out Oswald. Ruby killed Oswald to prevent the Mafia's role in the President's death being exposed.

THE FBI AND THE CIA

Even before Oswald left for the USSR, he was under FBI scrutiny. The reason for his dishonourable discharge from the Marines – for wanting to be a Russian – was public knowledge, so the CIA would have the perfect fall guy: a lone assassin working for the dreaded Russians, which would play extremely well with the media.

THE UNUSUAL SUSPECTS

KGB

The KGB knew that if Oswald was ever brought before a court, his communist background and links to the KGB would emerge. If this happened, the Soviets would be suspected of organizing the Kennedy shooting, so they employed Ruby to ensure Oswald never went on trial.

MOST CONVINCING EVIDENCE

If Oswald had killed Kennedy for political reasons, then why did he never proudly take credit? Instead, he insisted until his death that he had been set up – hardly the actions of a fanatic. His murder by Jack Ruby – preventing the truth from ever coming to light – was far too convenient.

MOST MYSTERIOUS FACT

The CIA reportedly experimented with LSD on troops in Atsugi, Japan, as part of their mind-control tests in 1957. Oswald was serving with the Marines there at the time.

SCEPTICALLY SPEAKING

Of course Oswald shot Kennedy and therefore it is not impossible that an outraged American might want to take revenge. If you listen to some of the conspiracy theories about him you might also believe Oswald sunk the Titanic and stole your newspaper this morning.

H

ANASTASIA

It was the perfect life of a fairy tale princess, brought to a tragic end by the blood thirst of revolution. Anastasia Romanov lived in an elegant world of finery and privilege, basking in the dying golden light of the legendary Russian dynasty. But political fires were being kindled by Bolshevik philosophies that demanded change. The absolute rule of the tsars, compounded by the inability of Anastasia's father, Tsar Nicholas, to rule a changing world, prompted revolution. She and her family had to pay the ultimate price – a cold execution at the hands of Bolshevik soldiers.

But did Anastasia die with the rest of her family, as ordered by Vladimir Lenin? Or did she somehow escape the claws of the ruthless Bolshevik leader, to be the final survivor of the Romanov dynasty?

Born June 5, 1901, into the grand opulence of the Petrodvoretz Palace on the outskirts of St. Petersburg, Anastasia grew into a playful and intelligent girl, never afraid to display her cutting wit on the political lackeys who populated her father's dinner table. Her nickname, not surprisingly, was "shvibzik", which was Russian for "imp". But the idyllic life inside the palaces did not reflect the harder world outside.

The Bolshevik threat, spearheaded by Lenin, gained strength among the people and Tsar Nicholas helped Lenin's cause by ordering soldiers to fire on protestors. Finally in 1917 the Russian Revolution swept the Tsar from the throne, and he and his family were exiled.

Nicholas, his wife Alexandra, their daughters Tatiana, Olga, Anastasia and Marie, along with the sickly son Alexis, were sent to live in a house in Ekaterinburg, deep in Siberia, where they lived rather comfortably, well out of Lenin's way. But a paranoid Lenin, fearing a return of the old Tsars, ordered the execution of the Romanovs.

Around midnight on July 16-17, 1918, soldiers told the Romanovs they were being moved to a new prison, and they were to gather for a group photograph before they left. Once the family was standing together, the soldiers opened fire, apparently killing them all. Those that survived the initial volley of bullets were stabbed to death by the soldiers' bayonets.

Years later someone appeared claiming to be Anastasia, with an incredible story of escape from certain death. Was it truly her? How could it be?

THE STRANGE PART

In 1991, 73 years after the Romanov execution, the remains of the family were dug up in Siberia, partly to give them a proper burial, and partly as an act of contrition by the Russian government. The bodies of both Anastasia and her brother, Alexis, were not found.

THE USUAL SUSPECTS

Vladimir Lenin

By ordering the cold blooded murder of the now politically impotent Romanov family, Lenin foreshadowed the paranoia and insecurity that would become the trademark of the Communist regime. Lenin undoubtedly feared them as powerful symbols, since his own revolution owed much of its success to the strength of symbols in propaganda. He feared his own weapon being used against him. Today the Romanovs are remembered fondly as the tragic victims of a madman's paranoia. It's interesting to note that Lenin's soldiers were so rigid in obeying Lenin's orders they felt the need to shoot Anastasia's dog as well.

Anna Anderson

In 1922, a Polish woman working in a factory in Germany announced that she was the long-lost Anastasia, saying she escaped the executions in Siberia because she had gems sewn into her clothing, and that a kindly German soldier had brought her to safety. This claim was quickly denied by the woman's own grandmother, and the fact that the woman had spent time in an insane asylum hampered her credibility.

Even so, old associates of Anastasia who met this Polish woman were shaken by the physical similarities, which ranged from old body scars, similar ear formations, and even identical handwriting. Her eyes were also the brilliant shining blue characteristic of the Russian royal family. She also possessed uncannily detailed knowledge of the Romanovs. When a German court felt she could not fully prove her identity, she moved to New York, changing her name to Anna Anderson. She died in 1984.

THE UNUSUAL SUSPECTS

The British Monarchy

George V ruled Great Britain at the time of the murders. A member of the House of Windsor, the House originated from the House of Sachsen-Coburg and Gotha, of Germanic descent. With possible links to the Bavarian Illuminati (the Duke of Gotha was a member), the British Crown may have played a role following Illuminati orders. With heavy Illuminati presence in the Russian Revolution, and the House of Windsor's strong ties in the Scandinavian region, this wouldn't be surprising, would be distateful.

Also suspected: fellow Romanovs; members of the Russian aristocracy; Bavarian Illuminati.

MOST CONVINCING EVIDENCE

The similarities between Anna and Anastasia were plentiful, from congenital defects to childhood scars. A forensic specialist, Dr Moritz Furtmayer, compared photographs of Anna and Anastasia in 1977. He discovered 17 identical tissue formation points in their ears. Under German law, only 12 are needed to confirm a person's identity.

MOST MYSTERIOUS FACT

After murdering the Romanovs, the Bolshevik soldiers counted the bodies and were horrified to discover that they were missing one.

SCEPTICALLY SPEAKING

DNA testing confirmed that Anna Anderson was not Anastasia, which remains the final word on the matter. Through the hazy eye of history, the Romanovs are now seen to be the last vestiges of a golden age, and to imagine that some part of that magic escaped an assassin's bullet is appealing. The mysterious allure of the story of Anastasia's supposed escape has become a favourite of mystery writers and romantics everywhere, even ending up as a highly-modified animated film for children. But romance and realism rarely meet. Anastasia perished in a flash of gunfire, another young life snuffed out in the name of politics.

THE HOLY GRAIL

The legends of King Arthur and the Holy Grail, the cup that Christ drank from at the last supper, were largely set into their current forms in the Fourteenth Century, a time when French and German romantic poets were busy writing epic sagas based on common stories.

King Arthur and his round table of holy knights are a historical pastiche that misses the truth – the kind of plate armour that Arthur's knights are associated with was not invented until centuries after his time. Similarly, the idea of a glowing golden chalice humming with the divine power to heal the land and raise the dead, is actually a complete distraction from the true Grail.

The idea of the Holy Grail comes from a deliberate misinterpretation of the root term "Sangreal" on the part of the Catholic church. Splitting the term into "San Greal", and from there to "San Graal", or "Saint Grail", the derivation of the idea of the Holy Grail is plain. However, if the word is split into "Sang Real", the true Latin meaning becomes clear – the Blood Royal. The Holy Grail is nothing more and nothing less that the royal line of descent founded by Jesus Christ.

Jesus was not born of a virgin, but in the normal manner. He was rescued from the cross by friends and was married to Mary Magdalene. They had three children, a daughter and two sons, and they settled in France in exile, far from the reach of the Romans. When Joseph of Arimathea arrived in England, legend says that he brought the Grail with him, rather than a cup, he brought his nephew Justus, Jesus's oldest son. Over the years, the exiled Hebrew royal family bred with local nobles, and the line became the Merovingian Kings of France. Even King Arthur's name is likely to be a nickname – Artos means the Bear. The real Arthur was a warlord related to the Merovingians – the Bear King, inheritor of the Blood Royal.

Through the centuries, the Holy Grail – the Blood of Christ – passed through the Merovingians to the Templars and the Crusaders, and into some of the royal bloodlines of Feudal Europe from the French Stuarts to the Scottish Sinclairs and certain noble houses of Greece and Italy. Interestingly, the Grail heritage is not part of the Germanic House of Saxe Coburg-Gotha, reputedly now known as the Windsors, the royal family of Great Britain . . .

THE STRANGE PART

It is alleged that the name Britain comes from the term B'rith-ain, or The Land of the Covenant. Further more, the idea of Merrie England is in fact derived from St Mary the Gypsy, Mary Jacob, who came to Europe with Mary Magdalene. She had a widespread cult in early Europe, and is best known in the form of Maid Marian and the Merrie Men of Robin Hood. These little known "facts" only go to show the extent of the Holy Bloodline in Britain.

THE USUAL SUSPECTS

Meonia

The secret mystical order charged with protecting the fate of the British Isles knew all about the truth behind the Grail and manipulated history and Royal dynasties accordingly. It is open to conjecture if the organisation had any involvement with Princess Diana's marriage into the Windsor clan – though Diana did have ancestral links to the Meonia organisation.

Priory of Sion

This French version of Meonia is a more surreal organisation. If they exist, they are almost certainly closely involved in the Holy Grail conspiracy.

The Catholic Church

There is no doubt that the Church has the most to lose if the Holy Grail ever became widely recognized as the line of Christ. By encouraging the romantic interpretations of the Holy Grail, and by constantly suggesting the idea of Jesus' birth and death being holy miracles, they safeguard their authority as derived from Godly favour. If it were ever known that the Christian faith was founded on a priestly hijacking of the power of the Hebrew kings, it would end in disaster for the Church.

THE UNUSUAL SUSPECTS

The Atlanteans

It has been suggested that Jesus was not of the line of David at all, but actually the descendant of the high priests of Atlantis. Jesus' revolutionary messages of love and acceptance for fellow humans is a direct throwback to his Atlantean teachings. His bloodline is holy because the people of Atlantis were genetically and spiritually advanced to a level never attained before or since, and the people who retain that heritage are still gifted with unusual powers and intelligence – *Homo Superior*. Frightened by the implications, jealous *Homo Sapiens* priests and rulers killed Jesus, and the knowledge that the Holy Grail is the *Homo Superior* mutation has been suppressed ever since.

MOST CONVINCING EVIDENCE

The long bloodlines in the Bible are there to prove Jesus' lineage as a royal descendant of David. The book of Matthew actually gives a line of descent from David the King down to Jacob being the father of Joseph, husband of Mary. The title of Christ denotes Jesus' royal status, and we should think of him properly as King Jesus. The whole concept of immaculate conception and divine succession was invented by the Catholic church in the Fourth Century AD to justify their power, stealing the authority of the royal line for themselves, by the "Grace of God".

MOST MYSTERIOUS FACT

Although the House of Windsor does not share in the Grail heritage, Princess Diana was supposedly descended from the royal House of Stewart. Although it is generally said that Queen Elizabeth II is royal and Diana married into the family, in fact the truth was just the opposite; it was Diana who was descended from Jesus Christ.

SCEPTICALLY SPEAKING

If the Holy Grail is the *Homo Superior* mutation, and if it was passed into the royal families of Europe, there would be thousands of people worldwide with the gene, and any actual differences would have been noticed by medical science.

HITLER

Nobody is in any doubt that Adolf Hitler, leader of the Nazi party, was one of the most evil and dangerous men to have come to power in all of human history. The legacy of death and suffering that he left behind him is staggering. Approximately six million Jews were slaughtered, primarily in death camps, as part of his "Final Solution" – almost two thirds of their world population. It is also important to remember he murdered a large proportion of Europe's population of gypsies, Seventh Day Adventists, Jehovah's Witnesses and Socialists.

During World War II, some sixty million soldiers were mobilized across Europe, the Americas, Russia and the Far East. Almost a third of them were killed. The total death toll for the war is estimated around 52 million people – 18 million soldiers, 16 million civilians killed in military action, and 18 million people murdered in the death camps. Hitler lurked behind all this death, the lynch-pin of the entire war. These facts are horrific enough that surely no conspiracy can compete – but there are suggestions that Hitler's ultimate goal was not to unite Europe under his rule at all, but simply to cause widespread death and destruction to appease his Satanic masters.

The Brotherhood of Death is the name given to a rumoured worldwide coalition of primarily Satanic organisations. Each organisation has, as its logo, the skull and two crossed bones, the emblem we most commonly associate with pirates. The German branch of the Brotherhood of Death was allegedly the *Thule Gesellschaft*, or Thule Society. Centred on a semi-mythical land from ancient times, the legend of Thule shares certain features with that of Atlantis. The land of Thule is supposed to have been the cradle of the Aryan race.

In 1919, disgusted by the way that the German government had "thrown away" World War I, Hitler joined the Thule Society, which at that time was led by Dietrich Eckhardt. When the Brotherhood of Death began their ambitious plan to reshape society in a more controllable form, their end goal was the surveillance and monitoring of an increasingly isolated and malleable population. Europe was identified as a potential flash-point for a useful war. Germany, having just lost a major war, was ripe for destabilisation, and Hitler, whom Eckhardt believed to be the Antichrist, was chosen as the obvious leader to initiate the gigantic conflict and death required. This would scar the human psyche so deeply that people would become paranoid and withdrawn, and once isolated they could be manipulated into giving up autonomy to the Brotherhood and its evil masters.

The Brotherhood of Death believed firmly that contact with ancient powers of spiritual evil – the Devil – was not only attainable but very desirable, and that by following the dictates of their master, they could achieve great earthly power. They used sexual perversions and practices to fuel their magical operations, which made their spells and rituals phenomenally powerful and opened channels of communication to the forces of evil.

By tapping the power of evil, the Thule Society was able to manipulate the consciousness of the German people and bring the Nazi party to prominence. By appealing to the basic human psychological programs of hatred, fear and greed, the Nazi party was able to divert the current of evil into the minds of usually decent people, and foster the political climate that led to Hitler's rise. Once he was in power, it was frighteningly simple to steer the world into a gigantic war, with the death camps providing the incredible amounts of magical energy needed to change human consciousness for ever.

THE STRANGE PART

Eckhardt's final act was said to be Hitler's initiation through an astonishingly sadistic black magic ritual which left the Nazi leader impotent. From then on, Hitler was forced to seek sexual fulfilment through sadomasochistic release, and it was this blow that forced him into beoming the greatest monster we have seen this century.

THE USUAL SUSPECTS

Satan

If ancient powers of spiritual evil are behind the Brotherhood of Death and the *Thule Gesellschaft*, then that rather implies the Devil. Given the Devil's well-known propensity for misdirection, it seems likely that in the event that his plans succeed, the Brotherhood will lose out along with everyone else.

Bavarian Illuminati

This age-old German secret society is often thought to control everyone from the Mafia to the Knights Templar. The Illuminati were the power behind many occult orders in pre-war Germany and may have been Hitler's ultimate puppet-master. It is recorded that Heinrich Himmler was closely involved with societies linked to the Illuminati.

THE UNUSUAL SUSPECTS

The Elders of Zion

The least credible and perhaps most offensive theory is that the Elders of Zion were responsible for the actions of the Nazi party. By causing a massive depopulation of Jews, the England-based group would have less difficulty in claiming to be the inheritors of Moses' wisdom. The horrors of the Holocaust would also breed sympathy for all causes even tangentially related to Judaism.

MOST CONVINCING EVIDENCE

On his deathbed, Dietrich Eckhardt is said to have announced: "Follow Hitler; he will dance, but it is I who have called the tune. I have initiated him into the Secret Doctrine, opened his centres of vision, and given him the means to communicate with the powers." Given that society continues to get more fragmented, violent, and subjugated by television, despite the fact that it is in no-one's interests, not even those of the world governments, the Brotherhood of Death could be said to be doing a particularly effective job.

MOST MYSTERIOUS FACT

The USA too has a society with the logo of the Brotherhood of Death – Yale's Skull and Bones society, rumoured to have been started in the 1800s as a US lodge of a German university-based society. President Bush was belonged to this group, as did many important figures in American society and political circles.

SCEPTICALLY SPEAKING

To dismiss the holocaust and the evils of the Nazi empire as a simple tool for generating magical energy seems somewhat offensive to those who died. In addition, the circumstances surrounding the rise of the Nazi party are well understood in sociological terms – tragic, but hardly mysterious.

THE MAN IN THE IRON MASK

The mystery of the Man in the Iron Mask has been a focal point for doe-eyed romantics and for serious historians since the Seventeenth Century, generating countless theories about the identity of the masked prisoner. The interest continues even to this day, hence the recent film, *The Man In The Iron Mask*, starring teen heartthrob Leonardo Di Caprio. But the world is still no closer to discovering who this tragic figure was and, as the years pass, the chances of discovering his (or her) true identity continues to fade.

Little is known about the prisoner. What little information that exists in French official documents paints a deliberately sketchy picture: he was arrested in 1669, and was imprisoned first in Pignerol, a fortress high in the French Alps. He was transferred in 1681 to Exiles, which lay close to Pignerol, and in 1687 he was moved yet again to the southern French coastal island of Saint Marguerite. His stay on the island lasted 11 years until he was sent to the Bastille in Paris. Finally, the prisoner died in 1703, an undoubtedly welcome release.

Throughout his entire imprisonment, there were reportedly only two instances of witnesses who were not prison officials actually seeing the prisoner. During his move from Exiles to Saint Marguerite, the prisoner was seen wearing a steel mask. With the move to the Bastille, this cumbersome disguise was replaced with a more humane mask of black velvet. It has also been discovered, through official correspondence between a government minister and Saint Mars, (the prisoner's jailer) that the prisoner was not to be allowed to communicate with anyone, by spoken or by written word. If he did, he was to be executed on the spot.

What terrible secret could this man have possessed that demanded such secrecy? Historians have wondered why he was even kept alive: if the knowledge he held was of such danger to the King and government, wouldn't it have been politically safer simply to kill him? And why such a concern over people seeing his face? Did he resemble someone well-known to the French populace, which would have to make him very famous indeed, bearing in mind the primitive state of print media during the Seventeenth Century? Once again, simply killing him – an option not in disuse in the French court of the time – would have made more sense.

The mystery of the Man in the Iron Mask is as unfathomable now as it was three hundred years ago. What is known is that a man paid a horrible price for an alleged crime – or deadly secret – that history can only guess at.

THE STRANGE PART

Saint Mars, the man appointed to jail the mysterious prisoner, held that position from the first day of his incarceration until the prisoner breathed his last in 1703. With the turnstile approach to political appointments of the day, this constancy is intriguing.

THE USUAL SUSPECTS

Louis XIV

Many fingers point towards the King of France. The masked prisoner could have been the twin brother of Louis, rumoured to have been conceived first but unfortunately born last. He didn't know his own true identity and, to clear up any messy succession issues, Louis imprisoned his brother. Other theories suggest that he could have been an elder brother, the result of an extramarital affair of Louis' mother. Another theory states that the prisoner was a doctor who attended Louis XIII's autopsy, who unfortunately discovered the late king incapable of siring children, thus endangering Louis XIV's right to the throne. Following the same thread, the prisoner could have been the true father of Louis XIV, recruited on account of Louis III's inability in the bedroom.

Count Antonio Matthioli

He may have been the prisoner, wearing the mask for the most pointless of reasons – because it was the fashionable thing to do in Italy at the time.

Louis Oldendorff

A Lorraine nobleman, Oldendorff was the leader of the Secret Order of the Temple. The rules of this society would not allow them to replace him while he still lived. After he died, another man was made to wear the mask, thus maintaining the illusion of Oldendorff's imprisonment, and keeping the Order from selecting a new leader.

Also suspected to be the prisoner: Richard Cromwell; the Duke of Monmouth; Vivien de Bulonde.

THE UNUSUAL SUSPECTS

Hidden Daughter of Louis XIII and Anne

Terrified of not having a son, the elder Louis may have hidden away his newborn daughter and replaced her with an infant boy changeling. When she grew up and discovered her identity, Louis XIV (the changeling) had her imprisoned.

Moliere

As beloved as the playwright was both by the French public and by Louis XIV, Moliere made many enemies because of his lack of religious beliefs and general disdain for the French establishment. He especially angered the Company of the Holy Sacrament, a strong and influential Catholic group. The theory follows that Moliere's death was staged in 1673, with the playwright becoming the Man in the Iron Mask as punishment.

Nicholas Fouquet
Fouquet was allegedly imprisoned for discovering hidden knowledge that Christ didn't die on the cross, but survived, leading to a secret bloodline of direct ancestors.

MOST CONVINCING EVIDENCE

The fact that the prisoner wasn't simply killed indicates that there must have been a royal connection. Anyone else would have been garotted and left to an unmarked grave.

MOST MYSTERIOUS FACT

Despite the back-stabbing of French politics, the gains that could be made by revealing who this prisoner was, and the methodical examination of records, there is no indication of who the prisoner was. It was a universally-kept secret, by all parties involved.

SCEPTICALLY SPEAKING

The identity of the Man in the Iron Mask is so well-hidden one can surmize it's simply because he didn't exist at all. The vision of such a figure would go far towards quelling any dissidence to the King's rule. The prospect of lifelong imprisonment does that sort of thing . . .

THE MURDER OF CHRISTOPHER MARLOWE

Fate can play cruel tricks on the gifted and Christopher Marlowe (1564-1593) was undoubtedly gifted. At one time he was England's leading playwright, thanks to such works as *Doctor Faustus*. If the hand of history had dealt more kindly with him it is unlikely that this giant of the

Elizabethan theatre would ever have been overshadowed by that relative upstart Shakespeare.

Marlowe was much more than just a talented writer. In his short but tempestuous life he experienced both wealth and poverty, was tried and briefly imprisoned and managed to kill a man in a brawl. Marlowe met an untimely end when he was stabbed in the eye in a Deptford tavern. The official story is that he was killed as the result of an argument over an unpaid bill, but conspiracy theorists never pay too much attention to the official version. There is another side to Marlowe. He was a spy.

England in the Sixteenth Century was a turbulent place. The country was troubled by enemies at home and abroad. The defeat of the Spanish Armada had ended the King of Spain's plans for a purely military conquest of the country, so he turned to espionage and began attacking England by more subtle means. The internal threat centred on religion. For many years there had been conflict between Protestants and Catholics, with prominent figures on both sides dying at the stake. Although the official attitude in 1593 was toleration, there was an active and dangerous Catholic underground with strong links to foreign powers.

To counter these threats it was necessary for the English Crown to operate an efficient counter-espionage system. Elizabeth I's spymaster was Francis Walshingham, who recruited Marlowe at Cambridge University (for generations afterwards Cambridge remained a fertile breeding ground for spies and double agents). Marlowe's public profile and wide network of connections made him a useful, if somewhat unreliable, agent. He infiltrated many secret societies and organisations while performing this role.

Given his secret life, his murder may not have been the simple affair it has been portrayed as. The question remains in many people's minds – was Marlowe killed to end the career of one of Elizabethan England's James Bond equivalents?

THE STRANGE PART

Fierce argument rages over whether Marlowe was killed by England's enemies, by its defenders or by some other clandestine organisation with a grudge against him. It is strange to say the least, that although he was stabbed in a crowded tavern, no witnesses ever came forward and no one was ever punished for the murder.

THE USUAL SUSPECTS

Dr John Dee

After Walshingham died in 1590, Britain's top spymaster was Dr John Dee. When not running England's cloak-and-dagger activity, Dee dabbled in astrology, necromancy, contacting angels and alchemy. The transmuting of base metals into gold is a neat way of explaining the funds that passed through his hands and were provided by various paymasters. The doctor was not over-troubled by scruples and if he felt that Marlowe had become a double-agent, would have had no problems having him silenced permanently.

Spanish Secret Agents

Marlowe may have been involved in an elaborate attempt to infiltrate the Catholic underground and thwart the plans of the Spanish spies who were working through it in England. By posing as a double-agent he may have been attempting to gain their confidence and secrets. If he was exposed, they would certainly have had reasons for wanting to take their revenge and prevent him from passing on any information he had obtained.

THE UNUSUAL SUSPECTS

William Shakespeare

The theatre can be a cut-throat business and in the days before copyright and Arts Council funding a great many bitter feuds developed between playwrights. Shakespeare was a member of the School of Night – a shadowy organisation which included spies, writers and representatives of the aristocracy among its ranks – and certainly had the connections to arrange for the elimination of one of his main literary rivals.

The Masons

Among the many secret societies that were flourishing in Elizabethan England were the Freemasons. It has long been suspected that Marlowe drew on Masonic imagery in his plays and was almost certainly a member of the order. While being a Mason probably helped to advance his career as a playwright, would also have given him access to insider information in his role of spy. Marlowe may have made the foolish mistake of breaking his oath of secrecy to the organisation. His murder may have been the consequence of underestimating just how much Masons value silence.

MOST MYSTERIOUS FACT

The threat of having an eye plucked out if you betray your colleagues forms the part of the initiation oath into several secret orders – including the higher ranks of Templars and Freemasons – so it is more than a little odd that Marlowe was killed by a stabbing to the eye. The nature of his death may point towards it being a ritualistic murder.

MOST CONVINCING EVIDENCE

Marlowe's arrest, under the pretext that he had murdered a man, provides strong evidence to support the idea that he was a spy. Even though it was a trumped-up charge used to detain him, the fact that he had the power and influence to be acquitted quickly suggests that he had friends in high places – or that he bought his freedom by switching sides and becoming a double-agent.

SCEPTICALLY SPEAKING

Spies shun the light and when they assassinate people they do it in dark alleys and not crowded taverns. Failing to pay your bar bill or clear your gambling debts tends to cause offence even if you are a spy. Marlowe had a talent for getting himself into trouble and it's quite feasible that he could have got himself involved in the fatal fight thanks to an overuse of clever words and irony – a *faux pas* that is still punishable with physical violence in some South London pubs today.

WOLFGANG AMADEUS MOZART

Genius may bring its blessings, but it also brings its fair share of enemies. No one knew this more than the brilliant composer, Amadeus Mozart. A child prodigy by the age of five, his musical gifts brought him more pain than joy. While his work is heralded today as the finest that classical music can offer, in his time he was openly reviled, with several of his contemporaries plotting his destruction. History may have given him fame but in his lifetime he knew no such comfort. Mozart, perhaps the greatest composer ever known, died penniless, his remains buried unceremoniously in a common grave in Vienna.

Born in Salzburg, Austria in January, 1756, Mozart quickly displayed his musical gifts: by the age of four, his father had arranged harpsichord lessons for him; by five, he was composing his own music; by the time he was six, his father took the young Mozart on a performance tour of Vienna and Munich. By the time he was 15, he was concertmaster of the Archbishop of Salzburg's orchestra. The future seemed to belong to the extremely gifted young man.

But there were personality conflicts between the Archbishop and Mozart – the fact that Mozart wasn't paid for three years may have been one reason. In 1781, he left the prestigious (but poorly paid) position and went to seek his fortune in Vienna. There, the poor relationship he had had with the Salzburg court continued with the Viennese composers. This became so bad that Mozart's father complained to Emperor Joseph II that the other composers were deliberately ensuring that a composition of his son's was not being performed.

Yet Mozart persevered, despite his difficulty in getting paid and his inability to spend money wisely. His marriage to Constanze Weber was fraught with financial difficulties and tragedy – of their six children, only two survived past childhood. Mozart was not a favourite with the Viennese court, and his work received lukewarm response from the public, if it was played at all. By 1790, Mozart's debts were staggering, and his health was extremely fragile. The following year, he was secretly commissioned, by a mysterious stranger, to compose a Requiem. After finishing writing *The Magic Flute*, Mozart threw himself obsessively into writing this mournful piece. But fate (or a force more sinister) intervened, and Wolfgang Amadeus Mozart died on December 5, 1791 in Vienna; the Requiem was unfinished and the stranger who commissioned it disappeared into the shadows of time. Mozart was only 35.

THE STRANGE PART

The identity of the stranger who commissioned Mozart's final work has never been revealed. Theories point to an anonymous woman in black or to a man dressed all in grey. No one ever came forward to admit to commissioning the Requiem. Mozart was obsessed with the piece, and many feel that this obsession drove him to illness and, finally, his deathbed.

THE USUAL SUSPECTS

Antonio Salieri

A court composer, it has been widely rumoured (and even cited as fact in the film Amadeus) that Salieri was terribly jealous of Mozart's gifts and upset by his ribald way of life. Salieri may have commissioned the deadly Requiem himself, knowing full well Mozart's fragile health and the cost the work would exact upon him. Salieri may have felt that with Mozart dead his own work would receive the attention he felt it deserved.

Count von Walsegg zu Stuppach

The Count was an amateur musician who may have wanted more glory than his talent would allow. The theory runs that the Count disguised himself as the mysterious stranger, hoping to pass off the finished Requiem Mass as his own work. To ensure that Mozart would not dispute this, he planned to have Mozart poisoned.

Unknown Viennese composers

Mozart's work easily outshone the work of his contemporaries: Handel himself said that Mozart was the greatest composer that ever lived. However, with Mozart's hit and miss approach to success, coupled with the cut-throat world of court commissions and appointments, perhaps someone simply decided to even the field a bit. If Mozart's health had been better and if he had learned to manage his life better, he would have been unstoppable.

THE UNUSUAL SUSPECTS

The Masons

Mozart was a Freemason, but his dissolute lifestyle may have been considered a liability they no longer wanted to suffer. It is also rumoured that they were none too happy with his Masonic-inspired opera *The Magic Flute* for giving away one too many secrets.

DISGRUNTLED BLACK MAGICIAN IN THE COURT OF EMPEROR JOSEPH
A story survives of an army general in Joseph's court complaining about Mozart's lack of court decorum to the Emperor. The Emperor replied that he could get a general any time he wished, but he would never get another Mozart. This could have led to someone in the court using black magic to kill Mozart, leading to the confusion among doctors concerning his death.

MOST CONVINCING EVIDENCE

While "miliary fever" was diagnosed as the cause of Mozart's death, the truth was that the attending doctors were unsure why he died. He suffered a range of apparently unconnected complaints, from toothaches to lethargy, but nothing pointed conclusively to one cause of death or another. The official diagnosis of "miliary fever" was perhaps nothing more than a face-saving way for the doctors to say they simply didn't know.

MOST MYSTERIOUS FACT

Mozart was initiated into a Viennese Masonic Lodge at the age of 18, with his father joining shortly thereafter. Curiously, despite the connection, Mozart was denied membership to the Viennese Society of Musicians. Also interesting to note was that his last public performance was a cantata for the dedication of his Masonic Lodge's new temple.

SCEPTICALLY SPEAKING

Mozart was a sickly man almost from his birth, plagued with one ailment after another. The question isn't why he died when he died, but why he didn't succumb sooner. Modern physicians have suggested that Mozart died of uremia caused by kidney disease. As for jealous rivals killing him, why murder a man whose work was never played?

RASPUTIN

The Russian royal family at the turn of the century was completely dominated by the charismatic power of a defrocked monk turned psychic healer and fortune-teller Grigori Yefimovich, known as Rasputin. The former holy man possessed the power to maintain the health of the Tsar's son, Alexei, who was dangerously anaemic. The hold this gave him over the Russian royal family is well-documented, and Rasputin used his influence to great personal gain.

That the "Mad Monk" greatly destabilized the Russian imperial government is a matter of historical fact. He used his influence to put his followers in positions of power and authority, demanded extortionate bribes in return for persuading the Tsarina Alexandra, the Empress, to favour certain courtiers, business people or plans of action, and charged great sums for dispensing his "healing" among the lesser nobility. He was already a national scandal by 1911, and by 1915 had become the Tsarina's chief advisor.

He also had a voracious sexual appetite, and would frequently demand sexual intercourse from both men and women as part of the payment for his services – often insisting that he sleep with the teenage child of a supplicant, if such were available. He also had no end of groupies available, partly because of his power, and partly because of his 13-inch erection. His exploits outraged the general public, but the royal family was totally under his spell. Reports from the time suggest that his powers of healing and precognition were both entirely genuine. Letters from Alexandra to Rasputin also hint that he was having an affair with her.

Finally, a cabal of Russian nobles decided Rasputin's influence was corrupting the state, and that he had to die. Led by Prince Feliks Yusupov, the cabal lured the healer to a private party hosted by Yusopov, where he was murdered, on December 30, 1916. It was too late to save the reputation of the royal family, and shortly afterwards the revolution swept away the old order.

THE STRANGE PART

The tale of Rasputin's death certainly lends credence to his healing powers. Arriving at the party, the holy man was placed in front of a banquet laced with enough cyanide to kill a dozen normal men. One conspirators, a medical doctor called Lazovert, prepared the poisoned food. When the monk became suspicious that Yusupov was not eating but failed to show any ill effects from his feast, the Prince panicked, and shot him at close range. He was also shot by Grand Duke Pavlovich, the Tsar's nephew. Enraged but still seemingly mobile, Rasputin chased Yusupov out of the house and into the courtyard, where a gang of conspirators beat him to a bloody pulp with hefty iron chains. Dr. Lazovert examined the monk, and declared him to be alive, so they wrapped him in the chains and dumped him in a hole cut into the ice of the River Neva.

THE USUAL SUSPECTS

Spiritual Avatar

Perhaps the most common theory is that Rasputin genuinely did possess the healing and precognitive powers that history has granted to him, including the ability to mesmerize women. He used these powers to gain his position of authority, and it was his sexual prowess that led to his being murdered. The powers were derived from the fact that Rasputin was in fact a spiritual avatar or genuine saint.

St Germain

Rasputin was in fact the immortal known to medieval Europe as the Count de St. Germain, smoothing the way for the Russian revolution so that history could follow its proper course. When he found himself stuck in the water and unable to tunnel out, Rasputin/St Germain decided that the best course of action was to feign death and lie low. He was dug out of the Neva by the conspirators, and hastily buried. From a shallow grave, he found it relatively easy to tunnel out. His enemies were certain he was dead, so he was free to make his escape. Rumour suggests that St Germain may now be in Los Angeles, having spent the 1980s in Eastern Europe bringing Communism to an end.

THE UNUSUAL SUSPECTS

Alien Invader

Rasputin's unnatural vitality was not a result of psychic ability at all. The healer was actually an alien, a rogue member of a small exploration team who decided to indulge himself in a few years of orgiastic amusement. Because his physiology was different to ours, the assassination was almost ineffective. In the end, it was lack of exposure to direct sunlight that killed him, not the low temperature or lack of oxygen.

MOST CONVINCING EVIDENCE

Rasputin's frozen corpse was finally retrieved several miles down-river from where it had been dumped. He had shaken loose of his chains, and had been trying to claw his way out of the ice from the inside when he had finally succumbed – after having been totally submerged in freezing water for at least six hours.

MOST MYSTERIOUS FACT

Perhaps the oddest feat of Rasputin's survival is his capacity to consume such a huge dose of cyanide. Equally as strange though is an artefact that surfaced in Paris in the 1960s – Rasputin's mummified penis. One observer described it as "like a blackened banana, about a foot long". There is no record of any of the conspirators castrating their victim, however.

SCEPTICALLY SPEAKING

It is just about possible that the poison was old and ineffective, that the gunshots failed to hit any vital organs, that the beating was mostly surface damage, and even that the cold of the river Neva slowed tissue damage from oxygen starvation so much that Rasputin was able to revive for long enough to lock his fingers in the ice. But if he was so precognitive, why did he not foretell the danger of taking Yusupov up on his invitation?

JACK THE RIPPER

The mystery surrounding the Jack The Ripper murders in 1888 has fascinated and tantalized criminologists, conspiracy buffs and Hollywood producers for more than a hundred years. Theories and counter-theories have arisen, mutually exclusive "authentic" diaries, confessions and notebooks have been discovered and published. It is doubtful whether anyone will ever be able to provide a definite answer.

On Friday August 31, Polly Nichols was murdered. She was followed by Annie Chapman on Saturday, September 8, then by Catharine Eddowes and Elizabeth Stride on Sunday September 30, and Mary Kelly on Friday November 9. Their throats were cut and their bodies mutilated, with internal organs often removed with surgical precision and carried away from the scene of the crime. Mary Kelly, who was three months pregnant, was found naked, with her clothes piled tidily on a chair nearby. It is also possible that there was an earlier victim – Martha Tabram, who was murdered on Tuesday, August 7. Elizabeth Stride may not have been killed by the Ripper. All six women were prostitutes in the East End of London. Some commentators add three more women to this total.

The Ripper used a fairly consistent Modus Operandi. When the victim lifted her skirts she was grabbed and throttled to unconsciousness, then laid on the ground. Once the woman was lying down, her throat was cut, and in most cases one of the victim's internal organs was removed, presumably as a trophy. The degree of precision exhibited in this procedure suggests that the Ripper had medical training; in one instance, a kidney was removed frontally, without damaging any of the other organs. This would require some skill in an operating theatre, and would be very hard indeed at night, in the dark, with the pressure of being in a public place with the corpse of someone you have just murdered.

Scotland Yard's files show that two notes were received by the Central News Agency from a person claiming to be the Ripper, one entitled "Dear Boss", and the other "from Hell". Both were strangely-written, and took a boastfully gloating tone. Most researchers into the matter doubt that either were actually written by the murderer. There was also a chunk of diseased kidney sent to a Whitechapel vigilance committee with a letter that claimed the organ was from Katharine Eddowes. While there was no way of knowing for certain, the damage to the kidney was consistent with the effects of the particular disease from which Eddowes suffered.

THE STRANGE PART

On the night of September 30th, police officers found a piece of Catharine Eddowes' apron that the Ripper had used to wipe his knife. This was very close to a doorway which had the message 'The Juwes are the men That Will not be blamed for nothing" written over the door. Senior police officers felt this would spark anti-Semitic riots, and erased the message. The odd phraseology and strange spelling has sparked suggestions that it was actually a Masonic message, and the police erased it to hide the fact.

THE USUAL SUSPECTS

PRINCE ALBERT VICTOR

The grandson of Queen Victoria, Prince Albert Victor (known as "Eddy") was a mentally subnormal youth, described by one royal commentator at the time as "a gleaming goldfish in a crystal bowl". Eddy seems likely to have been an occasional homosexual – a criminal offence in Britain at the time – and died in 1892. Rumours suggested the cause of death was syphilis. His madness is supposed to have been the spur that led him to murder prostitutes, and fear of scandal led to a conspiracy hushing up the Prince's guilt. An alternative theory suggests that he may have got one of the prostitutes pregnant. When she tried to blackmail the government, she and her friends were killed by royal agents in a manner that would distract investigators from the real reason for the deaths.

DR. FRANCIS TUMBLETY

An American doctor, Tumblety was strongly suspected by John Littlechild, head of the Secret Department at Scotland Yard during the investigations. The doctor fled back to the USA, and Scotland Yard sent detectives to interview him.

THE UNUSUAL SUSPECTS

JILL THE RIPPER

Some theorists have suggested that the murders were actually the work of a crazed midwife, Mary Pearcy, who was executed in December, 1890 for slitting the throats of her lover's wife and children. She may have been trying to exact some sort of terrible revenge on other women for some previous real or imagined insult or injury.

INTERDIMENSIONAL INVADER

Victorian London was also plagued with another notorious Jack – Spring-Heeled Jack. This strange figure, wearing armour, cloak and a helmet, could allegedly jump over buildings. He was seen by hundreds of witnesses and hunted for by a vigilante force led by none other than England's most famous soldier Wellington. Some feel that Spring-Heeled Jack was an interdimensional invader and the true Ripper.

MOST CONVINCING EVIDENCE

In 1970, Dr. Thomas Stowell claimed to have found documents that showed Prince Albert Victor's doctor, Sir William Gull, knew his patient was the Ripper, and placed the blame on the madness caused by Syphilis. After the night in which Stride and Eddowes were killed (known as the "Double Event" thanks to a phrase in the second note to the Central News Agency), he was locked up, but he escaped to kill Mary Kelly before being securely incarcerated until his death.

MOST MYSTERIOUS FACT

It is interesting that the days the murders took place on cycle through the days of the weekend – Friday for Nichols, Saturday for Chapman, Sunday for Eddowes (and Stride) and then back to Friday for Kelly.

SCEPTICALLY SPEAKING

Unfortunately, Dr. Stowell died shortly after publishing his theory, and his notes and papers were burned, so his claims cannot be verified. More importantly, court diaries show that Eddy was not in London on any of the murder dates. There is no evidence to indicate any Masonic involvement either, just pure speculation.

P

ANTARCTICA

Desolate but beautiful, Antarctica is a dangerous environment and an environment in danger. It is a place of massive contrasts but the greatest contrast that this mysterious continent may yield is that our perception of it as an uninhabited may not be true. Conspiracy theorists believe the truth about who lives in Antarctica is being hidden from the public.

The antennae of conspiracy enthusiasts have been twitching in anticipation of some strange truth being revealed ever since information began to leak out concerning the exploration of the continent by Nazis with links to mystical orders such as the *Thule Gesellschaft*, and Ahenerbe, the SS occult bureau.

When Admiral Byrd led a US military expedition force of more than 10,000 men to Antarctica in 1947 the mystery deepened. The force returned after just three months having suffered heavy losses on their mysterious mission. Even fifty years later, it is almost impossible to obtain any of the unclassified information concerning this inexplicable polar misadventure by the US military.

While debate rages over just who Admiral Byrd's men might have been fighting, most conspiracy theorists agree that underneath the ice of Antarctica is the remains of an advanced civilization destroyed by some great cataclysm. It is alleged that it is this fact that the Nazis stumbled upon and this fact that sinister forces are conspiring to keep secret from the rest of us.

THE STRANGE PART

Antarctica is governed by a treaty, signed by various powerful countries, that prevents any development or exploitation of its vast natural resources. Given that our governments do not generally have a good track record on defending the environment, this could be seen as a little curious. It has been suggested that the real purpose of the Antarctic Treaty is to eliminate the chance of any commercial organization stumbling on to the truth by digging through the two-mile thick crust of ice.

THE USUAL SUSPECTS

Nazis

In 1938, Nazi Germany made the most extensive survey of Antarctica to date, claimed it as their territory and renamed it Neuschwabenland. It is known that inner-orders of the Nazi Party placed a special importance on Antarctica and that the Germans maintained a presence there throughout World War II. In 1946, German U-boats were spotted off the coast of Argentina heading towards the ice-bound continent. Conjecture has it that elements of the German High Command escaped justice to set up a base among the ruins of a lost Antarctic civilization.

The Jason Society

The Jason Society was, apparently, set up by President Nixon, in 1973. A secret organisation, its ultra-classified purpose was to run a project called "Secret Earth" and some claim that it is the group charged with exploiting the remnants of an advanced civilization found beneath Antarctica and in one or two other locations across the globe. Unlike many other groups behind conspiracies, it seems that the Jason Society may have a semi-benevolent purpose for keeping us all in the dark over Antarctica. It is suggested that the Society's aim is to discover enough about the vanished Elder Race to prevent us from sharing their fate.

Also suspected: MJ-12; Project Phoenix; the US National Security Council; the United Nations; and a cabal of Freemasons.

THE UNUSUAL SUSPECTS

Ancient Space Aliens

If there are ruins of an ancient culture buried deep in Antarctica's forbidding wastes, some argue that it is of an alien and not human nature. They feel that the conspiracy has developed to prevent widespread knowledge of alien involvement in Earth's history.

The Knights Templar

If civilization was established in Egypt by survivors fleeing Antarctica following the catastrophe that covered it in ice, their knowledge of their original homeland may have been preserved in certain secret traditions. The Knights Templar trace their lineage to ancient Egypt, so they may have inherited this information. If this is true, they may wish to control Antarctica and exploit the advanced technology below its surface in order to further their plans for world domination.

MOST CONVINCING EVIDENCE

The single most startling piece of evidence that gives some weight to the conspiracy theory concerning Antarctica is the Piri Reis Map – a genuine document that was drawn up in Constantinople in 1513. It clearly shows not only the western coast of Africa and the eastern coast of South America, but it also shows the ice-free coast of a country called Queen Maud Land.

Antarctica was not discovered until 1818, and the astonishing accuracy of the map was not revealed until the Fifties when ground-penetrating radar technology allowed geologists to see the land beneath the ice for the first time. The map was drawn up from earlier charts, but no one is able to offer a convincing explanation of how it can possibly show what it does. Other similar charts exist, suggesting there may be some truth to the idea Antarctica could be have once been home to the civilisation that has become popularly known as Atlantis.

MOST MYSTERIOUS FACT

In 1998, a vast earthquake was reported to have occurred in Antarctica measuring up to 8.1 on the Richter scale. This fact hit global news services, preparations were made and the entire east coast of Australia was put on alert – the authorities feared it could be hit by a huge tidal wave. Medical authorities, the police and the army called the alert off when the expected tsunami did not arrive. What makes all of this mysterious is that there are no plates at the South Pole and there is, therefore, no logical explanation as to what could have caused such a massive quake.

SCEPTICALLY SPEAKING

There is very little scientific evidence for Antarctica having been ice-free enough to support a civilisation at any point during the last 15 million years. No archaeological evidence has so far been found to suggest an advanced culture ever existed on the continent.

BERMUDA TRIANGLE

The Bermuda Triangle – also known by the more intimidating name of the Devil's Triangle – is an area of the Atlantic Ocean that is generally accepted to fall within a triangle formed by Bermuda, Puerto Rico, and Fort Lauderdale, Florida.

This mysterious area was first given its famous nickname by the writer Vincent H Gaddis in 1964. He wrote a magazine story entitled "The Deadly Bermuda Triangle" which drew upon centuries of seamen's legends concerning the Devil's Triangle and the many unexplainable disappearances of ships and planes that had occurred within its boundary.

The Triangle has been known as place of odd happenings ever since the Fifteenth Century when Christopher Columbus made an entry in his log concerning "a great flame of fire" that crashed into the ocean as his compass went wild and his crew saw strange lights in the sky. The area's notoriety was added to over the following years by a number of odd incidents – most notably with the disappearance of the crew of the Mary Celeste in 1872.

However, some of the oddest incidents that have enshrined the Triangle took place more recently. The most famous case is that of Flight 19 – which was featured in the film Close Encounters of the Third Kind. On December 5th, 1945, five of the Navy's Avenger torpedo bombers on a routine practice mission vanished. A Martin Mariner, with its 22-man rescue crew, was sent out to find them – they also disappeared without trace. Added to this have the been the loss of more than 50 ships, such as the massive USS Cyclops, and the tanker SS Marine Sulphur Queen, which vanished in calm seas with her 39-man crew.

THE STRANGE PART

No wreckage from Flight 19 was ever recovered – despite a massive search – which suggests that something more than a mysterious five-plane crash or ditching into the sea is involved. The fact that absolutely no sign of any remains was spotted is typical of the disappearances said to occur the Bermuda Triangle, where even massive ships vanish without a trace and without sending a distress call. Of course, conspiracy theorists believe that the authorities know that something mysterious is going on and have attempted to cover it up.

THE USUAL SUSPECTS

ALIENS

Aliens top the list of those conjectured to be behind the disappearances in the Triangle and the need for the truth to be covered up. It is alleged that an alien race – probably those nasty little Greys – have an underwater base in the area of the Triangle. There are certainly plenty of reports of UFOs rising out of and diving into the ocean near Puerto Rico. As our unwelcome visitors have a thing about their privacy, they tend to dispose of anyone who crosses over into what they regard as their territory.

NORTH AMERICAN AIR DEFENCE COMMAND

Extra-terrestrials are not the only ones alleged to have undersea bases in the Bermuda Triangle. Some conspiracy theorists hold to the idea that the North American Air Defence Command, also known by the acronym NORAD, has a vast submerged complex running ultra-secret technology that interferes with the signals that aeroplanes and boats rely on for navigation. If any plane or ship spots evidence of the NORAD base, they are meant to be "vanished" by the US military.

Also suspected: MJ-12; United Nations; and the ancient alien space deities Cthulhu and Yog-Sogoth.

THE UNUSUAL SUSPECTS

CHRONONAUTS

Some feel it is not the Greys behind the missing pilots, sailors and passengers, but humans from the far future travelling back in time. The Chrononauts of this hypothesis take advantage of a gravitational time-space anomaly in the area to gather living evidence of the past. Of course, if anyone uncovers this fact, the Chrononauts can travel back into the past to change the timeline and prevent the evidence from being discovered.

Atlantean Ruins

Conjecture has been made that the Bermuda Triangle is situated above the sunken remnants of the ancient civilisation of Atlantis. The reason why so many ships and planes have vanished is that, buried among the supposed ruins of Atlantis, are huge crystals emitting powerful, random beams of energy. It is this energy that zaps unfortunate craft passing overhead. One or two even believe that some Atlanteans themselves remain below the waves and are actually responsible for the disappearances.

MOST CONVINCING EVIDENCE

Aside from the disappearance of more than 50 ships and 20 planes in the Triangle during the last century, and the fact that it is one of only two places on Earth where a magnetic compass does not point to true north, there is other evidence of strange goings on. Carolyn Casico, a licensed pilot, flew a charter flight to Turk Island in the Triangle. When she was seen flying over the island, Carolyn was heard over her radio saying: "I don't understand. This should be Grand Turk but there is nothing there. The shape is right but this island looks uninhabited." She circled the island a few times before heading out to sea and vanishing.

MOST MYSTERIOUS FACT

Before they vanished off the face of the Earth and into the limbo of the lost, the last message received from Flight 19 consisted of the letters "FT" repeated over and over again. No one has ever been able to make sense of what the pilots were trying to convey with their strange last words.

SCEPTICALLY SPEAKING

Storms, freak weather, tidal waves, explosive cargoes and poor navigators are all plausible reasons for many of the accidents behind the supposed mystery. Some sceptics argue the number of craft lost is not out of the ordinary, given the size of the area and amount of traffic passing through it. Added to all of this is the fact that many of the ships and planes said to have disappeared mysteriously in the Triangle were not in the Bermuda Triangle at all.

THE HOLLOW EARTH

There should be nothing more solid and dependable than the very surface of the Earth we walk upon, but many researchers in the conspiracy field believe that the interior of the Earth is populated by several bizarre groups. They feel that below a 1,000-mile-thick crust the Earth is hollow and illuminated by an inner sun.

It has long been felt that the entrance to the strange subterranean world of the hollow Earth is to be found at the poles. Everything, from the spectacular light displays known as Aurora Borealis and Aurora Australis – a side-effect of the inner sun – to gravitational and radio anomalies, has been cited in support of this idea. It is also known that some Eskimo tribes claim that they originated from much further north – from a warm land with perpetual daylight.

Some theorists believe that the hollow nature of Earth has been known by the initiates of some secret societies from the dawn of history. These organizations have been manipulating the scientific community and people in power so that the rest of us remain convinced that nothing lies below the Earth's surface other than rock, some patches of oil, and a molten core. It is a fact that the inner teachings of more than one secret society claim that the Earth is hollow, lit by a central sun, populated with an advanced race and connected to the outer Earth by a serious of tunnels. Have these secret societies been engaged in a plot to hoodwink us to the true nature of our planet?

THE STRANGE PART

Despite the full weight of the scientific community, the idea that the Earth is hollow and could be populated has never been totally quashed. Every few years another scientist breaks ranks and risks the wrath of academia and the end of his career by investigating the theory. The amount of scorn and ridicule these poor fellows are subjected to seems out of all proportion if the hollow Earth is only an invalid, crank idea.

THE USUAL SUSPECTS

NAZIS

It is well-known that many high-ranking Nazis totally believed in the fact that the Earth was hollow. It is recorded that, in the Thirties, Nazi expeditions were sent to Antarctica and Tibet to try and find a way to contact people living under the Earth. Indeed, Herman Goring even conducted rocket experiments based on the theory. Some people believe the theory that members of the *Thule Gesellschaft* and other Nazis escaped into the hollow Earth at the end of the war and have established colonies there. Obviously, the authorities need to prevent this frightening information from becoming known to the public.

ALIENS

Alien races, ranging from the well-known Greys to the less-exposed, Aryan-looking species nicknamed the Nordics, and the Orions (reptilians behind most of Earth's walking serpent legends) are all alleged to have bases in the Earth's interior. Our governments are reported to be aware of this, but are powerless to act against the extra terrestrials and so keep the rest of us ignorant of their presence.

THE UNUSUAL SUSPECTS

TERRAS

According to Dr Raymond Bernard – who acquired his PhD from New York University in 1932 – the Earth is hollow and its internal space is populated by the Terras. Members of this race of 12-foot-tall beings are purported to have descended from the original Atlanteans, to live on a diet of uncooked vegetables and to fly UFOs when they journey to the surface. Dr Bernard formed a colony in Ecuador for people who shared his beliefs that the authorities were suppressing the truth about the hollow Earth and the friendly Terras who want no more than to save humanity from an impending nuclear holocaust.

DEROS

First identified in reports made by a decidedly odd fellow named Richard Shaver in the Forties, the Deros is one of several races that inhabit the hollow interior of the Earth. In Shaver's world view, the Deros are descended from the original alien inhabitants of the Earth who were forced to live underground by the consequences of a solar disaster that took place 12,000 years ago. The Deros are masters of a superior technology that can control the minds of men and is used to enforce a conspiracy of silence about their subterranean world. Apart from a desire to prevent the truth concerning the hollow Earth coming out, the Deros also seem to have an unhealthy interest in surface-dwelling woman and sadistic sexual practices.

MOST CONVINCING EVIDENCE

Legends concerning underground kingdoms and the creatures that live within them have appeared as part of almost every culture over the last 6,000 years, but it still seems odd – to say the least – that more than one government has invested funds in investigating the idea that the Earth is hollow. In the Nineteenth Century, the US government first sent American military hero Captain John Cleves Symes to the South Pole to find an entrance into the hollow Earth and establish a colony there. Before World War II, it is known that Nazi Germany sent out more than one exploratory team in search of a way into the alleged world below. It is also rumoured that Admiral Byrd's mysterious military expedition to Antarctica in 1947 had more than a passing interest in the hollow Earth theory.

MOST MYSTERIOUS FACT

On November 25, 1912, American researcher and author Marshall B Gardner submitted an application to the United States Patent Office to obtain a patent on the theory that the Earth was hollow. Eighteen months later, after suitable bureaucratic delay, paperwork and investigation, 18 months later the US government decided to grant Gardner the United States patent 1096102: The Hollow Earth Theory. This is probably the first time that a conspiracy theory was ever officially endorsed by a patent.

SCEPTICALLY SPEAKING

Short on anything resembling hard evidence and strong on the Too Bizarre To Believe factor, the hollow Earth conspiracy theory fails to stand up to the combined weight of established geology, history, cosmology and common-sense. If entrances to the hollow Earth existed, modern satellites would have spotted them.

MONTAUK POINT, NEW YORK

Many conspiracy theories earn the tag TBTB – Too Bizarre To Believe – and Montauk certainly has a strong claim to this label. Labyrinthine, truly mind-boggling and with an incredible scope, the Montauk machinations and weirdness were first brought to light by the pioneering work of journalist Peter Moon and two people who had been involved in the strange goings-on at Montauk – Preston Nichols and Alfred Bielek.

The conspiracy surrounds Camp Hero – officially, a deserted Air Force Station at Montauk Point on Long Island, New York State. Camp Hero was a US Army base established before World War II. It later became the Montauk Air Force base and was officially active until 1969. However, since then new telephone lines and high capacity power lines have been installed and many witnesses have observed advanced military electronics equipment being tested in the area. Power usage for the derelict facility is measured with a gigawatt meter, which means it consumes enough power to run a small city.

Conspiracy theories suggest that the subterranean levels of this base continue to house a centre for research and experimentation into electromagnetic mind-control as well as manipulations of time and other dimensions. These experiments date back to 1943 and the infamous "Philadelphia Experiment" when Albert Einstein and Hungarian-born physicist Janus Eric Von Neumann worked on US government experiments that ripped holes in the fabric of reality during attempts to make a Navy vessel invisible to radar.

It is alleged that during the Philadelphia Experiment a battleship disappeared from sight and from our normal timeline. When it reappeared, the crew onboard had suffered devastating psychological damage and terrible physical repercussions. Some sailors rematerialized in the hull of the ship or suffered third-degree burns. After the war, Montauk, and other associated bases and laboratories in the Long Island area, continued research into what sounds like the most outlandish science fiction. When a US Congressional investigation into these secret projects decided to shut them down in the Sixties, it was not just the base that was underground. Montauk continued to run without governmental approval, receiving its funding from mysterious sources.

THE STRANGE PART

In 1984, the officially empty Montauk Air Force Base was given to New York State for use as public park land. Even though the property is under the care of the New York State Parks System, no part of it has ever been opened as a park. Significantly, the deeds transferring the base to New York State make it explicit that the US government still holds all rights to any and all property beneath the surface. Given that plans from the US Army Corps of Engineers provide evidence of the existence of at least four levels of subterranean facilities beneath Camp Hero, maybe there is something to the conspiracy buff's claims of a massive underground centre conducting research at the borders of established science.

THE USUAL SUSPECTS

National Security Council

Montauk is often alleged to be run by an inner cabal of the National Security Council of the US. All of the members of the cabal are also thought to be members of the Grand Orient Lodge of Egyptian Freemasonry who are using the advances made through research carried out at Montauk to further their aim of global domination.

Aleister Crowley

Possibly the most important occultist of the century, self-styled "wickedest man in the world" Crowley is known to have visited the Montauk area of

Long Island shortly after the end of World War I in which he had been acting as an intelligence officer. Quite what his interest in Montauk was is open to speculation, but it is worth noting that his pupils included ground-breaking scientists such as Jack Parsons – the man behind NASA's Jet Propulsion Laboratories, and an associate of Janus Eric Von Neumann.

THE UNUSUAL SUSPECTS

NAZI SCIENTISTS

Nazi submarines were often spotted off Montauk during the war and many Nazi scientists went to work for the American military after the conflict finally ended. Montauk has had a large Aryan community since the Thirties and some conspiracy theorists believe that the experiments at Montauk were infiltrated and taken over by ex-Nazis, with a view to using the awesome powers that are being developed to further their own evil schemes.

TIME TRAVELLERS

Given that many of the experiments at Montauk seem to involve time travel, some feel it is fair to assume that the real force behind the conspiracy are time travellers from the future. Stranded, in what is to them the past, they have taken over the experiments started by Einstein and Von Neumann in the hope that they can build a machine to take them back to their home time.

MOST CONVINCING EVIDENCE

For what is officially claimed to be merely a derelict military facility, within a designated state park, there seems to be a lot of security around Camp Hero. Picnicking women and children have been accosted and threatened at gunpoint by unidentified military personnel for venturing into its vicinity. Other people wandering through the park near to the supposedly abandoned Air Force Station have been told they have violated top secret and restricted areas, and could be arrested. Non-uniformed armed guards from seemingly shadowy government and military agencies have a track record of performing some very unconstitutional activities in the area. If there is no conspiracy at Montauk why is this happening?

MOST MYSTERIOUS FACT

The land that the Montauk Air Force Base is built on – and possibly under – should, under the terms of American law, belong to the Montauk tribe of Native Americans who were the original inhabitants of the area. Despite huge amounts of evidence to the contrary, the US Federal Court has declared the Montauk tribe extinct in order to prevent the remainder of the tribe claiming the land. It should be noted that the Montauk Indians record numerous strange legends concerning the area, and can remember when the site of Camp Hero was actually home to an ancient and rather odd stone pyramid.

SCEPTICALLY SPEAKING

While there's plenty of fascinating conjecture, there's little independent, hard evidence to back up some of the wilder aspects of the Montauk conspiracy. It seems understandable that the US government – or dark forces within it – might test ultra-advanced technology at a secret base, but when there are places such as Area 51, there's no logical need to operate out of a base only 100 miles from New York City.

THE MYSTERY OF OAK ISLAND

Tiny Oak Island, located in Nova Scotia, Canada, has been called many things over the last 200 years: the Money Pit; a cleverly protected trove of pirate treasure; and a deathtrap. In 1795, 16-year-old Daniel McGinnis was exploring the island when he discovered a depression beneath an ancient oak tree. Thinking that it looked as if someone had just dug a hole and refilled it, McGinnis enlisted the aid of two friends, and they began to dig, sure they were about to discover glittering piles of pirate treasure.

Four feet into the earth, they came across a layer of flagstones. At a depth of ten feet, they encountered a platform constructed of oak logs, embedded in the shaft walls. Another ten feet down, the boys encountered another oak platform, discovering yet another at a depth of thirty feet underground. Since the logs were impossible to remove, the boys abandoned the project.

With capital provided by Simeon Lynds, an affluent businessman who had enticed investors to finance a proper excavation of the pit, the boys returned in 1803. Digging deeper, they encountered more oak platforms, but also found something that was far more interesting: a large, flat stone with cryptic lettering etched across it. A later translation of this mysterious cipher yielded this message: "Forty feet below two million pounds are buried".

Moving past the stone, the excited workmen then ran into the problem that has plagued Oak Island excavations ever since: water. While the shaft had been dry up to this point, water began slowly seeping through the soil. It became so bad that the workers were removing two buckets of water for every bucket of earth. At a depth of 98 feet, the crew hit what sounded like yet another oak platform, but since the day was coming to an end, they stopped work. Returning to their work the next morning, the treasure hunters were horrified to find that the pit had filled up with water.

Undeterred, they dug another shaft 14 feet to the side of the water-filled Money Pit. Digging down 110 feet, they attempted to create a side tunnel towards the original shaft and reach the hoped for treasure that way. Two feet away from their goal, however, water once again poured through the walls of the side tunnel. Soon, the new shaft was as waterlogged as the first. Lynds' team gave up shortly thereafter.

In 1849, another crew attempted the Money Pit, armed this time with a horse-powered mining drill. They discovered more layers of wood, and for the first time, layers of loose metal. They also discovered what looked like bits of an old watch chain. Sure that the Pit contained chests of treasure, they pushed forth, but were once again foiled by water pouring into the shaft. Curious as to where the water was coming from, the crew excavated the nearby beach, making a startling discovery. They found a system of five carefully-constructed drains that fed water into a sump and then down a 500-foot tunnel directly into the Money Pit. Digging below the 90-foot mark broke a hydraulic seal in the Pit, causing water to run into it at a rate of 600 gallons a minute. Since the water was coming directly from the ocean, it was absolutely impossible to drain. Disheartened, the crew gave up.

Over the years, several expeditions have tried to pierce Oak Island's mystery, including such celebrities as Franklin Roosevelt, Errol Flynn and John Wayne. More mysteries were unveiled, including cement vaults, bits of cryptic parchment, and hidden caverns dug to the north of the original Pit.

Six people have died trying to unlock the mystery of Oak Island, but to this day, she jealously guards her secrets.

THE STRANGE PART

In 1971, when a camera was sent down Borehole-10X, a shaft sunk to the north of the original Pit, it encountered a hideous sight in a newly discovered underwater cavern. Floating in the dark, silt-laden water was a human hand, apparently cut off at the wrist.

THE USUAL SUSPECTS

Captain William Kidd

The infamous pirate, Captain Kidd, apparently littered the world with hidden piles of treasure. Several stories of Kidd's treasure seem to point towards Oak Island.

The Spanish

One theory states that a damaged Spanish galleon, loaded with treasure, may have stopped off at Oak Island to effect repairs and store its cargo of treasure, safe from pirate attack, so that it could be picked up later on the voyage back to Spain.

Francis Bacon

Since no original manuscripts have been found of Shakespeare's play, many argue that the Bard's plays were written by none other than Francis Bacon. Bacon may have buried the incriminating plays on Oak Island, to be discovered in the future.

Also suspected: The Vikings; the French and/or the British colonial troops.

THE UNUSUAL SUSPECTS

THE INCA AND MAYA

To avoid plundering by Europeans in the Seventeenth and Eighteenth centuries, the Inca and Maya, aided by compassionate Europeans, may have moved some treasures north to Oak Island.

THE KNIGHTS TEMPLAR

Fleeing persecution in Europe, the Knights may have spirited away the Holy Grail to Oak Island for safekeeping. There are two pieces of evidence in support of this. First, a formation of rocks on the island, when connected by lines drawn on a map, form a giant Christian cross 250 metres long. Secondly, Henry Sinclair, a suspected Knight, arrived in the area in 1398.

MOST CONVINCING EVIDENCE

The ingenious engineering of drains and hydraulic seals seems to indicate something valuable is indeed buried there.

MOST MYSTERIOUS FACT

In 1970, an investment group called the Triton Alliance commissioned a geological study of Oak Island. That report has, mysteriously, never been made public.

SCEPTICALLY SPEAKING

Just how did the original architects of Oak Island plan to retrieve their treasure? Obviously they didn't. And why advertise it with engraved stones? Doesn't that defeat the purpose of hiding it in the first place?

DENVER, COLORADO

Denver International Airport is usually only noteworthy for being the most important airport in the US State of Colorado, so it seems a very unlikely setting for a globe-spanning conspiracy. However, in recent years many conspiriologists have been researching its possible mysteries, in the belief that solving them may help expose the existence of the New World Order, the destruction of the Earth by comet impact, and the true nature of the MJ-12 organization. So far they have only provided concrete evidence that the airport also houses a massive and mysterious underground complex.

Certainly, the airport has a wealth of occult and conspiratorial symbolism within it design: its runways seem to form swastika patterns, and its numerous murals are truly mind-boggling – one shows the destruction of city and forest while a small girl holds a Mayan Tablet predicting the end of the world. The most bizarre is an image of the mystical Nazi symbol of the Black Sun, which is in the floor of the airport's Great Hall. Any conspiracy theorist with knowledge of Freemasonry can tell you that "The Great Hall" is an important Masonic term – which may help explain why the Hall also features a Masonic Capstone.

Some feel it is very significant that Air Force Space Command is stationed at the Schriever Air Force Base close to Denver International Airport. Among the publicly acknowledged duties of Air Force Space Command is the control of the Milstar satellite communications system, that links mobile ground forces, ships, submarines and aircraft together to create a unified fighting force of incredible power. It is also responsible for other satellites that orbit the earth at altitudes of more than 23,000 miles and communicate on super-high frequencies. It is possible that this satellite network will allow forces across the world to be controlled effectively in the event of either a nuclear war or a global catastrophe.

Air Force Space Command also runs the Defense Support Program satellites, which are a key part of North America's early warning system. However, instead of purely detecting missile launches, space launches and nuclear detonations, Space Command may also provide early warning of UFOs and comets approaching Earth. It is rumoured that Denver was chosen as the base for Space Command because computer models show that its position and high altitude make it the perfect area to create safe underground buildings capable of resisting any type of disaster.

THE STRANGE PART

There was a lot of opposition to the building of the Denver International Airport from people in the locality. Officials high-up in the Clinton administration became heavily involved in the project and they seem to have used their influence to ensure that the airport was built. Furthermore, the CIA may have stuck its nose in – Rodney Stitch, the author of *Defrauding America*, has claimed to have access to a tape showing a CIA agent paying the mayor of Denver to get the airport built. Why was this top-level pressure applied to build the airport and its underground bunker system?

THE USUAL SUSPECTS

The New World Order

Even before the bizarre details of the construction of Denver International Airport began to surface, rumours in the conspiracy field suggested that when the New World Order was established America would be split into two administrative divisions – the Eastern Sector and the Western Sector. The control centre for the Eastern Sector was to be based in Atlanta and the Western Sector's control centre would be located in Denver. To conspiriologists, this just makes the wording "New World Airport Commission" on the Masonic capstone of the airport even more ominous.

The Freemasons

It is hard to doubt that Denver International Airport is heavy with Masonic imagery, which leads some conspiracy researchers to believe that the obvious answer to the mysteries must lie with the Freemasons. As the Masons in America have a long history of constructing buildings and even whole cities packed with secret Masonic messages, they may have designed the airport as a form of subliminal propaganda to demonstrate their ownership of the building and its associated underground complex.

THE UNUSUAL SUSPECTS

NASA

One of the more paranoid conspiracy theories about Denver is that NASA, working in conjunction with the National Security Agency and Air Force Space Command, has built the underground complex at the airport. It is part of ORPHEUS – NASA's project to build a network of underground bunkers so that a chosen few can survive the disastrous comet impact that NASA predicts will hit the Earth in a few years' time. The murals were incorporated as a subtle warning to the rest of us as to the nature of our gruesome fate – death from above or slavery when the forces of NASA, NSA and Space Command take control of the globe in the aftermath of the disaster.

QUEEN ELIZABETH II

It is not too surprising to discover that Queen Elizabeth II owns land in Colorado – she is the richest woman in the world, after all. Her recent large purchases of real estate in the Colorado, however, conducted under the guise of a variety of front companies, has raised quite a few eyebrows. Is she planning to relocate to Denver in the advent of some disaster that wipes Britain off of the map? If, as some conspiracy theorists believe, she is the real power behind groups like the New World Order, she may have ordered the construction of the underground base as the HQ for her secret forces. Her Colorado land-buying spree is designed to allow for the building of other powerbases in the state.

MOST CONVINCING EVIDENCE

The artists who created the weird airport murals allegedly admitted that they had been asked to design them to incorporate specific themes and images. The person responsible for their commission is rumoured to have been Wilma Webb, wife of the mayor of Denver who conducted a Masonic dedication of the airport and was subsequently appointed by President Clinton to the Department of Labour.

MOST MYSTERIOUS FACT

The site of Denver International Airport was originally an American Indian burial ground. The mayor of Denver had to meet with Indian elders and a shaman to appease the spirits of their ancestors. The "tent-like" terminal structure was also designed to appease possible anger from the Indian spirits.

SCEPTICALLY SPEAKING

Underground bunkers are not an uncommon part of emergency forward planning and there is no reason why one should not be built at an airport.

No self-respecting secret society planning world domination would base itself under an airport in constant daily use by thousands of people and then advertize its existence via extensive use of cryptic symbols.

THE PENTAGON

The Pentagon is one of those buildings that everyone has heard of and everyone recognizes immediately. Home to the US Department of Defense – the body that controls the strongest armed force that this globe has ever seen – it is a striking piece of architecture perceived world-wide as a symbol of American might.

The building itself has lent its name to the US military machine, a name that is almost synonymous with conspiracy. From rumours of military-constructed UFOs to germ warfare experiments performed unwittingly on American citizens, the Pentagon has become a byword for dark designs and grotesque, secret plots. Its place in the conspiracy field has even permeated through to the mainstream entertainment media. In Steven Spielberg's blockbuster movie *Raiders Of The Lost Ark* it became the repository for the Ark of the Covenant, while from the first episode of The *X-Files*, it has been the base from which Fox Mulder's nemesis in the global conspiracy – Cancer Man – operates.

Home to more than 29,000 military and civilian employees, the Pentagon is a city within the capitol city of Washington DC. The official story is that the Pentagon building was the idea of Brigadier General Brehon B Sommervell, Chief of the Construction Division of the US Army. He came up with it in the summer of 1941, allegedly as a temporary solution to problems posed by the rapidly-expanding War Department and a shortage of space. The Pentagon was also designed to bring the Department's 24,000 personnel, who were then scattered among 17 different buildings in Washington, under one roof.

The only reason admitted by the military for the building's unique five-sided construction was that the original site chosen for the Pentagon was a tract of land known as Arlington Farms. As five roadways bordered the site, this supposedly dictated the concept of a pentagonal building.

However, the President himself – Franklin Delano Roosevelt – decided that the building be moved three-quarters of a mile down-river to a new location known as Hell's Bottom, where the final design of an open-air pentagram surrounded by five concentric pentagonal rings traversed by ten corridor spokes was implemented.

Some conspiriologists believe that the structure itself is more than the headquarters of the US national defence establishment and the nerve centre for the command and control of the world's strongest military force. Where others see only thousands of tonnes of steel and concrete that go to make up one of the world's largest office buildings, conspiracy buffs have spotted links between the building's odd shape and ancient secret societies and their plots to subjugate America and the rest of the globe

THE STRANGE PART

Even at the time of its construction, there was a degree of speculation about the symbolism inherent in the Pentagon's five-sided shape. Many noted that it has not only five sides, but the five points needed to construct a five-sided star – a design that has huge significance in almost every occult and mystic tradition. The five-pointed star contains the Phi-ratio and the Pythagoreans – an ancient cult based around the study of mathematics – claimed a pentagon held the secret of life and reflected the "divine design" which orders and controls the universe. Why did the normally conservative US military adopt such a radical, symbolic design and spend more than 83 million dollars, in a time of war, on building it?

THE USUAL SUSPECTS

THE FREEMASONS

It has long been established that Washington DC was laid out to a Masonic groundplan. Its elaborate geometry was even modified by the well-known high-degree Freemasons and founding fathers of America – Thomas Jefferson and George Washington. Given that the five-pointed star is a very important Masonic symbol, several conspiriologists have suggested that the Pentagon also has Masonic origins. They claim it was designed as both a Masonic temple and a sign of Masonic control over the US and its military.

SATANISTS

The Devil and his human minions are no longer the main force behind conspiracies – as they were in the witch-burning days when America was founded. Even so, fundamentalist Christian conspiracy theorists still detect the Devil's hand at work in the design of the Pentagon. For evidence they point towards the fact that for centuries the five-sided star has been a symbol used in the worship of Satan. It comes as no surprise to find that some believe the devil inspired his secret army of followers to create the Pentagon as his base of operations on Earth. They also feel that the original name of the marsh it was built on – Hell's Bottom – is also significant.

THE UNUSUAL SUSPECTS

NAZI OCCULTISTS

There is some circumstantial evidence to suggest that notable German Nazi scientists such as Werner Von Braun were working on secret projects in the US in 1938. It is also rumoured that they were in contact with an occult underground, which contained amazing characters like Jack Parsons – a follower of Aleister Crowley and the world's first solid-fuel-rocket scientist. Some conspiracy theories have it that secret occult orders infiltrated the US military and forced it to build the Pentagon. When operation Paperclip brought more than 400 Nazi scientists and thousands of assistants to the US after the end of World War II, the Nazi occult take-over of the US military was complete. Nazi scientists could rule supreme from their specially-designed headquarters.

MJ-12

Every organization – even one as powerful and ultra-secret as MJ-12 – needs a base from which to operate. Some believe that MJ-12 pre-dates the Roswell crash and was operating under a different name via the US military before World War II. They also feel that the Pentagon was specially designed because the mathematical properties of the Phi-ratio make it the perfect shape for sending and receiving messages in hyperspace.

MOST CONVINCING EVIDENCE

It is on record that President Franklin D Roosevelt did not like or approve of the design of the Pentagon, yet he was helpless to prevent it being built the way it was. If the President of the US cannot prevent a building being erected, what mighty force was controlling its construction?

MOST MYSTERIOUS FACT

It takes exactly seven minutes to walk between any two points in the Pentagon. In the mystical study of numbers and their relationship to the physical world, seven is the number of perfection and is symbolic of control over both spiritual and mortal realms.

SCEPTICALLY SPEAKING

Sometimes a building is just a building. The Pentagon is not the only controversially-designed office block in the world. If it were not the home of the US military and countless conspiracies, it would probably not attract any significant speculation.

THE SPHINX

The Great Sphinx of Egypt first became an icon of the Western world when Napoleon's soldiers "rediscovered" it in 1798. Ever since that time it has exerted an intense fascination upon many of the people who have studied its enigmatic gaze. An air of mystery has always surrounded the statue that has the body of a male lion and the head of a human. Conspiracy theorists have not been the only ones to speculate on its true age, meaning and the hidden chambers it is supposed to be watching over.

Located on the Giza plateau, six miles to the west of Cairo, the Sphinx faces due East, a short distance from the trio of famous large pyramids. Carved from a relatively soft, natural limestone that outcrops on the Giza Plateau, the Sphinx was generally believed to have been made some time after 2540BC. Recently, noted geologist Robert Schock and Egyptologist John Anthony West have agreed that weathering patterns on the Sphinx are consistent with water erosion rather than erosion produced by wind and sand. The only time this water erosion could have occurred was around 10,000 years ago when Egypt's climate was temperate and damp.

Not surprisingly, the idea that the Sphinx could be 10,000 years old has been attacked by orthodox Egyptologists who would look very stupid and have to rewrite every book on the subject if West and Schock are correct

Suppression of evidence by the archaeological establishment is not the only conspiracy in which the Sphinx features. Many of the mystical traditions which underpin secret societies such as the Freemasons, speak of chambers under the front paws of the Sphinx, that contain a Hall of Records placed there by survivors of an Elder civilization. In the Forties, famous American psychic Edgar Cayce predicted that by the end of the Nineties someone would discover this Hall of Records.

Conspiracy theorists naturally became excited when workers restoring the Sphinx located a doorway in its side; in 1995 a team renovating an area near the Sphinx uncovered a series of tunnels which seemed to go under the Sphinx. John Anthony West's team used seismograph technology that detected hollow, regularly-shaped chambers a few meters below ground between the paws and to either side of the Sphinx. It looked as if the conspiriologists' belief, that secret societies had held knowledge of an underground complex at Giza for centuries, was about to be proved correct.

THE STRANGE PART

A team from Florida State University undertook a survey around the Sphinx during April 1996 and found "rooms and tunnels" in front of it. Several other teams working on similar projects have made claims that back this up – including a team from Waseda University in Tokyo that found proof of a tunnel orientated north-south under the Sphinx. With all this material in support of an underground complex on the Giza plateau, it is odd that the Egyptian authorities banned any excavation of the chambers or even further public remote sensing studies. Is there a conspiracy to suppress an outstanding truth that lies buried below the Sphinx?

THE USUAL SUSPECTS

Masonic Egyptologists

The Grand Orient Lodge of Egyptian Freemasonry teaches, at its highest degrees, that the wisdom and traditions of the lodge come from Atlantean survivors. Members believe the Atlanteans built the Sphinx in pre-history and later founded the Egyptian civilization. Clearly, the Grand Orient Lodge is a centuries-old organization with a powerful reach. Many believe it controls a network of Masonic Egyptologists who ruthlessly try to suppress the truth about the origins of the Sphinx and any secrets that it may hold.

National Security Agency

The American National Security Agency is known to have used the services of remote viewers – psychics with the ability to see what is at any given point in the world after being given a map reference – via the Stanford Research Institute (SRI). Given the prominent SRI role in investigating the Sphinx, some conspiracy theorists conclude that the NSA has taken an interest in the possible secrets, from a lost civilization, that lie below the rock of the Giza Plateau. Perhaps the NSA wants to be the first to exploit those secrets when the Hall of Records is secretly opened and its knowledge recovered.

THE UNUSUAL SUSPECTS

NASA

Many of those who have been involved in the official investigation of the Sphinx have strong links to NASA such as former NASA consultants Dr James Hurtak and Richard Hoagland – a noted UFO conspiriologist. Hoagland believes that there may be a connection between Giza and Cydonia – the region of Mars where the mysterious "pyramids" and "face" are located. Is NASA using its former advisors to conduct an investigation into the mysteries of the Sphinx?

MOST CONVINCING EVIDENCE

Aside from the fact that Sphinx was created 10,000 years ago by a civilization we have no record of existing, and appears to be sitting on top of an underground complex, the way that the Director of Egyptian Council of Antiquities, Dr Hawass, banned John Anthony West from the Giza Plateau is more than a little suspicious.

MOST MYSTERIOUS FACT

Huge Millennial celebrations are planned to take place on the Giza Plateau on New Year's Eve 1999. While it is not too surprising to discover that a wide range of cults will be there in expectation of a major mystical event as the Millennium dawns over the Sphinx and the Great Pyramid, conspiracy buffs find it odd that one of their favourite conspirators – former US President George Bush – will also be in attendance. A member of the secret Skulls and Bones society and possibly other notable organizations such as MJ-12, Bush will not be going to hear Kula Shaker in concert, or so that he can join with New Agers in chanting to ancient gods.

SCEPTICALLY SPEAKING

Most of the evidence for underground chambers is based on the interpretation of seismographic data and could turn out to be nothing more than natural anomalies in the rock. It is understandable that the Egyptians do not want excavations to take place, with the risk of damage to the Sphinx, on the off-chance of discovering the remnants of a fabled lost civilization.

TIBET

Even to non-conspiracy buffs, the mention of Tibet can conjure up images of a land beyond the normal confines of time, where Buddhist mystics remain concealed from view in inaccessible mountain monasteries. The Himalayas – meaning "home of the snows" in ancient Sanskrit – have given us many legends, including that of the Yeti and the miraculous city of Shangri-La. Yet some conspiriologists believe that not all of the strange stories emanating from the mountainous realm of Tibet are mere fables.

Ever since the first Western explorers managed to make the perilous journey to Tibet, they have carried back with them persistent rumours of Shambhala – the "Hidden Kingdom" where a community of semi-divine beings lives in seclusion, guiding the destiny of mankind. In 1933, J Hilton wrote his best-selling book *The Lost Horizon* in which Shambhala becomes

Shangri-La; the English language was given another word to describe a paradise on Earth.

Despite pulp novels and bad movies, the belief in Shambhala has persisted and even grown, as conspiracy theorists unearthed evidence of the strange role it may have played in World War II. It has become well-known in recent years that the Ahnenerbe – the occult research section of the SS – conducted two extensive trips to Tibet on the orders of Himmler. It is believed that they were searching for allies and assistance from the alleged inhabitants of the Hidden Kingdom.

After the war, Tibet was crushed under the heel of an invasion by Communist China, but rumours regarding Shambhala have been harder to suppress than Tibetan liberty. They continue to inspire a belief that deep within the Himalayas lies an advanced mystical order whose members are behind a conspiracy to keep the location of the Hidden Kingdom secret while guiding the course of history from their remote mountain retreat.

THE STRANGE PART

Whether or not the Nazis found fabled Shambhala remains a matter of conjecture, but it is certain that they found strange allies while exploring Tibet. When the Soviet army advanced on Berlin during the final days of World War II, troops discovered a cellar containing the bodies of several Tibetan monks wearing green gloves who appeared to have committed suicide as part of some arcane ritual. Over the next few days, hundreds more Tibetan bodies were recovered – all wearing SS uniforms, without any identifying papers, and all wearing green gloves. The fact that this element of the war tends to be glossed over in history books only helps convince some conspiriologists that a massive cover-up of the role of Shambhala is taking place.

THE USUAL SUSPECTS

Order Of The Green Dragon

German academic, philosopher and occultist Karl Haushoffer – creator of the term geopolitics and an important influence on Hitler – travelled extensively in Tibet and Japan. It was while he was studying mysticism in Asia that he was initiated into the ultra-secret Order of the Green Dragon.

This clandestine organization had links to Tibet and is rumoured to have received its orders direct from Shambhala. It may have been the force that helped forge links between the Nazis and the Hidden Kingdom.

The Yellow Hats

The Yellow Hats – called Dugphas in Tibet – are proponents of the most esoteric branch of Tibetan Buddhism that fully acknowledges the reality of Shambhala. Certain conspiriologists feel that the promotion of the secret lands of Tibet as the "source of happiness", is nothing other than propaganda to mask a sinister plan from the hidden masters of the Yellow Hats for world domination. While Tibet's remoteness and subjugation by the Chinese may not make it an obvious base from which to dominate the globe, in conspiracy circles these obstacles are merely seen as part of an elaborate cover story, created to prevent effective scrutiny and investigation.

THE UNUSUAL SUSPECTS

The Elder Race

The mysterious builders of monuments such as the Sphinx, the Elder Race may not have completely disappeared from Earth. According to a selection of conspiracy theorists, the Elder Race relocated to the safety of Tibet's mountains when the Earth underwent a serious of global cataclysms thousands of years ago. Currently the rulers of Shambhala, members of the Elder Race are working secretly to prepare humanity for the next stage in its evolution. Quite how helping out the Nazis would have achieved this is open to speculation.

The Hollow Earthers

Alongside legends of Shambhala, there are mentions of the underground realm of Agharta – linked in the conspiracy genre with plots to hide the truth about the Hollow Earth. The inhabitants of this strange subterranean realm, that is recorded in the inner teachings of Tibetan mysticism, have been identified by some as having links to the alien culture hinted at in the thinly-veiled works of fiction written by HP Lovecraft. While little is known as to the aims of the conspiracy conducted by the dwellers of Agharta, few doubt it would be designed to benefit those living on the external surface of the Earth.

MOST CONVINCING EVIDENCE

The current Dalai Lama, like his predecessors, is convinced of the physical reality of Shambhala, but the strongest evidence of its existence may come from the interest shown in it by the Nazis during the war. In the midst of a raging global conflict it is more than a little strange that the SS found the necessary resources and time to transport transmitters to Tibet so that Berlin could be in radio contact with the area.

MOST MYSTERIOUS FACT

Occultist, sometime secret agent and conspiracy-buff favourite, Aleister Crowley, undertook a record-breaking ascent of the Himalayas early in the century in what some see as a search for Shambhala. His quest was later duplicated by famous mystic George I Gurdjieff and, most mysteriously, in 1942, by a covert US team sent by the Office of Strategic Services – the forerunner of the modern CIA.

SCEPTICALLY SPEAKING

You have to doubt the power of any alleged conspiracy operating from Shambhala after it failed to prevent Tibet being overrun by the Chinese. Furthermore, it has not made much headway in freeing Tibet from Communist domination. Besides, if Shambhala actually existed, modern satellite technology would have revealed it ages ago.

STONEHENGE

Standing alone and majestic as a reminder of long-lost civilizations, the ruins of Stonehenge present an enigma to which there will probably never be a definitive answer. There is no dispute that Stonehenge is a Neolithic architectural marvel, but its true purpose remains totally hidden. Stonehenge continues to stand in a modern world over-run with cell phones, satellites, and trans-Atlantic air travel, as a primitive testament to the ingenuity of early man.

Located about 80 miles from London, near Salisbury Plain, Stonehenge is thought to have been constructed in three phases about 3,500 BC. It was in the third phase, thought to be around 1800BC, that the giant stone monoliths we associate with Stonehenge were transported to the site. These sarsen (an extremely hard type of sandstone) blocks were molded and lifted into 30 upright stones with accompanying lintels, set in a circle. (17 of the original 30 are still standing today.) Other stone designs were set in place inside the structure, including five triathlons (a pair of upright stones supporting a lintel stone). There is also a rectangular arrangement of "station stones" situated outside the ring.

Stonehenge is a focal religious point for Druids, who perform ceremonies there to this day, marking the summer solstice, as well as more private ceremonies. But they did not build the monument, since Stonehenge's creation pre-dates the founding of the Druidic religion.

Why Stonehenge was constructed remains a mystery, as does the identity of its original builders. Whatever prompted its construction, it's clear that Stonehenge was very important – it may still play a role in man's sophisticated world today. Perhaps the supposed "primitive" builders knew something we have forgotten, much to our peril.

THE STRANGE PART

The mechanisms by which the stones were moved have intrigued archeologists and historians, considering the primitive level of technology at the time. The bluestones are thought to have come from the Prescelly Mountains in Wales – over 200 miles away. The sarsen stones originated from the relatively nearby Marlborough Downs – but at 25 tons per stone, the 20 mile distance is still formidable. Yet with all the work that went into Stonehenge's construction, archeologists have found little detritus around the site. Most ancient construction sites are a potpourri of discarded materials, Stonehenge is remarkably – perhaps suspiciously – clean.

THE USUAL SUSPECTS

The Beakers

A Neolithic people named after the type of pottery they produced, the Beakers have been thought to have begun the construction of Stonehenge.

As the years passed, the monument's use may have varied from generation to generation. It has been suggested that it may have been used simply to hold animals, with a religious ceremony involved either in the slaughtering of livestock or in thanksgiving. Over time, Stonehenge's role as a religious centre may have intensified with the original holding pen design of the site merely kept on in its new role as a holy temple.

The Egyptians

Stonehenge could also have been designed with astronomy in mind – the positioning of the stones correlating to the positions of the sun, moon and stars throughout the year. Others believe that the axis of Stonehenge is built to correspond to the path of the sun, and that by using the Aubrey holes it is possible to predict eclipses. Such a focus on astronomy points towards the advanced Egyptians, who may have travelled to England in the distant past.

Also suspected: Ancient Greeks; Phoenicians.

THE UNUSUAL SUSPECTS

Merlin

The Arthurian Magus may have erected Stonehenge, either for his own personal study of the heavens, or as a coronation site for the young king Arthur. He would have moved the stones into position using magic, presumably of the levitating sort.

Ancient Astronauts

Stonehenge may have been built by ancient, extra-terrestrial visitors as a visible landing site/landmark, or may have been built by primitive man to honour the beings from the stars.

Also suspected: Atlanteans; giants; dwarves; energy vortexes that have been created by ley lines.

MOST CONVINCING EVIDENCE

Stonehenge shares at least two significant elements with other places of worship, including several European cathedrals. First, it has an underwater spring running beneath it, which is taken as a sign of divinity in many faiths. Secondly, in a more mathematical sense, the square root of three can be found as a recurring proportion in its construction. This too is found in many places of worship, from Europe to Egypt.

MOST MYSTERIOUS FACT

Stonehenge, next to Avebury and Glastonbury, is considered one of the most magical places in England, reportedly because it is built along powerful ley lines.

SCEPTICALLY SPEAKING

Just because something is old does not mean it is significant. Take a look at Cliff Richard.

P

THE TRILATERAL COMMISSION

Formed in 1973 by private citizens from North America, Europe and Japan, the Trilateral Commission was born to create closer ties between the three geographical areas and to share leadership responsibilities on a more global basis. One of the principal founders of this was David Rockefeller, the wealthy American banker. Apparently inspired by Prof. Zbigniew Brzezinski's book, *Between Two Ages*, in which Brzezinski proposes an alliance between North America, Western Europe, and Japan, Rockefeller went about trying to establish such an organization in reality.

With a membership supposedly gleaned from the elite echelons of society, the Trilateral Commission is said to be composed of some 335 prominent figures in the media, politics, academia and business. Its membership is supposed to include such dignitaries as Paul Volcker, erstwhile head of the Federal Reserve System; Akio Morita, chief executive officer of Sony; Count Otto Lambsdorff, leader of Germany's Free Democratic Party; Henry Kissinger, and Bill Clinton. Top executives of such companies as AT&T, Pepsico and the Chase Manhattan Bank, among many others, are also members.

The Trilateral Commission meets once a year, in Spring, to discuss world problems and hopefully to come up with solutions. The Commission is nothing more than the political power behind the formation of the New World Order, according to conspiracy theorists who believe that the Commission has one aim: to wipe out all political sovereignty on Earth and place its people under the rule of one government and one bank. Others see the Trilateral Commission as a group that is merely trying to ensure that global financial interests (such as those of AT&T and the Rockefellers) are protected. While hiding behind a mask of benign kindness, the Trilateral Commission's real aim is not to protect the interests of the lower classes but to convince people, subtly, that they must bow to the needs of the banks and corporations . . .

THE STRANGE PART

Given that the Trilateral Commission's membership includes some of the most important and powerful names in the worlds of politics, business and the media, many conspiracy theorists find it had to believe that their role is purely consultative. The theorists feel that US presidents, world leaders and other members of the globe's power elite would not find time in their schedules to attend something which only serves as a talking shop – especially when the mysterious lack of media attention on the Commission means that they do not even get the chance for a photo opportunity.

USUAL SUSPECTS

The Freemasons

Theories abound that the Freemasons control the agenda of the Trilateral Commission, shaping its decisions and influences on global policy to ensure total Freemason domination of the Earth. By slowly moving the world into the straitjacket of the New World Order, the Freemasons, could by crushing all dissent under the tight rules and brutality of the NWO, finally achieve their ultimate goal.

The Illuminati

Another mysterious, shadowy group that is feared to be behind the scenes in all governments, the Illuminati is another candidate for running the Trilateral Commission. Like the Freemasons, the Illuminati's goal is total global domination.

Also suspected: The Bilderburger Group, another alleged 'discussion group' based in Geneva, Switzerland, and apparently partly financed by the Rockefellers.

UNUSUAL SUSPECTS

Aliens

According to this view, an un-named alien power is trying to take over the planet. It is working in conjunction with the Trilateral Commission, the Bilderburger Group, and the Council of Foreign Relations. Clearly, conquest will be much simpler for the aliens once all governments, and all armies, have first been absorbed into the single New World Order. Those who work with the aliens will be spared the horrors that are due to befall the rest of us.

SHIRLEY TEMPLE AND BARBARA WALTERS
Both are members of the Trilateral Commission, which only adds to a feeling of apprehension concerning the aims of this organization. While many media celebrities are members, perhaps to gain their compliance in indoctrinating the masses, it's interesting to note that no athletes or pop stars have been asked to join the Commission. The reason for this remains a topic of debate among conspiracy buffs.

MOST CONVINCING EVIDENCE

There is a curious lack of media attention surrounding meetings of the Trilateral Commission, which seems extremely odd considering the profiles of many attendees. In a world where the President of the United States is bombarded with flashbulbs and microphones when he does something as innocent as walking his dog, it's interesting to note that when he attends a meeting of the Trilateral Commission, it barely merits a mention on the evening news. Despite the Commission's insistence that it is merely a "discussion group" and that all of its discussion papers are available to the public, this shadow over its activities is disquieting. Considering how President Clinton could not control the media circus over the Lewinsky affair, where does the Trilateral Commission get its power to muzzle the media when it sees fit?

MOST MYSTERIOUS FACT

Some conspiracy theorists have found it interesting that the Commission renews itself every three years – an important mystical number – reinvesting itself to carry on its mission. Its current renewal comes to an end in the year 2000, a date that is both ominous in many people's books and all too near.

SCEPTICALLY SPEAKING

If there were going to be a New World Order, would the Trilateral Commission even have to exist as a public entity? While it can be argued that the best place to hide is in broad daylight, which could be the Commission's credo, why create such an organization that would inevitably lead to suspicion and fears of conspiracy? In an age of encrypted communications and underground government bunkers, there is no need for the power brokers of the world to meet in full view of a suspicious public to discuss their future enslavement. There is every evidence to suggest that the Trilateral Commission is nothing more than an excuse for rich people to get together, swap stories, drink expensive wine, and maybe sneak in a few rounds of golf. Perhaps world domination isn't their goal: maybe just getting away from the office is.

THE GUNPOWDER PLOT

"Remember remember the fifth of November – gunpowder, treason and plot." It seems as if every schoolchild grows up having to learn the famous phrase, but few of them ever see beyond the fireworks and bonfires and think of it is as the most famous political conspiracy in English history.

Given that the Gunpowder Plot was exposed before it was successfully completed, there is a tendency to view it as a failed conspiracy – one which has been fully investigated, resolved and consigned to the pages of dusty history books. However, some conspiriologists have nagging doubts over the whole matter and feel that the Gunpowder Plot we are taught about as children is only the visible tip of a much larger conspiracy.

The bare facts of the Plot are well known. Guy Fawkes was caught red-handed in a cellar underneath the Houses of Parliament the night before King James was due to preside over the State Opening of Parliament. His fellow conspirators were soon hunted down. Those who did not die resisting arrest were tried, found guilty of treason and sentenced to death. Within a week of their trial they had all been hanged, drawn and quartered.

The accepted theory – usually the one you need to be deeply suspicious of – is that a small group of Catholic fanatics, working alone, planned to kill King James I, hoping in the confusion after his death that they would be able to put a Catholic on the throne of England. However, for many conspiracy buffs, those who were exposed and punished as conspirators were little more than the fall-guys for the true plotters whose aims may have had very little to do with restoring Catholicism to Britain.

THE STRANGE PART

One of the most significant aspects of the Gunpowder Plot is the spectacular nature of its failure. It seems incredible that any group of conspirators – especially a group as amateurish as the one led by Guy Fawkes – could have gained access to a cellar under the Houses of Parliament, smuggled in several tonnes of explosive undetected and then have been magically caught almost in the act of lighting the fuse. Incredible – unless there was another unseen level to the conspiracy.

THE USUAL SUSPECTS

Robert Cecil, Earl of Salisbury

Cecil was England's spymaster and his speciality was uncovering plots – or as some suspect, uncovering plots that he had set up in an attempt to frame enemies of the state and make himself look good. Cecil had met Guy Fawkes' main co-conspirator Robert Catesby previously, when he had uncovered the Essex plot and spared Catesby from execution. Conspiriologists believe that Catesby was recruited by Cecil as a double-agent to operate a plot that would be uncovered at the last minute, boosting not only Cecil's prestige but allowing for a ruthless crackdown on Catholics.

The English Nobility

When James was crowned King of England in 1603 he united two countries that had been at war far more often than they had been at peace. It is inconceivable that this unification could happen without upsetting plenty of people – as soon as James arrived in London he began appointing Scottish nobles to positions of power. Among the displaced English nobles were members of the mystical order known as Meonia – including Sir Walter Raleigh – who were known to have links with some Gunpowder Plot conspirators, including Robert Catesby and Thomas Wyntour.

THE UNUSUAL SUSPECTS

The Tobacco Lobby

Sir Walter Raleigh had first introduced tobacco from the New World a generation earlier and the fashion for smoking it had spread like wildfire throughout England – making some merchants who dealt in tobacco very rich indeed. One of the few men who had not succumbed to the demon weed was James I, who published his famous rant A Counterblast To Tobacco. There was a rumour that the King was intending to introduce a series of punitive taxes on tobacco to raise some much-needed cash. If these had been introduced they would have seriously damaged the financial interests of several powerful people in England and Virginia, so the Gunpowder Plot may have been one of the first times that big business decided to flex its muscles.

The Scottish Nobility

James I of England was also James VI of Scotland, and Scotland, at this point in history, was as torn apart with plots and treason as any soap opera plot could ever become. Plots, conspiracies and assassinations were commonplace and one of the most favoured ways of disposing of an enemy or rival was death by explosion. James I's father had been killed by this method and the King himself had ordered the destruction of his enemies be carried out with explosives. James had plenty of enemies in his home country who wanted him out of the way and would not have minded the Catholics taking the blame.

MOST CONVINCING EVIDENCE

Two of the other major plots exposed during James I's reign which led to the downfall of Sir Walter Raleigh – the Main plot and the Bye Plot – shared certain common elements with the Gunpowder Plot. They both failed, they were both uncovered at the last minute thanks to Cecil, and they both left the establishment and the King stronger and more firmly in place.

MOST MYSTERIOUS FACT

On December 28, 1604, King James I attended the society wedding of the Earl of Montgomery to Robert Cecil's niece. Bizarrely, among the other guests attending this glittering social function was Guy Fawkes. If Guy Fawkes was the Catholic fanatic painted by many historians, with a burning desire to murder James I, then why did he not simply bring a knife to the wedding and attempt a more straightforward assassination? It seems more than a little strange that three of the key figures of the Gunpowder Plot were attending the same wedding.

SCEPTICALLY SPEAKING

Sometimes the official explanation is the one that is not only obvious, but also correct. Catholic countries, such as France and Spain, certainly had an interest in destabilizing England and were known to work through underground networks of priests to ferment unrest. Maybe this is one conspiracy that really is as simple as it seems.

MALCOLM X

If you were a controversial political figure in America during the Sixties, it was highly probable that your life would end in a hail of bullets. Malcolm X, the fiery leader of the Organization of Afro-American Unity, who outraged white America with his pronouncements on racial matters, was yet another man cut down in his prime because of the dangerous power of his beliefs.

Malcolm X was born Malcolm Little in 1925. His father, a Baptist minister, was murdered by white racists six years later and family was broken up and put into care. Although he was a bright student, Little's dreams of becoming a lawyer were crushed when a teacher explained to him that he was only a "nigger", and should consider becoming a carpenter instead. Disillusioned with education, he drifted into a life of petty crime. While serving time for burglary, Little began to read about the Nation of Islam. The NOI's beliefs of black self-reliance and the need for racial separation intrigued Little, and when he was released, in 1952, he joined the Nation of Islam, dropping his surname because it was a vestige of slave ownership, and replacing it with a simple "X".

Malcolm X rose quickly through the ranks of the Nation, becoming the organization's chief spokesman. But after his inflammatory comments about the Kennedy assassination, its leader, Elijah Muhammed, suspended him from the NOI. Malcolm X took this opportunity to create his Organization of Afro-American Unity, and did not return to the Nation when his suspension was over.

Where Martin Luther King believed in non-violence and the integration of the black man into white America, Malcolm X angered white society by stating that blacks were superior to whites in all ways. He travelled the world, speaking in the Middle East, and generating support for a United Nations resolution condemning both South Africa and the United States for human rights violations in their treatment of blacks. Such views, as well as animosity from the Nation of Islam, made Malcolm X a man who was widely hated. This hatred came to a head on February 21, 1965 at the Audubon Ballroom in New York.

At the beginning of the meeting, a fight broke out in front of the stage where Malcolm X was speaking. As he tried to calm things down, a group of five assassins stood in the audience and shot him. Malcolm X died shortly afterwards, another figure cut down in America's cull of leaders who threatened the Establishment in the not-so-groovy Sixties.

THE STRANGE PART

Even though there was a hospital across the street from the Audubon Ballroom, it still took close to half-an-hour for an emergency crew to arrive, following X's shooting.

THE USUAL SUSPECTS

The FBI

J Edgar Hoover, the cross-dressing head of the FBI, distrusted Malcolm X because he represented a force of black power that had no place in Hoover's view of America. One counter-intelligence program sponsored by the FBI was designed to keep a "black messiah" like X from uniting the black movement. With Malcolm X growing closer to Martin Luther King, the FBI could have decided that killing X was the only way to prevent a united black front from arising.

The US Government

The prospect of a UN resolution condemning the US along with South Africa for human rights violations seemed a clear possibility. This would have been seriously embarrassing for the US. By taking out the chief proponent for this resolution, Malcolm X, the States could then spin-doctor the whole messy business away.

THE UNUSUAL SUSPECTS

The Mob

In an effort to clean up black neighbourhoods and institute a lifestyle of clean living, Malcolm X verbally attacked the drug trade. This threat to the profits that could be made from the despair of the ghetto may have sealed X's fate.

The Nation Of Islam

The schisms between the Nation of Islam and Malcolm X's own group ran deep, with some people feeling that X was unfairly criticizing Elijah Muhammed and other Nation leaders, such as Louis Farrakhan, if not outrightly blaspheming. This could have resulted in a murder that had both political and religious overtones to its motive as some in the Nation of Islam openly fanned this hatred of X.

MOST CONVINCING EVIDENCE

Leon Ameer, a member of the Organization of Afro-American Unity, stated on March 13, 1965, that he had proof of a government connection in Malcolm X's death. Unfortunately, Ameer's body was found the following morning before he could back up this claim. His death was attributed to an epileptic fit, even though past medical examinations had found no hint of epilepsy.

MOST MYSTERIOUS FACT

Of the three men who were convicted of Malcolm X's murder, one was unable to walk and was at home on the day of the assassination.

SCEPTICALLY SPEAKING

In the US, if you're black and speak out about human rights, you're a radical asking to be shot. If you're white, you're a humanitarian and get asked to Rotary dinners. No conspiracy is needed to explain this awful truth.

NIXON, WATERGATE AND E HOWARD HUNT

Watergate is the most famous political conspiracy of the modern age. The exposure of attempts to cover up a failed conspiracy led to Richard Milhous Nixon becoming the first US President to resign from office. It gave new meaning to the term "Deep Throat" – now an anonymous source of classified information as well as a sexual act – and no current political scandal is complete unless it is given the "-gate" tag.

In 1995, when renowned conspiriologist and film maker Oliver Stone produced Nixon – starring Anthony Hopkins as the unfortunate President – he was not the first theorist to speculate that Watergate was only the visible surface of a much larger and more sinister plot. Like Stone's other conspiracy-fuelled opus, JFK, the film was condemned by those it portrayed and by the establishment – a sign taken by Stone's fellow conspiriologists to suggest that it may have contained a great deal of truth.

The facts regarding the outer layer of Watergate are well-established and form the basis of the official version of the scandal that is even taught in schools – one of the few conspiracies that the education system acknowledges. In the early hours of June 17, 1972, James McCord – a man with links to the CIA – led a group of four anti-Castro Cuban exiles in an attempt to burgle the Democratic National Committee Headquarters. The burglars were discovered and arrested as they attempted to tap the telephone system in the Watergate office and hotel complex in Washington DC.

Charges were also eventually laid against two more people: G Gordon Liddy, finance counsel to the President and the power behind Nixon's Committee to Re-elect the President (CREEP); and E Howard Hunt, a former White House aide and ex-CIA operative. Over the next few months, what initially appeared to be a third-rate burglary quickly escalated into a full-blown political scandal. Nixon's involvement in the conspiracy to cover up a conspiracy led to America's gravest constitutional crisis and climaxed with his resignation as President on August 9, 1974.

However, in the national aftermath of distrust following Watergate, conspiracy theorists began to examine the details of the case. They discovered an assortment of facts that suggested the real reason behind the downfall of Nixon was a conspiracy to hide the truth about the assassination of President John F Kennedy.

THE STRANGE PART

On the Watergate tapes that provided the damning evidence of his involvement in the cover up of the original burglary, President Nixon says: "Look, the problem is that this (Watergate) will open up the whole Bay of Pigs things again." John Ehrlichman, Assistant to the President for Domestic Affairs, who served 18 months in prison for his part in the conspiracy, has admitted that "Bay of Pigs" was Nixon's code phrase for the John F Kennedy assassination.

Dorothy Hunt, the wife of one of the key players in Watergate, E Howard Hunt, may have been blackmailing the White House and have demanded more than a million dollars to keep silent about information that would "blow the White House out of the water". Many conspiratologists believe that there is photographic evidence to suggest that Hunt, a long-time CIA agent, was one of the famous "Three Tramps" photographed on the grassy knoll immediately after the shooting of JFK.

THE USUAL SUSPECTS

James Jesus Angleton

Director of CIA counter-intelligence from 1954 to 1974, James Jesus Angleton is suspected by many of being the mastermind behind JFK's assassination. His uncharacteristic refusal to help Nixon cover up the White House involvement in the burglary definitely helped seal Nixon's fate. Was Angleton willing to sacrifice a President to hide his involvement in the "whole Bay of Pigs thing"?

THE MAFIA

It is well established that the Mafia and their Cuban allies had strong links to the CIA and probably played a part in the death of John F Kennedy, so it is probably more than coincidence that four anti-Castro Cuban exiles were among the Watergate burglars. If the role of high-placed mobsters in the JFK conspiracy were in danger of being exposed by Watergate, they would have a solid motive for wanting Nixon to take all of the blame.

THE UNUSUAL SUSPECTS

FEDERAL RESERVE BANK

Lee Harvey Oswald's widow has pointed the finger to the US Federal Reserve Bank's mysterious role in the JFK affair. A private corporation that controls the creation of all American money, the Federal Reserve Bank (FRB) is owned in part by the Rockefellers. Given that the hugely-influential Trilateral Commission was set up by David Rockerfeller in 1973, some have conjectured that the FRB had the financial and political muscle to stage Watergate to depose Nixon – a possible obstacle in its plans for world domination.

HOWARD HUGHES

In 1972, eccentric millionaire Howard Hughes asked the White House to send the team that eventually bungled the Watergate burglary to break into the office of a Las Vegas newspaper editor, Hank Greenspun. Their task would have been to steal certain papers that formed allegedly devastating blackmail material. Given that some have linked Hughes and his fellow oil barons with Nixon and a plot to kill JFK, his role in Watergate is suspicious to say the least.

MOST CONVINCING EVIDENCE

In December 1973, a United Airlines flight crashed near Chicago Midway Airport. On board was E Howard Hunt's wife Dorothy. One of Hunt's fellow Watergate conspirators, Charles Coulson, made a statement to Time magazine claiming that "the CIA killed Dorothy Hunt". Unfortunately his claim may not have been pure paranoia – the pilot of the flight was found to have a quantity of cyanide in his blood that could only have been there if he had been poisoned. Another odd element to the crash is that Dorothy Hunt was carrying more than $250,000 in "hush money" when she boarded the plane, but only $10,000 was recovered with her body.

MOST MYSTERIOUS FACT

A mysterious letter written by Lee Harvey Oswald on November 10, 1963 has been the source of much heated debate. In this note Oswald asks a "Mr. Hunt" for a job within his organization. More than one researcher has come to the conclusion that the letter supplies additional evidence for Hunt's role in the JFK affair.

SCEPTICALLY SPEAKING

Watergate traumatized the American psyche and its scars run deep. The events, which started with that "third-rate burglary", have been described as the root cause in America of the current distrust of government as well as the tendency to believe in conspiracies. Hardly surprising, then, that Watergate set off further speculation into the JFK assassination.

PEARL HARBOR

There are cross-roads in time – nexus points – when the actions that take place have the potential to shape the course of history on a grand scale. The events that took place before dawn on Sunday December 7, 1941, at Pearl Harbor form such a nexus point. They influenced not only the course of World War II, but also the way world history unfolded.

The infamous "sneak attack" by Japanese forces on Hawaii resulted in 2,403 American deaths, 1,178 wounded servicemen, 18 ships, including three battleships, were sunk and 188 aeroplanes were destroyed with a further 162 suffering severe damage. By contrast, the Japanese lost only 29 planes, five midget submarines and 64 men. The direct result of this allegedly surprise attack was a US declaration of war on Japan, which immediately led to Hitler supporting his Asian allies – an act that finally brought America into the war against the Nazis.

However, some of America's most respected historians have joined forces with the conspiriologists they usually refer to as "delusional paranoids". Both groups suggest that the real reason why Pearl Harbor should be remembered is because it was the tragic outcome of a massive conspiracy to ensure that the US joined Britain as a full combatant in World War II.

By 1941, the US President, Franklin D Roosevelt, was faced with a massive and seemingly insurmountable political problem. He wanted America to become involved in the war with Germany but US public opinion was unsympathetic – Americans felt it was a European affair, and that Britain, Russia and Germany should be left alone to sort it out without any American lives being put at risk. Conspiracy theorists, and some historians, feel that Roosevelt knew Pearl Harbor was going to be attacked, but allowed it to happen as it would give him the perfect excuse for declaring war on Japan – an action that his intelligence services had told him would provoke an identical response from Germany on the US.

THE STRANGE PART

In 1941, Roosevelt had been warned by his admirals that cutting off the supply of petrol to Japan was likely to involve the US in a Pacific War. In July Roosevelt cut off those petroleum supplies and began to withhold intelligence information about Japanese activities from Army and Navy officials based in Hawaii. The governments of Britain, Holland, Australia, Peru, Korea and the Soviet Union all warned the US that a surprise attack on Pearl Harbor was coming, so it is even more odd that this information was not passed on to the military in Pearl Harbor.

THE USUAL SUSPECTS

Franklin D Roosevelt

The most obvious suspect in the conspiracy is the President himself. It is no secret that he wanted to bring America into the war with Europe, but was being held back by domestic political concerns. His position meant that he had the power to manoeuvre events in such a way that the US would not have to fire the first shot and be seen as the aggressor.

Anglo-American Cabal

There is a widespread belief, at least in certain sections of the conspiracy field, that there is a powerful Anglo-American cabal in operation determined to keep the "special relationship" in existence. Believed to involve members of the American and British intelligence services, as well as major figures from business and finance and top politicians, the cabal may also have counted Roosevelt as a member. He could have been instructed to cover up the impending attack on Pearl Harbor so that the US could be brought into the war to defend Britain.

THE UNUSUAL SUSPECTS

The American Banking Community

At the time of Pearl Harbor, Britain was in debt to America under the terms of the lend-lease agreement. If Britain were defeated by Germany there would be no chance of her ever repaying the vast loans she had taken out. Therefore, members of the American banking community had a vested interest in British victory and may have pulled strings behind the scenes to ensure America lent more than financial support to their client.

International League of Communists

American conspiracy theorists with a very heavy Right-wing bias have believed for some while that Roosevelt was secretly a communist. Their conjecture also makes him a vital member of an alleged International League of Communists, which conspired to take the US into a war with Germany. America's entry to the war would not be to save democracy in Britain and Europe, but to ensure that the world's first communist state, the Soviet Union, was not crushed by the might of the Nazi war machine.

MOST CONVINCING EVIDENCE

In 1932, a joint Army-Navy exercise saw Pearl Harbor being successfully "attacked" by 152 planes half-an-hour before dawn on a Sunday – catching the defenders completely by surprise. This was duplicated in 1938, so there can be no doubt that the military knew the potential risk to Pearl Harbor. Furthermore, the US had cracked the top Japanese Naval and diplomatic codes – a fact not lost on a top secret Army Board. In 1944 the Board reported: "Numerous pieces of information came to our State, War and Navy Departments in all of their top ranks indicating precisely the intentions of the Japanese including the probable exact hour and date of the attack."

MOST MYSTERIOUS FACT

The US Navy in Pearl Harbor was laughably under-prepared for the attack. Ships were tied up side-by-side and, despite radar operators in Hawaii reporting that Japanese planes were coming, no one took any action. Three American battleships were sunk in the attack, but by 1941 battleships were obsolete and the aircraft carrier was the pinnacle of naval power. It may be significant that no American aircraft carriers were based at Pearl Harbor during the attack – the majority of them were 3,000 miles away, safely stationed at San Diego, which is where a lot of American Navy people had wanted the Pearl Harbor ships to be located.

SCEPTICALLY SPEAKING

It is hard to be sceptical over many aspects of the Pearl Harbor conspiracy, but it is also hazardous to ever underestimate the levels of incompetence that can be achieved by the US military and its Commander-In-Chief – the President.

RUDOLF HESS

There are many strange stories surrounding World War II, but few are stranger than that of Rudolf Hess. In many places, the story of Hess reads more like a lost Monty Python sketch than the historical details of the activities of a high-ranking member of Hitler's Nazi Party.

Born in Alexandria, Egypt on April 26, 1894, Hess fell under the spell Adolf Hitler was weaving over Germany when he first saw him speak in

Munich. Hess joined the Nazi Party in 1920, becoming close to Hitler, whom he idolized. This idolatry led Hess to join Hitler in the Beer Hall Putsch of 1923 when Hitler attempted to take over the reins of power of Germany. Instead, they ended up in Landsberg prison.

Hess acted as Hitler's secretary in prison, taking slavish dictation as Hitler composed Mein Kampf. Released from prison in 1925, Hess followed Hitler as he built his Nazi powerbase, continuing to act as his secretary. As Hitler finally attained the power he so desperately craved, in 1932, he appointed Hess Chairman of the Central Political Commission of the Nazi Party. Hess was also made a General in the SS for good measure. As Hess continued to follow Hitler with the blind devotion of a puppy, he was rewarded with the position of Deputy Führer in 1933.

Hess was determined to do what he perceived best for his beloved Führer: he would negotiate peace with England, by himself, without telling anyone. Borrowing a Messerschmitt ME-110, Hess flew across the North Sea on May 10, 1941. He was headed for Scotland, to meet with the Duke of Hamilton, a casual acquaintance he had met at the Berlin Olympics in 1936. Hess parachuted into Scotland, met a bewildered farmer, and told him he had an important message for the Duke.

His peace plan was considered ludicrous by Churchill: that if England let Germany have Europe, then England would be left alone. Disowned by the Nazi Party, and considered half-mad by the British authorities, a disheartened Hess was thrown into prison. He was transferred to Germany for the Nuremberg Trials in 1945, where his mental instability was readily apparent. He was sentenced to life in Spandau prison, and reportedly committed suicide by hanging himself in 1987 at the age of 92. Or did he?

Theories have sprung up that the man who died in 1987 was not Hess, but a body-double. Questions have also arisen as to why a man so obviously incompetent was considered such a threat to British authorities.

THE STRANGE PART

Dr Hugh Thomas, who cared for Hess in Spandau, stated repeatedly that his patient was not Hess, citing the absence of the scars that Hess should have had.

THE USUAL SUSPECTS

The Nazi Party

Knowing Hess was more of a liability than an asset, members of the Nazi Party planted the seeds of the glorious peace plan in Hess' head, knowing he was foolish enough to attempt it, but hoping he would be shot down in the process.

Winston Churchill's government

There is a chance that Hess did die before the Nuremberg Trials, and was replaced by a British body-double. One possibility has Hess being severely interrogated and beaten to death by military investigators. Afraid of the consequences of Hess' death for British officers being held by German troops, the government quickly recruited a body-double to keep up the appearance that Hess was still alive. The double carried on the charade all his life and was murdered by the British in Spandau to ensure his silence. Another theory states that Hess had an actual, viable peace plan but Churchill was determined to wage war, so kept Hess imprisoned and unstable through drugged food. This theory sees M16, the British secret service, murdering the real Hess to hide the truth about the peace plan.

THE UNUSUAL SUSPECTS

Vril Society

This theory states Hess was kept imprisoned by the Germans because he held vital information about secret Nazi Antarctic bases operated by the occult Vril Society which included many top Nazis among its members. Although this sounds bizarre, it should be remembered that James Bond creator and member of MI6, Ian Fleming, recommended that master occultist Aleister Crowley should lead the interrogation of Hess.

MOST CONVINCING EVIDENCE

Karel Hille, a Dutch journalist, claimed to have files that had been stolen from M16 by none other than Sir Maurice Oldfield himself, ex-head of M16. The files proved that the man who died in Spandau was not Hess, but a body-double.

MOST MYSTERIOUS FACT

While in British prison, Hess kept complaining that he felt his food was being poisoned. This was just chalked up to Hess' instability, but if he were being drugged, his food would be the least conspicuous form of administering poison.

SCEPTICALLY SPEAKING

The world actually managed to jail a high-ranking member of Hitler's Nazi Party? No wonder no one believes it, since all the other Nazis went to work for the CIA.

SADDAM HUSSEIN

On the face of it, the Gulf War was a straightforward conflict. The traditional analysis of it stems from a view that Saddam Hussein is a classic megalomaniac dictator who tested the will of the world to halt his expansionist policies by invading Kuwait in August 1990. Britain and the US – backed by the much-trumpeted New World Order as mentioned for the first time by George Bush during the Gulf War – organized enough military and political power to successfully defeat him and free Kuwait.

Yet all is not what it seems when the conspiracy researchers turn their questioning gaze to the Gulf War – the largest international military campaign undertaken since World War II. A number of significant puzzles develop when certain questions are asked. For instance, why did the Allied forces stop when they easily could have driven into Baghdad? If Saddam is another Hitler why are we allowing him to stay in power?

Accusations and rumours that began as conspiracy theories have started to be accepted as mainstream facts. More than one revisionist commentator on international politics has begun to wonder if the Gulf War was set up and carried out for objectives other than freeing Kuwait.

THE STRANGE PART

It has become generally accepted that the US State Department gave a "green light" to Saddam to invade Kuwait. This happened when an Iraqi Ambassador raised the subject of how the US would react to a potential Iraqi invasion with American Ambassador April Glaspie, in August 1990 just before Iraqi tanks rolled across the sand.

While debate rages as to the exact details of what occurred at that meeting, whether by intent or accident, it seems certain that Saddam thought that the US would not object if he went ahead with his invasion plans. Given that a number of US Senators had recently visited Baghdad and declared support for Hussein – including at least one staunch Jewish liberal and champion of Israel – it is a conclusion he could be forgiven for making.

THE USUAL SUSPECTS

New World Order

The "new world order" was an expression first used in the Twenties by Colonel Edward House who believed in world government. President George Bush brought the phrase into the public spotlight when he described the coalition gathered against Saddam as a sign of an emerging New World Order. Most conspiriologists view the NWO as a form of One World Government that secret forces are working to introduce. For a New World Order to hold power over nation states it would need to be able justify its existence. The type of international operation of joint political and military force seen in the Gulf may be the first example designed to convince the population of the globe that the NWO is an idea whose time has come.

Military Industrial Complex

With the fragmentation of the Soviet Union, in 1989, and the spectre of a communist menace a thing of the past, people were beginning to question whether the US and its Western allies actually needed to keep spending billions on defence. Conspiracy theorists believe that the invasion by Saddam Hussein, in 1990, is just too much of a coincidence. They believe that he was put up to the attack on Kuwait by the Military Industrial Complex, so that he could be presented as the new enemy that needed opposing – hence justifying continued massive spending on armaments.

THE UNUSUAL SUSPECTS

KGB

It is well known that the Soviets and the KGB had developed a very close relationship with Hussein over the years. Some conspiracy theorists believe that the demise of the Soviet Union is merely a diversionary tactic to allow the KGB to develop plans for communist world domination – it was the KGB that arranged the Gulf War. By setting up Saddam as the main bogeyman, the KGB's strategists ensured that American attention would be focused on Iraq, leaving them free to pursue their machinations unmolested by the US.

Oil Companies

If nothing else, the Gulf War managed to push up the price of crude oil to the type of figure that oil companies had not enjoyed since the days of the 1973 oil embargo. George Bush made his fortune as an oil baron and with the connections that the petrol industry has with the intelligence community, some have speculated that financial gain may have been the true motive behind the staging of the Gulf War.

MOST CONVINCING EVIDENCE

It is odd that a UN-backed coalition of powerful nations – including the only country that can still justifiably be called a superpower – could not remove the dictator of one Middle Eastern state even after smashing his army within a matter of days. It is also strange that in subsequent years, no covert operation has assassinated Saddam. Nor has meaningful military action been taken to prevent him from continuing to develop his stockpile of chemical and biological weapons.

MOST MYSTERIOUS FACT

In the aftermath of the Gulf War, an intriguing book entitled *American Hero* was written by Larry Beinhart and published by Ballantine Books. Purporting to be fiction, it details how the war was the idea of a Republican dirty tricks expert designed to boost the popularity of George Bush. For a novel, its unearthed facts and extensive footnotes provide a damning level of evidence for the conspiracy view of the Gulf War. One question it raises is why did the American, British and Soviet Ambassadors all leave Kuwait two days before the invasion?

SCEPTICALLY SPEAKING

America has never shown that much inclination to come up with excuses for throwing its weight around, so purposely allowing the invasion of Kuwait seems highly fanciful. Maybe the reason why Saddam is still in power is that when it comes down to it, American military might is not all that it is cracked up to be.

JAPANESE BIO-EXPERIMENTS

Politics is a dirty business and an activity in which morality is quickly abandoned when there is an advantage to be gained. That said, surely even politicians would draw the line at doing deals with war criminals who experiment on live human subjects? The answer may be no.

Cryogenics, models of the spread of infection, and plague bombs are just three of the inventions that we in the West can thank Japanese war criminals for. Much like the deal made with Nazi scientists that guaranteed freedom from prosecution after World War II in return for access to technological breakthroughs in rocket technology, the Allies also let Japanese scientists from Unit 731, Japan's bio-warfare division, go free in return for useful information.

That was not the only arrangement that made with the Far East, though. Three leading figures from the war, Nobusuke Kishi, Yoshi Kodama and Ryoichi Sasakawa, were tried and convicted as Class A War Criminals – the most serious of the classifications – after the end of World War II, and put into prison. In 1948, all three were suddenly released, apparently without explanation. Recent release of US government documents has shown that the CIA was seriously involved with the trio.

For years, the biological warfare section of the Japanese World War II military continued its experiments in the US while the CIA was busy bribing Japanese war criminals to work on its behalf in the Far East. Unit 731 offered the US vital data gathered from vivisection experiments on enemy soldiers, and the unit continued its work after the War. According to the Associated Press, six ex-members of Unit 731 have spoken out in Japan, talking for the first time about some of their activities. One revealed that several dissections were carried out on live, conscious, unanaesthetized victims, saying that they invariably "let out a horrible shriek and then fell silent". Another gave details of releasing several poisons and disease cultures into public water supplies in Mongolia.

THE STRANGE PART

Kamikaze bombers were a major problem towards the end of the World War II. These pilots would crash their planes into warships, killing themselves and also large numbers of American servicemen. The usual presumption about the Kamikazes is that they were insanely loyal, cheerfully laying down their lives in the service of their Emperor. That may not have been the case. Reports on the work of Unit 731 suggest that a drug was developed there that suppressed fear and caused fervour and excitement. A drug that was slipped into pre-flight drinks given to the pilots to help get them in the right mood.

THE USUAL SUSPECTS

The American Government

Desperately keen to get its hands on useful technology that would help in the now-inevitable Cold War against the Soviet Union, the American government was prepared to deal with anyone. If freedom was the price that the horrendous butchers of Unit 731 required to hand over their secrets, then it was worth paying.

THE UNUSUAL SUSPECTS

Hitler

Having fled to South America with a small cabal of his top aides and strategists, Hitler would have been very keen to make sure that he still had access to human vivisection research, according to some conspiriologists. Without such research, he would not be able to breed his Aryan Master Race clone warriors. Hitler pulled strings with the US government – funding his campaign with stolen art treasures – to make sure that Unit 731 was allowed to continue.

MOST CONVINCING EVIDENCE

Kishi, who became Prime Minister in Japan, was strongly anti-Communist, and the Japanese press have accused him of being backed strongly by the US because of this stance. Kodama became a lobbyist for Lockheed and was a known CIA agent as well as being a major Yakuza gang lord. Sasakawa was shown to be a major funder of the Moonies, which turned out to be run by the Korean CIA – set up by the American CIA, in 1961. In other words, all three war criminals took US money to become CIA agents and spies.

MOST MYSTERIOUS FACT

Is Unit 731 still at work? The Japanese still lead the world in bio-technology advances and Dr Richard Seed, the US's aptly-named leading exponent of human cloning, has announced that he is setting up a human cloning lab in Japan.

SCEPTICALLY SPEAKING

Could the US government really have been so interested in the test results of some human dissection experiments that they were prepared to let war criminals go free? What use could they put that sort of data to anyway?

GEORGE BUSH

Anyone elected to the office of President of the United States of America becomes the centre of attention for an army of conspiriologists. George

Bush was something of an exception – even before he was elected as Ronald Reagan's Vice President, in 1980, he was already at the heart of several major conspiracy theories including Watergate, the Bay of Pigs and the assassination of JFK.

Officially, George Bush only worked for the Central Intelligence Agency from 1976-1977 when he was its Director. However, there is a large body of evidence to suggest that George Bush was working for the CIA as early as 1961. He was a member of the bizarre Skull and Bones Society at college – a known recruiting ground for senior CIA agents. Running his oil company meant visiting rigs across the world – perfect cover for an agent. His company was named Zapata which was also the codename for the CIA's Bay of Pigs operation; the two Navy ships repainted as civilian ships for the aborted invasion attempt were renamed Barbara and Houston – the names of Bush's wife and of the town in Texas where his company was based.

When the US government released nearly 100,000 pages of documents on the Kennedy assassination, in 1978, conspiracy researchers found a memo among them from the State Department to "George Bush of the Central Intelligence Agency". This memo warned of the possibility that anti-Castro groups in Miami might stage another invasion of Cuba in the aftermath of the JFK murder. President Bush has denied that he was the man in the memo and that it was intended for another "George Bush" who also had a similar address to him. Conspiracy buffs believe that the memo was sent to the CIA because of the previous invasion attempt and to George Bush because he was involved in the planning of other invasions, including the Bay of Pigs.

Another significant Bush link to the Kennedy affair lies with George de Mohrenschildt, a rich Russian oilman and long-time CIA agent who lived in Texas and helped Lee Harvey Oswald settle there after he left the Soviet Union. Shortly before he was due to testify before the House Select Committee on Assassinations, De Mohrenschildt was found dead of an allegedly self-inflicted gunshot wound. His personal address book contained the entry: "Bush, George H W (Poppy) 1412 W. Ohio also Zapata Petroleum Midland."

Given this type of security service background to investigate, it is not surprising that some conspiriologists believe that the then-Vice-President Bush was the force behind a conspiracy to assassinate President Ronald

Reagan in 1982, in an attempt to place himself in the White House a few years ahead of schedule.

THE STRANGE PART

The official version of events on March 30, 1982 is that Ronald Reagan was walking to his limousine when John Hinckley Jr surged forward and opened fire with a pistol. A bullet allegedly ricocheted off the limousine and injured Reagan, but failed to kill him. However, more than one witness – including CNN anchorwoman Judy Woodruff – reported that at least one shot came from a Secret Service agent who was stationed on the overhang behind Reagan's limousine. As one beneficiary of Reagan's death would have been Bush, conspiracy buffs have made him (or forces controlling him) the prime suspect in the Reagan shooting.

THE USUAL SUSPECTS

CIA

The traditional bad guys of the conspiracy world have certainly played a big part in the life of George Bush. It is possible the Agency wished to put one of their men into the White House early to help them strengthen their position in the drugs trade and secret wars they were conducting in Central America at the time of the Reagan shooting. The CIA may have already eliminated more than one President – JFK through an assassin's bullet and Nixon by the Watergate scandal – so would have little reason to doubt it could be done again without comeback.

Skull and Bones

It is well known that George Bush was a member of the Skull and Bones – a secret society at Yale college with initiation rites that involve lying naked in a coffin and providing fellow members with a list of blackmail material against you. Members of the Skull and Bones have a tendency to form the ruling elite of America and the society also seems to operate as an unofficial recruiting body for the US intelligence community. No one knows exactly what the true aim of the Skull and Bones is, but placing one of its own in the White House does not sound too unlikely a goal.

THE UNUSUAL SUSPECTS

MJ-12

Allegedly the true ruling power in America and the group behind the cover-up of the existence of UFOs and aliens, MJ-12 may have wanted to eliminate Reagan because he was unstable and could have exposed the group's existence. It is certain that Reagan came close to implying the reality of an alien menace when he made a speech suggesting that the USA and USSR would be forced to unite in a moment if the people of the world discovered that they had a common extra-terrestrial enemy. MJ-12 is rumoured to always include the current Director of the CIA on its controlling committee, which, if true, would have made George Bush a former member of the organization.

KNIGHTS OF MALTA

An allegedly Catholic organization, based around the Knights of the Hospital of St John of Jerusalem, which was created during the Crusades, membership of the Knights of Malta at the time of Reagan's shooting included head of the CIA, William Casey, and Reagan's foreign policy chief, General Alexander Haig. Confusion reigned in the aftermath of the shooting as to who, exactly, was in control of America while Reagan was disabled. When asked about this, Haig said: "I'm in charge now". Were the Knights of Malta behind the shooting as part of plot to install a President who was an ex-CIA man with close links to certain "Knights"?

MOST CONVINCING EVIDENCE

If you inspect the video footage of the shooting it is clear that from the position Hinckley was standing in when he opened fire, that he would have needed to shoot through a car door to hit Reagan where he did. This impossibility is explained by the "ricochet theory" which is as implausible as the infamous "magic bullet theory" in the JFK shooting.

MOST MYSTERIOUS FACT

Members of the Bush and Hinckley families were very old friends as both families had made their fortunes in the Texas oil boom. The families shared many connections, and it may be more than just a rather spooky coincidence that George Bush's son, Neil, was supposed to have had dinner with Scott Hinckley – John Hinckley's brother – the evening that John attempted to shoot President Ronald Reagan.

SCEPTICALLY SPEAKING

Anyone whose hero is Travis Bickle and is obsessed with Jodi Foster deserves the label "nut" and is probably unbalanced enough to attempt the lone assassination of a President. The facts that George Bush is connected to the CIA by a large number of supposed links and secret societies just help foster the illusion of conspiracy where there is no real evidence for one.

EUROPEAN UNION

Until fairly recently, only a few conspiriologists and those with Right-wing views that make Margaret Thatcher's European-Union-bashing seem tame, believed that the EU was part of secret plot to take control of the people of Europe and strip them of political rights. However, as the European Union has continued to grow in power – issuing a single currency and planning to expand into the former Eastern Bloc – more and more conspiracy theorists have been turning their attention towards it.

The official view of the history of the European Union claims that it grew out of an initial plan by France and Germany to pool all their coal and steel production under a joint authority as a sign of co-operation and friendship after World War II. However, even the European Steel and Coal Community of 1950 showed early grand plans. Its founding declaration reads: "The contribution which an organized and living Europe can bring to civilization is indispensable to the maintenance of peaceful relations. Europe will not be made all at once, or according to a single, general plan. It will be built through concrete achievements . . ."

Many thought the direct ancestor of the EU – the European Economic Community – would be a purely economic and technical organization. It was envisioned as covering such issues as common standards for tomato paste or safety in steel plants, so little or no provision was made for the inclusion of a democratic element in the Treaty of Rome, which founded the organisation in 1956. However, by the end of the Cold War, the EEC had evolved into the EU which is now responsible for more than 80 per cent of economic and social legislation – and it has a massive impact on the lives of all those who live within its borders.

THE STRANGE PART

There is now little doubt even among Europhiles that the European Union is eroding the importance of the centuries-old nation states that form its membership. It's also clear that the new ruling body is a long way from offering true democratic representation to its millions of citizens. These consequences of the current EU set-up uncannily echo the type of aims that many conspiracy theorists claim that shadowy organizations like the Illuminati have been struggling to achieve for countless centuries.

THE USUAL SUSPECTS

Priory of Sion

This mysterious, Europe-wide secret society, that has links with everyone in European conspiracy history from the Knights Templars to the Freemasons and the Illuminati, may be the true force behind the rise of the EU. Allegedly the guardian of the bloodline of Christ, the Priory of Sion may exist to establish a United States of Europe ruled over by a monarchical dynasty descended from none other than Jesus Christ. While a few of the wilder conspiracy theorists are not entirely certain about the Priory of Sion's role as keepers of a messianic genetic heritage, few of them disagree about the influence and power the Priory wields in the murky world of European and international politics.

The Nazis

It is interesting to note that Hitler's ultimate plan after he had defeated his opponents was to establish a "Europe of Regions". The plan for this proposed European Union – the *Europaischewirtschaftgemeinschaft* – was published in book form by the Nazis in 1942. Written primarily by Nazi

Economics Minister and war criminal, Walther Funk, the book – entitled The European Community – echoed Goering's talk of a post-war project for the "large-scale economic unification of Europe". Goebbels was also fond of saying that: "In 50 years Europe will be unified and people will no longer think in terms of countries". With these facts established, it is easy to understand why some conspiracy buffs feel that the EU is a dark plot run by a cabal of deep Nazi agents who infiltrated the governments of Europe at the end of World War II.

THE UNUSUAL SUSPECTS

The Vatican

The idea of a united Europe is not exactly a modern idea – it has existed in the past in the form of the Holy Roman Empire, as a confederation of European states where the real power lay with the Roman Catholic Church. More than one conspiracy buff, with an anti-Papal bent, has seen the hand of the Vatican at work within the EU and theorized that the church is trying to recreate its glory days by restoring the Holy Roman Empire under a new name. Of course, evidence of this conspiracy is hard to find; but then again most established religions have a good record of covering their tracks when pulling a fast one.

Aliens from Sirius

Some conspiracy theorists who have read the works of the mysterious Gerard de Sede believe that the EU is creating a United States of Europe so that the ancient Merovingian dynasty can sweep back into power in the Twenty-first Century. While the Priory of Sion believes the dynasty is linked to the family of Jesus Christ, followers of de Sede feel that the Merovingians are the descendants of extra-terrestrials from Sirius. So it is those aliens that are pulling the strings to get their distant family members back into the business of ruling lesser mortals.

MOST CONVINCING EVIDENCE

More than four decades after it was founded, the EU is less popular now than it has ever been. Fewer than half the voters in Europe think that their country's membership of the EU is a good thing, or that their country benefits from EU membership. While the majority of citizens disagree with the concept, they also think that European integration is inevitable. They also feel that a European policy elite brought about the institution behind closed doors in chancelleries and conference centres. Given that very few direct votes have been taken on the subject of the EU, its growth does seem more like the work of a conspiracy than the exercise of the European people's democratic will.

MOST MYSTERIOUS FACT

In 1973, Swiss Journalist Matthiew Paoli began investigating the links between the EEC, one of its bureaucratic entities – the Committee to Protect the Rights and Privileges of Low-Cost Housing – the Grand Lodge Alpina of Freemasonry and General de Gaulle (one of the prime movers behind the EEC). He published the results of his investigation as the book Les Dessous – Undercurrents – and left Europe in fear of his safety. On assignment in Israel, he was arrested by Mossad, found guilty of spying without trial, and shot.

SCEPTICALLY SPEAKING

If bureaucracy, centralized power and undemocratic decision-making constitutes a conspiracy, then all governments – and not just the European Union – deserve to be branded as conspiracies. Under these circumstances, it seems unfair for the conspiracy buffs to make the EU seem any worse than the rest.

THE CIA

Everyone is suspicious of spy agencies; what would be the point of a covert operations organization which freely admitted what it was doing? In the USA the CIA is up against a highly-liberal Freedom of Information Act – a problem that few of its counterparts in other countries have to deal with. It is the uneasy mix of information and misinformation surrounding the CIA that makes it such a popular target for conspiratorial speculation.

The accusation that most often lands on The Company's doorstep though, is that it sells drugs to people. Supposedly to Contras and rebels throughout South America in the first instance, to help raise cash for the anti-Communist cause and destabilize local countries. Then Africa was supposed to be the target of drug sales, to help raise independent finance for certain operational budgets that CIA chiefs didn't want Washington to know about even as expenses claims. More recently, the accusation is that the CIA was the force behind the American Crack Cocaine explosion of the Eighties.

The idea might seem quite a good one – at least to a particularly cynical and sadistic manipulator. Devise a new drug that is extremely addictive, extremely debilitating to the user, and can be sold for large amounts of money. Then distribute it to the dealers who service the ghettos and other poor black areas until there's a huge demand economy set up. Once it's firmly entrenched, simply hand over production to the locals, and let them get on with it. The result? Instant internal warfare in those poor quarters.

The overall plan sees the unfortunate citizens in the ghettos so totally distracted by Crack – being on it, looking for it, making it, selling it, fighting over its distribution, and finally killing themselves with it – that they wouldn't have any time left to hassle nice middle-class Caucasians. Strangely enough, the drugs wars have indeed kept the poor and marginalized more or less out of the way.

Despite the general opinion of the public, amateur and petty criminals such as junkies usually prey on their own social groups. The poor tend to rob other poor people, or better-off people passing through. It normally takes a bolder, more dedicated thief to go into good neighbourhoods and risk the greatly increased police presence, better burglar alarms, and other hindrances to easy pickings. Encourage such an addictive drug in the poor areas, and, with the police presence differential between bad areas (not many of them around) and good areas (plenty of them around), you keep all those potentially rebellious and troublesome marginal people safely out of the way, busy killing one another.

The San Jose Mercury published a series, in 1996, detailing supposed CIA involvement in the Crack trade. The series was well-researched and carefully thought-out, and made some pretty thought-provoking suggestions. The vast bulk of the American press responded with nothing but vitriol for Gary Webb, the reporter who had uncovered the story. *The Washington Post* and *The Los Angeles Times* both conducted thorough investigations of Web's investigation, and found nothing to substantiate his information. Even so, the CIA launched its own "full internal investigation" – described by the *The Los Angeles Times* as "the most intensive in their history" – the complete results of which were never published.

THE STRANGE PART

Retired CIA agents who were interviewed as part of the investigation described it as a joke. Duane Clarridge, Chief of Cover Ops for Latin America in the Eighties, called the questions "nonsense" and refused to answer. He was interviewed by questionnaire, and returned it blank. Very thorough . . . Others described the questions as "going through the motions". Former CIA officer Donald Winters said that the interview began with the CIA stating that it held "no substantive evidence that any of the allegations in the San Jose article had any basis" – hardly an aggressive questioning stance.

THE USUAL SUSPECTS

WASPs

The people that most consistently feel threatened by poor Afro-Americans are, as everyone knows, the White Anglo-Saxon Protestant middle classes. Many WASPs would do whatever they could to keep the ethnic "minorities" out of sight and out of mind. Many of them certainly wouldn't blink at introducing a new, highly-addictive drug to the ghettos.

The Freemasons

It is well-known that many members of a Certain Intelligence Agency are also high-level Masons. Some conspiracy theorists believe that the whole CIA is under the control of the Masons and that the drug conspiracy is only part of a larger scheme to keep the world firmly in their control.

THE UNUSUAL SUSPECTS

Christian Identity

More of a collection of lunatic sects than a true religion, the Christian Identity movement says that the real descendants of the Biblical Hebrews are actually the white Americans – rather like a US version of the British Israelites. This appeals very much to aggressive, ultra right-wing, survivalist-style groups. Links have been suggested between Identity members (including Larry Harris, the "Anthrax in Vegas" guy, and Eric Rudolph, accused of the Atlanta Bombing) and the CIA, which is allegedly funding such groups. Could it be that Christian Identity is currently the real faith of the chiefs of the CIA, and their agenda is to wipe out the black American community by any and all means available?

MJ-12

This UFO cover-up organization, alleged to be beyond the control of the US government and to be covertly working with the aliens known as the Greys, always includes top-level CIA men on its committee. Could drug-running by the CIA be a way of bolstering the MJ-12's Black Budget? Reverse-engineering alien flying discs isn't cheap.

MOST CONVINCING EVIDENCE

Although the full report remains unpublished, the CIA revealed that the investigation found absolutely no evidence to back up any of *The San Jose Mercury's* allegations. Now there's a shock . . .

MOST MYSTERIOUS FACT

Very few figures who were closely connected to the issue but who were not current or retired CIA members were questioned in the investigation.

Robert Owen, who called attention to potential links between the CIA and drugs back in 1985, wasn't even contacted, let alone questioned.

SCEPTICALLY SPEAKING

Such an operation would be very hard to keep hidden; the men and women of the CIA are still just that – men and women. It would take a particularly evil sort of zealot to decide that the best way of dealing with the problem of poverty-stricken black Americans was to infect them with a new drug. While such people do exist, the scale of such an operation would involve a very large number of operatives. Surely someone would have retained enough humanity to leak solid evidence of such a monstrous policy to the press?

NASA

America's space agency is, if all the various rumours are to be believed, one of the greatest sources of misinformation and suppression currently active in the world. It has got the low-down on everything from the alien presence surrounding the globe to a range of useful inventions that it is keeping out of the public grasp. NASA also frequently falsifies mission data in order to justify its huge budgets. Money received is siphoned off for mysterious research projects, conducted away from public scrutiny, using US taxpayers' dollars. No one is accountable, and no one on the outside knows what it is that all this cash is being used for. Alternatively, NASA could just be creaming off huge bonuses for directors, and covering up incompetence.

One particularly paranoid rumour suggests that NASA is in fact building a gigantic tunnel network under the US, code-named Orpheus. This is so deep underground that it can survive a direct strike from a massive meteorite without problems. Geothermal energy supplies heating, lighting, air circulation and microprotein cultures, so the network is self-sufficient. That way, when the big asteroid actually hits, NASA will be well-placed to survive with a small military set-up, and be in a position to take control after the disaster. To make sure all goes smoothly, the approach of this huge meteorite's approach is kept secret so that NASA will be the only organization prepared for the disaster . . .

One feasible-sounding element of this conspiracy is that the Moon Landing photographs were faked. They were taken inside a secret warehouse that was made up to look very convincingly like the surface of the moon. There are two possible reasons for this. First, NASA never went to the moon – the launch was faked, radio messages were provided by actors, and the actual landing itself was staged. This might have been to save money for Project Orpheus, or it might have been to provide the US government with a vitally-important propaganda victory over Russian Cosmonauts.

The second idea is that the moon landing went ahead and the film footage that was broadcast live was genuine. However, the photos that the astronauts took just did not come out, because Kodak underestimated the effect of solar glare on the plates. Faced with massive press demand for stills, NASA considered the financial and PR advantages of selling rights, and the embarrassment of admitting that they took the wrong camera equipment. They decided it was better to bluff it out, and mocked-up a lunar landscape for a photo-session on Earth.

THE STRANGE PART

Evidence keeps on leaking out that NASA knows much more than it releases officially. A former high-level NASA consultant is rumoured to have leaked copies of conversational transcripts from astronauts on the Space Shuttle Discovery. In this document, two of the shuttle pilots are supposed to discuss what appears to be "a huge glowing spacecraft flying around the Earth". Now former NASA specialist Dr Hoagland has made claims that NASA not only knows about extra-terrestrials, but also understands hyper-dimensional space and the true origins of human life.

THE USUAL SUSPECTS

The American Government

The most common explanation is that faced with the humiliating prospect of ruining a superb public relations scoop by having screwed up the photos, the American government told NASA to fake some photos and keep it quiet or else. If there is a UFO conspiracy, it seems likely that the American government controls NASA's involvement in the suppression of the truth.

The Freemasons

A lot of strange symbolism seems to be involved in NASA's space missions and it appears that astronauts have even been instructed to perform sacred rituals at appointed times facing in the direction of certain constellations. This is suggestive of the involvement of a secret society with an interest in mystical symbolism – step forward the Masons.

THE UNUSUAL SUSPECTS

Nazis

Many people already know that, at the end of World War II, America scooped up the cream of Nazi Germany's rocket scientists and put them to work on its space programme. However, there is the belief that some of the Nazi scientists held true to their earlier political views and that NASA is now run by a fascist elite with its own agenda.

The Greys

The real reason that none of NASA's UFO sightings have been made public knowledge is that the agency is actually controlled by aliens. Although the shuttle routinely flies through a ring of different alien craft, the knowledge is kept suppressed by the extra-terrestrials, who are building up slowly to revealing their presence. Gifts of technology keep the US government happy – and anyway, who better could you have running your space program?

MOST CONVINCING EVIDENCE

If you look at the shadows of the rocks in the moon landing photos, you'll see that they point in an arc of different directions – sure proof of a point-source of light just off camera. If the illumination was solar, as it would be on the moon, the shadows would all point in the same direction. They would also have higher contrasts to the earth around them, as there is no atmospheric scatter of light on the moon.

MOST MYSTERIOUS FACT

Comments about alien spaceships apart, there is a short, authenticated transcript of an in-flight shuttle conversation held when the craft was well outside Earth's atmosphere. In this conversation, one astronaut notices an unidentified object outside and asks his partner if he also saw it shoot past then dart off. Whatever it was, it was not a military jet or a weather balloon this time.

SCEPTICALLY SPEAKING

If NASA faked the whole moon landing – an impressive feat – then how did that American flag get up there? Did someone smuggle it along later? As an aside, for some of the other hypotheses to be credible, someone would need to explain exactly why a space agency should want to take over a post-apocalyptic world on its own.

THE NEW WORLD ORDER

There is, within society, a highly-organized cabal of world leaders, bankers, religious figures and business gurus who have a vision of a united Earth. These VIPs, along with certain powerful but secretive mystical adepts, and a smattering of seemingly ordinary people, form the leadership of the NWO, the New World Order. They – and their predecessors – have been manipulating world events for centuries in order to bring about their goal.

The NWO has several very specific aims in mind. The peoples of the Earth must be united under one governmental body, sweeping away nationalist divides and replacing patriotic bigotry with belief in the common bonds of humanity. There is to be one currency, one language, one fair set of laws, and one race. Religion is another major source of conflict, so it is to be abolished.

National armies will no longer be necessary in the New World Order, so they can be abolished too. Because pollution is destroying the biosphere, our consumption of industrial technology will have to be reduced, and we must get back to nature. Half of the Earth's surface will be given back to nature for "rewilding", so that we don't kill the planet. Finally, universal education, contraception and certain tax incentives will allow the planet's population to be reduced to just two billion, a third of its current size. It all sounds rather pleasant really, doesn't it?

Apparently not. There are those who believe that succumbing to the NWO's outrageous plans would just be the start of a servile bondage so vile that it can barely be mentioned. The fact remains that the NWO is prepared to use any and all means necessary to achieve its ends. The leaders of the New World Order clearly see that society is killing the world, and if two-thirds of the Earth's population has to be slaughtered to save the remaining third, then that is two billion lives saved, rather than four billion needlessly wasted, or so the reasoning goes.

The New World Order has long held a drive to terrorize and traumatise the populace into accepting one central government – this is an easier path than using reason. The first stage involves achieving a global infosphere of media networks that can be manipulated. With the advent of the Internet and satellite communications, this has been achieved. As part of the drive to scare us, the NWO is directly responsible for both World Wars, global warming, heroin, Crack, serial killers, Cancer, genetically modified food, daytime television, AIDS, Kurt Kobain, Hiroshima, and in fact everything else wrong with the world. They are the "Them" that we've all been talking about for so long. They are prepared to kill any and almost all of us, if They have to, in order to save us.

THE STRANGE PART

To help make the idea of one central government more palatable, the NWO created the United Nations, a prototype for the planned political structure. In addition, they divided the world into three significant power blocs, in the forms of NATO (the West), the Warsaw Pact (the Soviet states), and SEATO (everyone else). These blocs were designed to provide sufficient tension that people would wish for unification, while also showing that countries could work within organisations larger than themselves profitably.

THE USUAL SUSPECTS

The Illuminati

When Adam Weisshaupt founded the Bavarian Illuminati, in 1776, it was with the express purpose of taking over the world. They and he (thanks to the appliance of magic, Weisshaupt hardly ages at all) have been fronting the New World Order all this time.

The United Nations

Fed up of being caught between the US and Russia, the United Nations has decided that it is best suited to the job of running the world. Only the United Nations has the breadth of vision to represent all the peoples of the Earth fairly.

THE UNUSUAL SUSPECTS

Satan

The driving force behind the New World Order is the Devil. Once the NWO has come into power, it will elect the Antichrist as leader, and then the End Times (the "Tribulation") will be upon us.

The Greys

According to some, the Greys long ago took control of the highest authorities on the globe and are the real power behind the NWO. When it is established and large sections of humanity are disposed of, it will be much easier for them to run the planet.

MOST CONVINCING EVIDENCE

The launch of the Euro, a common pan-European currency, is another clear step to smoothing the way for integration. Despite the radically-different natures of the European economies, one currency with a fixed value is supposed to be sustainable, a move clearly aimed at eroding traditional sovereignty. Furthermore, the Euro is made up of dollars and cents, which is obviously to pave the way for a unification with the dollar early in the Twenty-first century.

MOST MYSTERIOUS FACT

Maybe someone is playing with the weather . . . El Niño is a well-documented cycle in the Gulf Stream, which occurs every seven years, bringing storms and troublesome weather. However, the extreme weather patterns of 1996, 1997 and 1998 have all been blamed on the El Niño current. The chances of a seven-yearly cyclical event accidentally repeating two years running are small, but for it to happen for a third consecutive year is beyond the bounds of coincidence.

SCEPTICALLY SPEAKING

Given the difficulty that most governments seem to have merely organising their own internal financial flow, it would be astonishing if such a group of people – all of whom are going to have their own vested interests – could organize events in the world at large to such an amazing degree. If the Devil is behind it all, what does he care if we are one nation or 200?

THE BILDERBERG GROUP

They meet once, sometimes twice a year, renting out remote and expensive hotels. The members of this secretive group include the power brokers of the world, from international financiers to heads of state. Their discussions are rumoured to affect everyone on the planet; allegedly the group chooses the political leaders of countries and just where the next war will erupt, yet the group is answerable to no one. Their members include such luminaries as David Rockefeller, Henry Kissinger, Bill Clinton and Tony Blair. They are the Bilderberg Group, and according to some, they are your masters.

Formed during the paranoid years of the Cold War, the Bilderberg Group was conceived by Joseph Retinger, an American who headed the CIA-bankrolled European Movement, whose contacts included a who's who of global governmental and military powers. Retinger believed in a world where peace would be brokered not by governments but by superpowerful multinational organizations.

After meeting with Prince Bernhard of the Netherlands in 1952, Retinger proposed a series of meetings to discuss world problems. This idea was well-received by other world leaders and the first meeting was held in May, 1954, at the Bilderberg Hotel in Oosterbeek, Holland. Since then, the subsequent meetings have retained the name "Bilderberg" as they are moved from one luxurious retreat to another in locations around the globe. The meetings still take place, and usually comprise 120 attendees, drawn from the key elite of the world, with one third of them being North American, the remainder European. The general makeup of each meeting has two thirds of the delegates being from the world of business, media and education, with only one third actually being politicians.

Journalists are not allowed on the premises, let alone allowed to report on the mysterious proceedings. The Bilderberg meetings are held under a complete media blackout, apparently with the complete cooperation of the media itself. So what are the Bilderbergers up to? Are they simply discussing topics on the evening news or are they quietly deciding just what those topics will be?

THE STRANGE PART

At the 1998 Bilderberg Meeting, held at the exclusive Turnberry Hotel in Scotland, security was so tight that two pipers who were employed to play for the delegates were horrified to see security forces take apart their pipes to ensure they weren't hiding explosives. The security forces did this not once, but every time the pipers arrived for an engagement. All cartons of milk delivered to the hotel were also torn apart and searched.

THE USUAL SUSPECTS

International Cabal of Greedy Businessmen

The aim of the Bilderberg Group may be nothing more than simple greed. With its concentration of business leaders and insistence on secrecy, the Group could merely be fine-tuning economic policy before disseminating it through members' contacts in their respective governments. By ensuring that everyone is singing from a common hymn sheet, the Group could simply be making certain that profits stay exactly where they want them – high.

THE NEW WORLD ORDER

With a high number of members who are bankers and financiers, it's no surprise that Bilderberg favours free trade, an attitude that tends to break down economic barriers and protectionist policies. Free trade has long been seen as a tool for solidifying the grip of the New World Order on an unsuspecting Earth – start by destroying economic barriers, and it's only a short step to destroying any sense of individual nationality.

With an eye to furthering the dream of a New World Order, the Bilderbergers would decide when and where wars would erupt, thus further destroying national borders and making money for those members who choose to finance such conflicts. With a One World Government, and attendant World Bank, the Bilderbergers would pick leaders who follow their plans. Clinton was only Governor of Arkansas when he attended a Group meeting in 1991, yet became President of the US two years later.

THE UNUSUAL SUSPECTS

THE GREYS

This theory has the Greys running the Bilderbergers in much the same way they are rumoured to run other secret societies, all in aid of weakening Earth and making it easier to conquer.

THE ILLUMINATI

The Bilderbergers could be nothing but a ruse to draw the suspicions of the media and public while the real decisions are made elsewhere – allegedly by the real group that runs the world, the Illuminati.

MOST CONVINCING EVIDENCE

In 1955, the Bilderberg Group discussed the need to create a tightly-bound European market. A year-and-a-half later, the European Common Market was established by the Treaty of Rome.

MOST MYSTERIOUS FACT

Vernon Jordan, a close friend and golfing buddy of Bill Clinton and key character in the Monica Lewinsky scandal, is a member of the Bilderberg steering committee. It was Jordan's influence that allowed Clinton into the compelling world of the Bilderbergers, and possibly the Presidency.

SCEPTICALLY SPEAKING

The wealthiest people in the world are actually the ones ruling it? Well, fancy that . . .

KGB

For many observers, the true death knell of the Soviet Union was heard in 1991 when an enthusiastic crowd toppled the statue of Felix Dzerzhinsky and the air resounded with the sound of it shattering into hundreds of pieces. For years his figure had looked across the square that bore his name towards the infamous headquarters of the KGB – the Lubyanka.

Dzerzhinsky was the mastermind behind the Red Terror that allowed the Communists to seize and hold on to power after the overthrow of the Tsar in the 1917 October Revolution. He created the Cheka secret police that over the years mutated into the Committee of State Security – more commonly known by the initials KGB – the most dreaded and pervasive intelligence-gathering network the world has ever seen.

The KGB (Komitet Gosudarstvennoy Bezopasnosti) was responsible for defending the Soviet Communist regime against all internal and external enemies. When the statue of its founder was destroyed, it was a symbolic of the breaking of the hold the KGB on every Soviet citizen, a hold that was maintained from cradle to grave. Throughout the Cold War, wherever there was a hint of conspiracy there was also a rumour of KGB involvement. Some conspiracy buffs go so far as to state that the world's largest covert organization did not even owe allegiance to communism, but existed only to serve its own mysterious ends.

In theory the KGB was responsible to the Soviet Council of Ministers, in practice it took its orders directly from the USSR's ruling politburo – if it took orders at all. With the collapse of the Soviet Union and the dismantling of the KGB in 1991, commentators were quick to describe the organization as "lost to history". Some conspiriologists are not so certain that KGB's awesome, globe-spanning power has been brought to an end.

To many it seemed suspicious that the KGB – which had controlled the Soviet population using fear and an extensive network of secret informers – had allowed the USSR to collapse with barely a pretence of opposition. Particularly as the KGB has a supervisory influence on the Soviet army. Conspiracy theorists believe that the apparent end of the Soviet Union and the KGB was merely a cover for an insidious KGB plot to consolidate its power and bring about an even stronger Russian empire.

THE STRANGE PART

Since the fall of the Soviet Union, Russia has been sliding into anarchy. One of the main beneficiaries of this has been Vladimir Zhironovsky – leader of the extreme nationalist Liberal Democratic Party. Millions of Russians have agreed with his statement: "What Russia needs now is a dictator, when I come to power I will be that dictator", voting for him in presidential and parliamentary elections.

With links to ultra-right groups in Germany, to the Russian mafia and even to Saddam Hussein, Zhironovsky is a potential Russian Hitler with a huge arsenal of nuclear weaponry at his disposal – an arsenal he has threatened to use. Perhaps the most worrying fact is that Zhironovsky was a secret KGB agent. Some of his former associates claim he is being prepared for power by the ex-leaders of the allegedly disbanded secret police and espionage agency.

THE USUAL SUSPECTS

Bavarian Illuminati

Even some orthodox historians are beginning to recognize the key role that several secret societies and occult orders had on the creation of Nazi Germany and Hitler. Behind many of these group is the spectre of the Bavarian Illuminati – whose modus operandi is to stay in the shadows, take control of other clandestine organisations, and then work through them. Could the Illuminati have followed an age-old pattern and subverted the

KGB? Given that Zhironovsky has close links to German right-wing groups with fascist origins it could be that the hand of the Illuminati is controlling the KGB and the Russian Hitler-in-waiting.

Freemasons

It is well established that the KGB infiltrated Masonic organizations as part of its attempt to place its agents in the British government and security services. However, it is suspected that the traffic was two-way and that the Freemasons penetrated deep within the leadership of the Committee of State Security and managed to take control of it. Some conspiracy theorists now feel the KGB and its plans to recreate a Russian Empire are merely part of a larger Masonic plot to achieve world domination.

THE UNUSUAL SUSPECTS

Teutonic Knights

The Germanic protégés of the Knights Templar, the Teutonic Knights once controlled the independent principality Ordensland that covered Finland, Prussia and large tracts of Russia. Once they lost their powerbase in the Fourteenth Century, the Teutonic Knights became a secret society determined to regain the lost lands. Some conspiriologists believe that the Teutonic Knights were the hidden power behind the Tsars and, that when the Russian Royal Family became hard to control, masterminded the revolution and infiltrated the new secret police. In this conspiracy scenario, the Teutonic Knights staged the disintegration of the USSR and the KGB in order to form a fascist state which would have more popular support and therefore be easier to control.

MOST CONVINCING EVIDENCE

Former president of the Soviet Union, Mikhail Gorbachev denies the accusation made by some conspiracy theorists that he instructed the KGB to create Zhironovsky's Liberal Democratic Party. However, he does admit the possibility that the former secret police are controlling Zhironovsky. Gorbachev has stated: "Can the KGB create a whole party? Zhironovsky is a remarkable actor; it is very important to find out who is directing him, who is behind him."

MOST MYSTERIOUS FACT

Zhironovsky's strongest foreign supporter is Saddam Hussein. As a thank-you to Zhironovsky for sending some of his "commandos" – a small band of ex-KGB operatives and soldiers – to Iraq during the Gulf War, Hussein made the Russian an honorary colonel in the Iraqi army and gave him a giant portrait.

SCEPTICALLY SPEAKING

There is very little solid evidence of the KGB surviving the disbanding process. History shows that anti-Semitism and severe economic woe are sometimes all the reasons that are needed to explain the rise of a megalomaniac, would-be world dictator.

MI6

MI6 is known across the globe as the British security service responsible for defending the realm from external enemies thanks to its portrayal as the employer of Special Agent 007 in the decade-spanning series of hit Bond movies. However, in the shadows where conspiracy theories thrive, there are many who see MI6's portrayal in the films as a force for good as no more than blatant propaganda. MI6, they feel, is an organization that is secretly dedicated to achieving world domination.

In theory, MI6 is neutral and does not align itself to any particular political party or ideology. Even the most hardened sceptic viewing modern history would have to admit it shows that one thing – MI6 could not be accused of is being neutral. There are many established examples of MI6 campaigning against a politician or organization that it feels is too Left-wing or that does not support the "special relationship" between Britain and America. The most famous case is the removal of Prime Minister Harold Wilson from power.

It had long been rumoured that MI6, in conjunction with its sister service MI5, had been behind the sudden resignation of Wilson in 1976. When the government was unable to prevent the publication of ex-MI5 agent Peter Wright's memoirs, the full details of the conspiracy to remove Wilson in a bloodless coup eventually became public knowledge. The devastating allegations point to a treasonable conspiracy undertaken by a cabal of intelligence officers to undermine and bring down the constitutionally-elected government of the United Kingdom.

There are also many other cases of MI6 blackmailing, smearing and recruiting Members of Parliament – not an activity the movies have ever portrayed James Bond undertaking as part of his remit to "defend the realm". One of the key figures seen to be involved with MI6's on-going attempt to subvert its own nation's democracy was director of CIA counterintelligence, James Jesus Angleton – mastermind of the Italian P2 conspiracy, possible mastermind of the Kennedy assassination and a member of the mysterious Knights of Malta.

Confirmed conspiratorial actions against the British government, undertaken with allies from the American intelligence community, have made many conspiracy theorists wonder just who MI6 actually works for. If MI6 is not loyal to democratically elected British leaders, they feel it may be engaged as a key player in a conspiracy to achieve global domination for a secret Anglo-American cabal.

THE STRANGE PART

There is no doubting that a network of "Atlanticist" groups exist and work behind the scenes of international politics. These round-table groups often share a common membership, which suggests that the American Council on Foreign Relations works closely with British groups such as the Royal Institute of International Affairs. Given that the leadership of MI6 and the CIA plays a prominent role in all of these groups, conspiriologists feel that it is not unfair to suspect the security services are working to a secret agenda on behalf of these organizations.

THE USUAL SUSPECTS

THE ROYAL FAMILY

More than one conspiracy buff has pointed the finger at the royal family as the cement that bonds the alleged Anglo-American cabal. They believe that the royal family has been working since the Nineteenth Century to promote the doctrine of "mystical imperialism" and world domination by the two largest English-speaking nations. Early steps in this process included inspiring Cecil Rhodes to set-up round-table groups and the Rhodes Scholarships at Oxford – which would mean the brightest Americans – including President Clinton – received their "education" in England. MI6 swears loyalty to the Crown, so its part in the conspiracy comes from following the direct orders of the Queen.

Rockerfeller Family

The Rockerfellers are one of the most fabulously wealthy families in the world and seem to be major players in the conspiracies behind international politics. With possible controlling interests in several banks and major corporations – including the Federal Reserve Bank which controls all money in the US – David Rockerfeller is also chairman of both the Trilateral Commission and the Council on Foreign Relations. Some conspiracy theorists believe that the Rockerfellers' aim is to create a superpower Anglo-American alliance dedicated to preserving and furthering their financial interests.

THE UNUSUAL SUSPECTS

Rosicrucians

The origins of the Order of the Rose Cross are a matter of heated debate in conspiracy circles. Whether they developed from an ancient Egyptian cult or were the idea of Giordano Bruno – a Sixteenth-Century philosopher burnt for organizing secret societies and teaching that life existed on other planets – there is no doubting the Rosicrucians are major conspiracy players. Given that they infiltrated British Freemasonry centuries ago, it is not impossible that they are the true controllers of the Anglo-American cabal.

Knights of Malta

Operating out of small office in the Vatican, the Knights of Malta have included members as diverse as General Reinhard Gehlen, Hitler's Chief of Intelligence, who later worked for the CIA, and General Alexander Haig – the force behind Nixon and Reagan's foreign policy and a friend of the Queen's. Some conspiriologists feel the Knights of Malta secretly control the CIA and via that organization, MI6. Just why the Knights of Malta would want to do this is open to question, but it is known that the Knights Templar regard them as their sworn enemies.

MOST CONVINCING EVIDENCE

People looking for evidence of MI6 trying to establish closer ties between Britain and America, have turned their attention to the British-American Project. Backed by companies such American Express, Apple Computers, British Airways, Coca-Cola, Monsanto and Philip Morris, it is officially a charitable trust which aims to bring together senior representatives from the intelligence services business, government, the media and the armed forces from the two countries. However, conspiracy theorists feel MI6's alleged links with the project means that it serves a more sinister purpose.

MOST MYSTERIOUS FACT

Recently disclosed British Government documents show that there were plans to turn the United Kingdom into the Fifty-first State of the US. Was the real reason MI6 chose to remove Harold Wilson from office because he scrapped these plans?

SCEPTICALLY SPEAKING

It seems unlikely that MI6 is competent enough at covert operations to be capable of masterminding an ultra-secret plot to shape world politics. If the organization can't even prevent itself from being publicly exposed as severely compromized by Soviet intelligence, it is doubtful that MI6 has the ability to successfully run a dozen top-level conspiracy organizations and two major governments.

MOSSAD

When the assassins' bullets fly from the smoking gun and change the course of history, it is usually inevitable that within hours both an official version and the conspiracy interpretation of events will be in circulation. However, on November 4, 1995, when Israeli Prime Minister Yitzhak Rabin was shot at a rally in Tel Aviv, it took more than a few hours for the first hints of conspiracy to surface. The reason is Mossad – probably one of the most feared and effective intelligence agencies in the world.

Until recently, Mossad's control over Israeli media was so strong that its very existence, like that of its sister agency the Shaback, was shrouded in secrecy. Everyone knew that the agencies existed, but in Israel none of their activities were ever reported and no one even knew who was in charge.

Mossad's tight reins of censorship may have loosened a little over the last couple of years, but it is certain that they played a strong role in preventing even the mildest hint of there being a conspiracy behind Yitzhak Rabin's death from reaching the Israeli public, for as long as possible. While CNN and even the BBC questioned the official version that the co-winner of the Nobel Peace Prize was not killed by a fanatical, lone gunman, the Israeli security services fought to keep such speculation from its own citizens. Not surprising, since much of that speculation focused on the possible role that Mossad may have played in murdering its own Commander-in-Chief.

Mossad was formed in 1951 to oversee the intelligence gathering and defence of the recently-created nation of Israel that was surrounded on all sides by hostile countries opposed to its very existence. Over the years, Mossad has developed an impressive track record of counter-terrorist actions, assassinations and covert operation success stories. Its infiltration of the security services of friends and foes has also meant that Mossad has become the prime suspect in many conspiracy theories. From the killing of media tycoon Robert Maxwell in 1991, to the death of Princess Diana and even the attempted assassination of Pope John Paul II in 1981 – there is no shortage of events in which Mossad may have played a part.

Resourceful, ruthless and fearless – how else could they have abducted Nazi war criminal Adolf Eichmann, stolen a MiG jet from Iraq and smuggled enough weapons-grade plutonium out of America to build a hundred atomic weapons – it seems that nothing is beyond Mossad. For conspiracy theorists, that includes possibly being the shadowy cabal behind Rabin's assassination.

THE STRANGE PART

The Shamgar Commission of Enquiry, which investigated the assassination of Rabin concluded that Ygal Amir was the lone killer of the Prime Minister. It also concluded that he was acting entirely alone when he shot Rabin twice in the back. In the Commission's opinion it was those two shots which killed Rabin, while a third shot wounded the PM's bodyguard. At his trial Ygal Amir testified that he loaded his gun clip with nine bullets, yet ballistic tests found eight remaining bullets after security forces seized Amir. This means Amir only had one shot at Rabin. Where did the other shots come from? If there were a conspiracy to assassinate Rabin and subsequently cover-up the identity of the killer, it would be impossible for Mossad not to be involved – but why would the agency kill its own leader?

THE USUAL SUSPECTS

The Israeli Right-wing

Rabin had made a historic peace deal with the PLO that gave away Israeli territory and earned the eternal hatred of Israeli Right-wing factions in the process. Mossad is not an organization known for its moderate views and many members of the agency have close links to the radical fringe of Zionist politics. The assassination of Rabin would not only be an act of revenge, but would ensure that the process of returning land to the Palestinians and the cause of peace in the region would both be set back for several years.

Saddam Hussein

The Iraqi dictator had a number of grudges against Israel and Rabin – including one assassination attempt on him, carried out by Mossad for the CIA that had led to the deaths of members of his family. If an Iraqi plot was responsible for the Israeli Prime Minister's death, Mossad would have to cover it up to prevent the possible chemical and nuclear warfare that could have ensued from its exposure. Some even suggest that highly-placed members of Mossad are actually in the pay of Hussein.

THE UNUSUAL SUSPECTS

KGB

Although consigned to the pages of history by the majority of commentators after it was officially disbanded in 1991, the KGB is held by many conspiracy buffs to still be playing an active role in covert actions across the world. The aim is to cause as much unrest as possible and so tie up American resources while the KGB attempts to rebuild the former Soviet Empire, unmolested by the attentions of the CIA. It is not impossible that the KGB also infiltrated Mossad in the same way it penetrated the CIA, MI6 and MI5.

CIA

The close links between Mossad and the CIA are well known and many feel that the independence of Israeli security has been compromized by the US. Some people argue that Mossad's attempts to regain its autonomy, by blackmailing President Clinton over the Lewinsky affair, brought about a swift reminder by the CIA of where the balance of power lay. This is considered a wild theory by many, as it is rare for anyone to credit the CIA with the level of competence needed to pull off this type of stunt.

MOST CONVINCING EVIDENCE

Everyone who saw the amateur video footage of Rabin's assassination witnessed the alleged murderer, Ygal Amir, shoot the premier in the back from five feet away. However, Chief Lieutenant Baruch Glatstein, of the Israeli Police's Forensics Laboratory, told a very different story at Amir's trial. Glatstein stated: "In the upper section of the prime minister's jacket I found a bullet hole to the right of the seam, which, according to my testing of the spread of gunpowder, was caused by a shot from less than 25 centimetres' range."

MOST MYSTERIOUS FACT

Before his death, Rabin was sent a letter stating that an Israeli mathematician had discovered a hidden code in the Bible that appeared to foretell the future, and that the name Yitzhak Rabin was encoded in the Bible, along with the words "assassin that will assassinate".

SCEPTICALLY SPEAKING

The combination of a lone gunman and a major political assassination seems to happen a lot, but surely at least one of them must be exactly what it seems to be, instead of a conspiracy? Maybe the legendary Mossad had an off-day and Ygal Amir was a lone nut who got lucky.

NSA

The National Security Agency is probably the organisation most feared by conspiriologists. MJ-12, the Mafia and the Greys are often seen as the most dangerous groups by outsiders, but in fact it is the NSA that is the most feared, the most suspected. The reasons are simple – it is the US spy agency responsible both for external and for domestic affairs. The most technologically-advanced intelligence agency in the world, these spooks watch American citizens and anyone else they have an interest in.

The NSA is routinely accused of just about everything, from stealing the gold in Fort Knox and replacing it with spray-painted lead, down to kidnapping scientists and computer engineers whose ideas could threaten the agency's technological superiority. The sheer secrecy of the organization helps these often-wild rumours to accumulate. However, one of the most persistent accusations to have been levelled at the agency is that it is deeply involved in an attempt to control the global banking system.

The NSA is known for its expertise in cryptography. In the early Nineties, the agency was behind the attempts to have a chip known as Clipper accepted as the standard for all computer encryption. This chip carried an in-built weakness, a back door that the NSA could use to decode any data encrypted using the Clipper. Your information would be perfectly safe from anyone, except the government.

The NSA may have succeeded in compromizing the banking industry – in the late Seventies, a firm called INSLAW (the Institute for Law and Social Research) developed an integrated database management system called PROMIS. This allowed huge ranges of databases to be combined into one usable, cross-referenced whole. Law enforcement agencies wanted PROMIS to track national and international crime, and major banking agencies such as the World Bank wanted to use it for an efficient international financial database. The US Department of Justice took the system on board, then refused to pay money owed, driving

INSLAW to bankruptcy. Despite court rulings in its favour, the company has still to receive payment for PROMIS.

A journalist named Danny Casolaro claimed to have uncovered evidence that the NSA had modified PROMIS to allow complete access to the contents on the NSA's demand. Apparently, the NSA and Mossad then sold modified copies of the software to banks, foreign governments and law enforcement agencies. The plan was to allow the NSA to spy on the entire legal, governmental and financial systems world-wide. A company called Wackenhut, based outside US jurisdiction on a small Indian Nation reservation in California, carried out this modification.

THE STRANGE PART

Deputy White House Counsellor Vince Foster apparently committed suicide in July 1993. His death was suspicious and he had been a control liaison for a company called Systematics, one of the fronts through which the NSA was selling the compromized PROMIS software. Systematics also laundered profits from covert operations, and gathered back-door information from PROMIS for sifting. A woman was with Foster hours before his death, and her hair colour matched the colour of hairs found in Foster's underwear. Pathologists discovered that Foster had died at the moment of ejaculation. Video surveillance tapes do not show Foster leaving the building – yet his body was found in a park in Virginia, a short distance from his car.

THE USUAL SUSPECTS

The Freemasons

Harry Truman, a 33rd degree Master Mason, suddenly created the NSA in 1952. It retains its old ties, and its forays into global control of the legal and banking systems are in fact carried out on behalf of the Freemasons. It was they who organized the murders of Foster and Calosaro, to hide their mastery of international banking.

THE UNUSUAL SUSPECTS

The Greys

It has been suggested that the NSA's power over cryptography comes, not from putting back-doors into computer programs, but from a mastery of advanced mathematics given to the agency by the Greys in return for a quota of US citizens that they can take and use for experiments every year.

MOST CONVINCING EVIDENCE

In Bob Woodward's book, *VEIL: The Secret Wars of the CIA, 1981-1987* on page 386, former CIA Director William Casey claims of his time in office: "There was penetration of the international banking system, allowing a steady flow of data from the real, secret sets of books kept by many foreign banks, that showed some hidden investing by the Soviet Union."

MOST MYSTERIOUS FACT

Journalist Danny Casolaro was murdered on the same night that he mentioned having discovered evidence to support his story, as was Alan Standorf, the NSA agent supposed to have passed him documents. Twelve days before his death, Foster's secret Swiss bank account was mysteriously emptied of its $2.7 million contents without his knowledge.

SCEPTICALLY SPEAKING

Why drive INSLAW to bankruptcy? It seems likely that it would have been easier just to pay a licence fee as the contract required, and then negotiate the rights to sell the software on to other parties, keeping everything discreet.

THE ROYAL FAMILY

The dramatic, ever-changing story of the royal family is perhaps the longest-running and most enjoyed soap opera the world has ever known. Watched and adored by millions around the globe, the everyday routines of the British royals have become the stuff of dreams and form the material for endless discussion. When a major life event occurs in the royal family, whether it's a wedding or a birth, it becomes an excuse for international celebration. They are the royal family, and their lives take precedence over the perceived mundanity in the lives of their fans.

In its current incarnation, the British royal family stems from the House of Windsor, a family tree that can trace its roots to Germany. Under the stern eye of Queen Elizabeth II, the Royal Family has endured much in the past few years, but the death of Diana, in 1997, put the spotlight on the family with a white-hot glare not seen before. A world mourning the loss of Diana, its most beloved princess, watched to see how the family would react. But even as the memorial flowers that had mounted against the security fences surrounding royal homes were finally swept away, the story continued to unfold. images of Diana and other members of the royal family are sold on everything from books and videos to commemorative tea towels.

But behind the smiles and waving hands, behind the castle gates and power of British tradition, just what is the royal family truly up to? What dark secrets lay hidden in their palatial closets? Are they really just nostalgic figureheads, or, like their plotting, politically-vicious predecessors, are they busy planning to seize power and create a renewed and glorious British Empire?

THE STRANGE PART

Newspaper reports routinely focus on the depravity of the Windsor clan – from toe-sucking in foreign locations to intercepted phone calls made by princes describing sexual fantasies. Either they all lack judgment, or they're putting up a cleverly-deceptive front.

THE USUAL SUSPECTS

The Virginia Company

Some theorists believe that the royal family heads the mysterious Virginia Company – an organization that aims to run the world. The fall from grace of the royal family could have been a cleverly-orchestrated public relations campaign to disguise their plans for world domination – which is nothing short of a re-establishment of the glory days of the British Empire. While they continue to project an image of reserved dignity and eccentricity, the royals secretly manage all major banking institutions and top-level security forces like the KGB. There are even rumours that the royal family planned the American Revolution, and that to this day, they still rule sovereign over America's shores.

British Shadow Government

The current royal family may be nothing more than it seems – an ongoing media circus. The constant engagements of royalty opening paint factories, giving speeches, or grabbing space in newspapers as they play polo may be designed to distract media and public attention from the activities of the British Shadow Government, an elite backroom conspiracy headed by ex-members of M16. As their forces quietly pass legislation in the House of Commons or test weaponry that will facilitate the coming of the New World Order, the evening news pacifies the populace by showing Prince Harry getting his knee scraped on a games field.

THE UNUSUAL SUSPECTS

Imposters

The current House of Windsor could be a family of imposters who lacked the apparently essential secret Bloodline of Christ. They orchestrated the murder of Diana because, as a Stuart, she alone possessed the true remnants of the Bloodline. Thought at first to be easily malleable to the policies of the Royal Family, Diana's strong spirit proved to be too much of a liability, and she was removed in a badly-managed assassination before she could inflict any more damage to the Windsors' plans.

MOST CONVINCING EVIDENCE

Queen Elizabeth II is among the richest women in the world, and is still head of the British Commonwealth, a glaring anachronism in the days of blurring national boundaries and international culture. Instead of being relegated to a secondary position of nostalgic tradition, she still exerts a considerable amount of power, but uses it discreetly, thus proving that there's more to the royal family than they would have us believe.

MOST MYSTERIOUS FACT

The current Duke of Kent is head of the British Freemasons, a secret society long thought to be involved in the backroom machinations of world government.

SCEPTICALLY SPEAKING

The fact that *Coronation Street* is still broadcast suggests royal intervention on a grand scale – but nothing else does.

THE VATICAN

The heart of the Roman Catholic faith can be found in the Vatican, the palatial home of the Pope, the spiritual leader of all Roman Catholics worldwide. The Holy See, with the surrounding Vatican City, exists as an independent papal state in Rome and is the headquarters of the Roman Catholic faith. It stretches over an area of 44 hectares, with an estimated population of 850 people. The Vatican is fully independent from Italy, with its own currency, its own radio station, and a police force.

But even the most seemingly benevolent of institutions can be corrupted by the addictive taste for power. With its unbreakable dual hold of tradition and religion on the world's millions of Roman Catholics, the establishment within the Vatican walls may have been corrupted by power, which has polluted the spiritual atmosphere with human greed. With the power and wealth that the Vatican has amassed over the centuries, politics are unavoidable and may have taken precedence over the need to care for people.

Few can say what secrets are hidden in the Holy See, but as the Vatican continues to put forth an altruistic image of goodwill, there may be an undercurrent of darkness that even many in the Holy See are unaware of.

THE STRANGE PART

When Pope John Paul I died, he had allegedly been in bed reading papers that connected the Mafia to the Vatican. When he was discovered, the papers has disappeared. Furthermore, no public death certificate was issued. John Paul was embalmed just 12 hours after he was found dead, even though Italian law clearly states that 24 hours must elapse before embalming.

THE USUAL SUSPECTS

The Mafia

Mafia influences have long been suspected of playing a part in many aspects of the Vatican, and the Mafia came under close scrutiny following the mysterious death of Pope John Paul I. After assuming the mantle of the papacy, the popular Pope allegedly began to uncover deep levels of corruption within the Vatican, including ties to the Mob. He was also reported to be set to revolutionize the Catholic Faith, including allowing birth control, and starting an investigation into the lucrative Vatican Bank – two moves that would upset staunch conservatives and insiders within the Holy See. John Paul was found dead in his bed on September 28, 1978. A new Pope was chosen, one who, not surprisingly, was far more conservative than his predecessor.

Also suspected: ultra-conservative Catholics; Grand Lodge Alpina.

THE UNUSUAL SUSPECTS

Aliens

Rumours have surfaced that the Vatican has a direct line to the Hubble space telescope, and was aware that the Hale Bopp comet carried a "companion", thought to be an alien spacecraft. Connections between the Vatican and this spacecraft are pure speculation, but reportedly the Pope was directly involved in the situation, receiving up-to-date emails on the subject. One of the reasons for such concern about life elsewhere is the Vatican's worries over whether the symbolic significance of the death of Christ – which absolved all humanity from the taint of original sin –

would also apply to aliens. Members of the Pope's staff have already considered converting any aliens discovered to Catholicism.

MOST CONVINCING EVIDENCE

In 1998, a young member of the Swiss Guard – an order dating back to 1506 comprising Swiss Catholic men sworn to defend the Pope – murdered his superior and his wife. While first explained away by the Vatican as a tragic case of madness, stemming from the murderer being passed over for a decoration, the incident began to take on more mysterious dimensions. Rumours arose that the murdered man, Alois Estermann, may have been a Stasi mole in the Vatican. What is even more interesting is that Estermann may have saved Pope John Paul II during the assassination attempt on his life in 1981, by blocking the line of fire to the wounded Pope with his own body. Was Estermann killed to reveal his Stasi connection, or did agents in the Vatican have him murdered to hide those potentially embarrassing ties?

MOST MYSTERIOUS FACT

For over 500 years, papal candidates had to undergo the test of the sella stercoraria. In this rather embarrassing ritual, candidates were forced to sit in a chair with a hole in the seat so that their genitals could be examined to ascertain that they were indeed men. Only once everyone was convinced of the candidate's masculinity was he allowed to become Pope.

SCEPTICALLY SPEAKING

Jesus Christ once explained the relationship between wealthy men, camels, needles and the entrance to Heaven. With all the wealth in the Vatican, from its Library and Bank, to the untold treasures secure in its vaults, it's apparent that they missed that particular Sunday School lesson.

S

FREEMASONS

Knock three times . . . The Masonic Rites underpin one of the oldest, and certainly by far the most successful, of the secret societies.

Potential candidates – those who would like to be admitted – have to find a known Mason and ask, on three separate occasions, to be considered for membership. Only after the third request is the Mason allowed to acknowledge having heard the plea. Admission to the Masons is rigorously policed, and while any member is free to admit their own membership, they may not reveal any other member's name, or any ritual or decision internal to the craft. In this way, the Masonic Rites have, for centuries, made sure that only the right people get in – but what sort of people are considered to be right?

Certain groups maintain that Masonry is working to take over the world. There is no doubt that many important or influential people – politicians, policemen, lawyers, cardinals and bishops, media tycoons, celebrities and so on – are Freemasons. In many cases, it is a matter of public record. Bill Cooper, a major conspiracy writer, claims (perhaps somewhat enthusiastically) that: "The Masons are major players in the struggle for world domination". He goes on to say that the infamous Italian P2 lodge, implicated in the murder of Roberto Calvi (discussed elsewhere), has connections with the Vatican and with the CIA. He also claims that P2 persuaded Pope John Paul II to admit Freemasons to the higher ranks of Vatican officials.

Whether this is true or not, many people believe that Freemasons discriminate in favour of each other in social and business life. This may even be true – after all, most people tend to trust their friends in business, and to spend time with them socially. The danger may be that the men in charge of Freemasonry are pulling the lodges in directions and their well-meaning members in a direction they may not wish to travel. Just why are they so secretive?

THE STRANGE PART

It may or may not be significant that the Masonic term for non-Masons is "Profanes", implying that the rest of us are less sanctified, or less holy, than they are. It seems a strangely intolerant term for what is a supposedly benevolent organisation.

THE USUAL SUSPECTS

The Illuminati

The mystery traditions in general, to which Masonry traces many rituals, frequently used the term "Illuminated" to refer to a person who was a member. This has been taken to signify a link to Adam Weishaupt's Illuminati, who were officially announced to the world on May 1, 1776 in Bavaria. The Illuminati were supposedly controlling world events for hundreds of years before that date, and are still in power now. Could the Masons be under the control of the Illuminati?

The New World Order

Because their numbers include so many powerful people, the Masons are suspected by some theorists of being lynch-pins in the New World Order, the movement towards a unified, global population with no religion, a centralized government and limited technology.

THE UNUSUAL SUSPECTS

Satan

The most popular accusation levelled at Masons is that they are in league with the Devil. The hidden nature of their rituals, along with the occult imagery employed, has led many Christian groups to denounce Freemasonry as working for the forces of Evil.

MOST CONVINCING EVIDENCE

From their very first round of Initiation, Freemasons are urged to "Seek the Light". Masons are continually exhorted to do this throughout their Masonic endeavours, and often say that they are "moving towards the Light". However, for some people, the light towards which Masons try to move is not necessarily the light of God, as most outsiders would expect, but the light of Lucifer, the angel who fell to become the Devil. "Lucifer, the Light-bearer" is a strange and mysterious name to give to the Spirit of

Darkness – Lucifer, the Son of the Morning. Some renegade, high-level Masons who left the organization when they discovered the truth about 'the light'.

MOST MYSTERIOUS FACT

According to some interpretations of Masonic doctrine, a Freemason can learn to control his emotions and energies, and to apply the power created therein for magical purposes:

"When the Mason learns that the key to the warrior on the block is the proper application of the dynamo of living power, he has learned the mystery of his Craft. The seething energies of Lucifer are in his hands, and before he may step onward and upward, he must prove his ability to properly apply energy. He must follow in the footsteps of his forefather, Tubal-Cain, who with the mighty strength of the war god hammered his sword into a plowshare."

Taken from *The Lost Keys of Freemasonry or The Secret of Hiram Abiff* by Manly P Hall, 33rd Degree, KT, published by Macoy Publishing and Masonic Supply Company, Inc, Richmond, Virginia.

SCEPTICALLY SPEAKING

The great majority of Freemasons are respectable, upstanding professionals and business people with busy careers and family lives, and every year the Masonic lodges donate a fortune to charity and charitable work. Many priests and vicars are Freemasons, and the order is open to all religions. It seems unlikely that so many decent people are in fact working for Satan, and it is certainly hard to imagine exactly how helping to organize a school jumble sale is playing straight into the hands of Evil Forces. Apart from anything else, Masons have no reason to support the dark side in the hope of gaining favour – most of them are already successful before they join. Not only are the Masons probably one of the oldest and most successful secret societies, they are also the most-blamed by conspiracy theorists, which seems a little unfair given that they are ostensibly an organization devoted to charity, brotherhood and the search for truth. But then, you don't know whether I'm a Mason or not . . . do you?

THE BAVARIAN ILLUMINATI

Adam Weishaupt was born in Ingolstadt, Germany on February 6, 1748. Educated by the Jesuits, he became Professor of Natural and Canon Law at the University of Ingolstadt in 1775, aged 27, and was initiated into the Masonic Lodge "Theodore of Good Council" in Munich, in 1777. He was a cosmopolitan man who despised the bigoted superstition of the priests of his time. He decided to establish an enlightened – or Illuminated – society to oppose injustice and this he did, forming the order that would become "The Illuminati of Bavaria" May 1, 1776.

Originally called "The Order of the Perfectibilists", its object was to allow its members to team up in order to "attain the highest possible degree of morality and virtue, and to lay the foundation for the reformation of the world by the association of good men to oppose the progress of moral evil."

In collaboration with a range of other influential figures, including Baron Von Knigge, Xavier Zwack and Baron Bassus, Weishaupt developed an order that became extremely popular. Before long, some 2,000 people had enrolled as members. Lodges of the Illuminati were located in France, Italy, Poland, Hungary, Sweden, Denmark, Belgium and Holland. The Bavarian authorities issued a suppressive Edict concerning the order on the June 22, 1784, which was repeated the following year in March and again in August. That same year, 1785, Weishaupt was stripped of his professorship and exiled from Bavaria.

Once it began to experience attempts at suppression, the order started to go into public decline and by the end of the century it had apparently vanished completely. The authorities illegally raided Xavier Zwack's home in 1786 and the documents that were seized were used to help suppress the order.

Most serious commentators take this decline at face value. *The Encyclopaedia Britannica* barely mentions the Illuminati, and the vast majority of historical sources follow suit, judging the order to be insignificant. Others feel that the Illuminati disbanded into Masonry, a movement that was infiltrated in much the same way as cancer takes over a healthy body. Since that time, they allege, the Illuminati have stayed within the Masons, seizing power and manipulating the whole order.

THE STRANGE PART

In 1906, the British Museum in London received a copy of a manuscript called *The Illuminati Protocols*. These first appeared in Bavaria in the late Eighteenth Century, and Joly used parts in an 1864 play. The copy the British Museum received was written in Russian. It is also interesting that both Adam Smith's capitalist treatise *The Wealth of Nations* and that great democratic treatise the American *Declaration of Independence* were written in 1776. It has been suggested that Weishaupt may have been the mysterious Black-Cloaked Man who presented Washington with the text of the declaration. It is also rumoured that the raid on Zwack's house was spurred on by the chance interception in 1784 by the authorities of a document telling the head of the French Illuminati, Robespierre, how to orchestrate the French Revolution in 1789. Warnings were ignored, and the revolution happened on schedule.

THE USUAL SUSPECTS

Freemasons

To achieve their goal, the Masons knew their real target – overthrowing all world government and organized religion in order to allow peace and liberty to prevail – had to remain concealed. So, in order to avoid promoting hysteria against themselves, and as a way of dealing with criticism and exposé, the Masons created the Illuminati as a front organization to take the blame for any perceived misdeeds or shortcomings. It is a strategy that has worked brilliantly for two centuries.

THE UNUSUAL SUSPECTS

Robert Shea and Robert Anton Wilson

In the Seventies, Robert Shea and Robert Anton Wilson published a cult set of books called *The Illuminatus! Trilogy*. This was a novel masquerading as the largest conspiracy theory ever seen, disguised as a grand exposé of the Illuminati. It is this book that has set the Illuminati back in the public mind. Of course, no one claims that the trilogy is anything other than a good work of fiction – or that Robert Anton Wilson is the current chief of the Illuminati . . . do they?

MOST CONVINCING EVIDENCE

In 1902 the Freemason William Westcott records receiving membership in the Order of the from Theodor Reuss. Similarly, the occultist Eliphas Levi strongly connected the Bavarian Illuminati with Freemasonry in 1913.

MOST MYSTERIOUS FACT

Among the list of notable members of the Illuminati is the name Marquis Saint Germain de Constanzo. This seems likely to be The Marquis de Saint Germain, the man most commonly suspected of being the only true immortal known in the world. He has cropped up as a sorcerer, an alchemist and a wise man throughout medieval history. Who better to help found the world's most successful Secret Society?

SCEPTICALLY SPEAKING

There is, when you get down to it, no real evidence whatsoever to suggest that the Illuminati were anything other than a short-lived Bavarian secret society – just a lot of hearsay. If it hadn't been for *The Illuminatus! Trilogy* the Bavarian Illuminati would still be an obscure sect lost in the footnotes of history.

THE KU KLUX KLAN

Nothing is more terrifying than organized hatred. The Ku Klux Klan has been among the most reviled of hate-fuelled organizations, spreading fear throughout the US against minorities and those who disagree with the Klan's strict, racist views. Hiding behind anonymous white hoods, Klan members have become infamous for their burning of the Christian Cross, their intolerance of racial integration, and their reputation for violence. In an age where so many inroads have been made to build bridges between races, the Klan still exists, proclaiming the power of white supremacy.

Rising in the ashes of the South, following the end of the American Civil War in 1865, the Klan came into being with a self-proclaimed mission to save the South from what it saw as the greatest threats of the time: blacks, Catholics, Jews, and the American Federal government, among others. First led by Nathan Bedford Forrest, the Klan fought to preserve what it considered to be the purity of the white man. This was known as the Klan's First Era, with Forrest acting as Grand Wizard.

By the Twenties, the Klan had grown in political power, and entered its Second Era. Through the turbulent civil rights battles of the Sixties, the Klan was implicated in murders and acts of violence against civil rights leaders and civil rights workers, especially in the South. Currently, the Klan considers itself in its Fifth Era, fighting not only for the white man, but to save all of Western civilization.

While the Klan is seen by many as nothing more than a hate organization run by ignorant men and women, it is possible that the KKK is far stronger, and has more influence, than is generally thought. Even today, when the civil rights battles of the Sixties seem a lifetime away, when racism is fought and decried by so many, the power of hate continues to glow with all the intensity of the Klan's trademark burning cross.

THE STRANGE PART

Woodrow Wilson, twenty-eighth President of the United States from 1913–1921, once claimed that the Ku Klux Klan saved civilization on the North American continent. Why did he make this odd statement?

THE USUAL SUSPECTS

The CIA and the FBI

The Klan has been implicated in the murders of popular black political leaders Martin Luther King and Malcolm X, apparently acting because both men posed a threat to the Klan's vision of America – a vision allegedly shared by many in the CIA and in the FBI. King's vision of peaceful racial integration was unpalatable, as was Malcolm X's more contentious view that blacks were superior to the white man in every respect. For refusing to conform to the Klan's ideal of a black man, both men were killed. In the case of King, Klan and FBI involvement seem particularly strong, since the FBI openly recruited Klan members before King's death.

Black Ops Race War

The KKK may be part of a race war directed against blacks and Jews, playing a role in the creation and distribution of the AIDS virus along with black ops government agencies. The Klan is also suspected of spreading false conspiracy rumours about ZOG (the Zionist Occupation Government), a purported Jewish plan to take over the US. Such rumours help deflect attention from America's true enemy – the Shadow Government and its black ops agents.

THE UNUSUAL SUSPECTS

The New World Order

The Klan may be a front for the NWO, secretly furthering the aims of the New World Order while openly pretending to fight its influence on every level. This would include Klan involvement in the phenomenon of black helicopters, which, it is alleged, the Klan uses to incite panic in the populace which, the Klan hopes, will provide an environment in which it is easy to stir up racial tensions.

The US Government

Despite the recent liberalism of the US Government, many leaders in corporate, government and military circles still favour a more conservative outlook, a viewpoint shared by the Klan. Funds could be diverted to the Klan, as well as weaponry and clandestine political support. This would explain David Duke's political career after he left the Klan.

Also suspected: the Bavarian Illuminati, the Order of the Green Dragon.

MOST CONVINCING EVIDENCE

The continued existence of the Klan in an age where hate groups are not tolerated suggests some high-level connection with the US government.

The American Constitution's guarantee of free speech as the right of every American is a guarantee that the US government has shown in the past it will ignore as it sees fit (in the McCarthy Era, for example). The Klan persists, and in the modern world, that poses the question of just who is looking out for its interests.

MOST MYSTERIOUS FACT

Theodore Roosevelt, President of the US from 1932-1945, once bankrolled WG Griffiths' Birth of A Nation – a pro-KKK film.

SCEPTICALLY SPEAKING

You don't need a conspiracy to explain the ignorance that lies behind race hatred. Anthropology classes probably would not be a hit with the Klan as the strong possibility that all humanity shares a common black ancestry might put a dampener on Cross-burning activities.

THE MAFIA

Since the start of the Twentieth Century, the Mafia has constituted a significant part of the organized crime underground in the US. In addition to its American operations, the Mafia is currently active in Italy, Southern France, Germany, and Russia. The facts of the Mafia's presence and its wide range of criminal activities – from prostitution and illegal gambling through to drugs distribution, contract assassination and slavery – are undisputed. What is less well known is the extent to which the Mafia is one unified organization.

The Mafia was first formed in the Ninth Century AD, in Sicily. The original Mafia valued loyalty above all and respected culture, family and heritage. Membership was only open to Sicilians and the organization's aim was to protect the interests of its members. As the centuries passed, the Mafia evolved the belief that justice, vengeance and honour were matters for the individual to look after, and not responsibilities that should be delegated to the current government – which was often put in place by invaders anyway. Secrecy was maintained through the tradition of Omerta, which said that betrayal of the society's trust was repayable by death.

Early in the Eighteenth Century, the Mafia started to become openly criminal. Money was extorted from wealthy Sicilians, who would receive a picture of a black hand. If cash were not forthcoming, arson, kidnappings and murder would follow.

The Mafia has been active in the US since the early Nineteenth Century, particularly in New Orleans. Word soon good back to Sicily that a lot of money could be made in the New World, and the organisation grew swiftly. In 1924, Mussolini cracked down on the Mafia in Italy and Sicily, and many members fled to the US. Ever since its super-profitable days of Prohibition, the Mafia has been spreading its influence throughout American political, legal and financial institutions, creaming off vast amounts of money in the process.

THE STRANGE PART

The Mafia in the US is commonly thought to be a collection of rival gangs, clans that are organized on a family structure and have little but hatred for each other. However, this may be far from the truth. While the different gangs do certainly compete, the heads of the 24 families regularly meet in a cartel called The Commission. At these meetings, they settle territorial and business disputes, and decide policy for the coming months. It is possible that the the Commission may also negotiate with government agencies, particularly the CIA, on areas of activity where mutual benefit can be derived.

THE USUAL SUSPECTS

The Network

Major world crime organizations are teaming up to maximize profits. Just like any legitimate big business, crime empires that merge activities can improve profitability. The Mafia has joined forces with the Triads, with the Yakuza and with drugs cartels. This alliance, known as the Network, also accepts junior members such as Jamaican Yardies and Algerian slave traders. Because different groups control different resources, they have much to offer each other. The American Mafia, for example, can provide access to the US banking industry, law enforcement and justice systems as required.

Established Government

To what extent are government and organized crime actually different? Paying tax or protection money amounts to much the same thing, and few criminal organizations have caused as much public death as the US did courtesy of Vietnam, or Russia did in Chechnya. Some conspiriologists believe that established governments actually control the Mafia as a way of having authority on the otherwise impossible-to-govern world of crime.

THE UNUSUAL SUSPECTS

The Freemasons

The Mafia has long held strong ties to Masonry through the shadowy Vatican lodge P2, that is said to be the most powerful Masonic lodge in Europe. When Pope John Paul I determined to clear the Masons out of the Vatican – having discovered over 100 among the priesthood – he was killed, supposedly by the Mafia. Could the Masons be the power driving the Mafia's relentless advance over the years? Certainly both groups own a lot of judges and policemen.

MOST CONVINCING EVIDENCE

The spread of the Mafia is truly staggering. In the US, the Mafia and officials from the government were maintaining an Illinois-based bank as a criminal enterprise, laundering money. The bank was run by a close Mafia associate, the Catholic Bishop of Cicero Paul Marcinkus, head of the Vatican Bank until 1991 working in association with a Congressman who was a controller of the CIA's Black Ops budget.

A documentary detailing this was made, but before the programme could be broadcast, State law enforcement officers threatened the makers, families were harassed, and one was falsely arrested.

MOST MYSTERIOUS FACT

The Mafia believes deeply in conspiracy theories. Some Mafia members even claim that the organization was originally formed to fight the mysterious "potere occulto" or hidden power they believe is rife in the world.

SCEPTICALLY SPEAKING

Organized crime is just that – organized crime. The last thing it wants to do, surely, is to take over the irritating trivia of everyday government, something that isn't necessary anyway, given the number of politicians already in the pay of Mafia Dons.

MJ-12

In 1947, the now-famous crash of an alien spacecraft at Roswell, New Mexico allegedly left the US military in possession of a partly-destroyed alien craft, along with several alien corpses.
The Roswell Air Force base announced the discovery in the world's press. The story was retracted three days later, when the President, Harry Truman, suppressed the information in the national interest, remembering the panic caused by Orson Welles' famous radio broadcast *The War of the Worlds*. He assembled a group of 12 military, strategic and scientific advisors to conduct a thorough investigation of the wreckage. This group was given security classifications above Top Secret, and named the Majestic Twelve, or MJ-12 for short. The craft was taken to the top secret Nevada test area called Watertown, now known as Area 51.

From here, MJ-12 oversaw a number of different projects. In 1953 and 1954, President Eisenhower instituted Project Grudge under the auspices of Majority Agency for Joint Intelligence, or MAJI. Grudge was given a security clearance of MAJIC (MAJI Clearance), the highest security classification of all.

The work of MJ-12 is alleged to have led to the US government signing a treaty with aliens to allow them to perform tests on animals and humans in return for technological information. MJ-12 also agreed to suppress all information regarding the alien presence, and cover up the evidence of their tests, an operation known as Project Garnet. A further operation, Project Delta, was set up for this purpose, and employs personnel to suppress, by any means necessary, evidence of alien presence. Project Delta provides the so-called Men in Black.

THE STRANGE PART

When an undeveloped film containing images of files purporting to be a Presidential briefing concerning MJ-12 turned up out of the blue in the post-box of a prominent UFO researcher, many people were quick to dismiss the documents as fakes. However, as more investigation was made into the claims of the so-called "MJ-12 documents" it became harder to dismiss them, as they identified the only days possible when all the 12 original members could have met for meetings – a level of detail unlikely in a hoax.

THE USUAL SUSPECTS

The US Military

Always known for being pragmatic, the military supports MJ-12 recognizing that although the aliens may not be a good thing, there is little that can be done to change matters. While research into weapons with which to fight the aliens continues, MJ-12 can only stick to its end of the bargain in order to prevent the invaders taking matters into their own hands. Better a few missing abductees and a few murdered UFO investigators than the human race enslaved.

MAJESTY

MJ-12 is not in control at all. That dubious distinction falls to the MAJI committee also known as MAJESTY – a combined council of the heads of the intelligence agencies, along with the President. MJ-12 is a group of consultants to MAJESTY, and has never known the whole truth. Information on MJ-12 has been released in order to muddy the waters, and obscure the truth about MAJESTY and the MAJI committee, the groups that really run Project Grudge.

THE UNUSUAL SUSPECTS

THE ELDER RACE

MJ-12 and the UFO story is only a cleverly-constructed decoy story to divert attention away from the real source of mankind's advances in science over recent years – technology recovered from the ruins of an advanced Elder Race that was wiped out by a massive, global catastrophe. Those behind the conspiracy want to hide the truth – both of humanity's origins and the fact that we may also one day share the fate of the Elder Race.

MOST CONVINCING EVIDENCE

Defense Secretary James Forrestal was allegedly one of the original members of MJ-12. Shortly after Roswell he appeared to have a mental breakdown, though few conspiriologists believe that he leapt through a window to his death from the 16th floor of a hospital, as was officially claimed. Especially as his personal journals – which were seized by the government – are still classified above Top Secret after 50 years.

MOST MYSTERIOUS FACT

The aliens who allegedly signed a treaty with MJ-12 claim that they have been genetically tinkering with humanity for millennia. They created Jesus Christ and have used a tachyon scanner that can view images from any time in history, to show his crucifixion. This time-movie has been recorded on to video, and the aliens hold its release in reserve, should they want to cause spiritual chaos.

SCEPTICALLY SPEAKING

While occasional documents have been found to back up the information regarding MJ-12 and its various projects, almost all this evidence includes errors. The people who suggest that the documents were deliberately made to look suspicious when first created, in order to minimize damage if they were leaked, are forgetting the fact that when first written, the supposed authors would have had no reason to know that such an elaborate conspiracy would ever be necessary.

THE ODESSA

The popular belief, reinforced by countless war movies and other forms of corporate-controlled media, is that the Allied Forces at the end World War II soundly defeated the Nazi Party. The evil had been vanquished, never to rise again. Or did many Nazis not only escape the grasp of the Allies, but also actually receive help from them? Could the Third Reich still be exerting influence over the world? Yes, according to the theories surrounding the Odessa.

Mid-way through World War II, sensing the way the wind was blowing, many Nazis (among them Otto Skorzeny, Reinhard Gehlen, and Martin Bormann) began to take steps to ensure their own survival. This metaphorical lifeboat was called The Odessa.

The Odessa splits into three divisions. The first division, headed by Skorzeny, developed a system for smuggling important members of the Nazi Party to safe havens across the world, including places like Indonesia and South America. The second division, the brainchild of Gehlen, (who had been head of Nazi Intelligence during World War II) was an organization of Nazi spies, that would set up shop in Munich and in time call itself "The Org". The third division handled perhaps the most crucial element in Nazi survival: the transport of money and gold, stolen from Nazi victims, out of a fallen Germany. This was also the work of Skorzeny.

But such grandiose plans, no matter how clever and ruthless the perpetrators, would not have succeeded without help. And here the tale of The Odessa takes a much darker turn – it appears that this help came from the US. In fact, it can be argued that without Nazi intervention, the CIA would never have existed and NASA would never have made it to the Moon. Perhaps the Nazi dream did not die – it may have simply changed address.

THE STRANGE PART

Captured by Allied forces, Otto Skorzeny did not face a war crimes tribunal, as would have befitted a Nazi war criminal. Instead, the Americans released him in 1947.

THE USUAL SUSPECTS

The OSS/CIA

Following the war, Allen Dulles of the OSS (Office of Strategic Services) in the US contracted the spy services of Gehlen, blatantly ignoring the US law that made the employment of Nazis illegal. Using American tax dollars, (rumoured to be around $200 million) Gehlen polished his ring of Nazi spies into The Org. Then, working alongside Dulles, who later became head of the newly-formed CIA in 1947, Gehlen was in a position to manipulate American domestic and foreign policy.

The US government

Under the notorious Project Paperclip, in which the US government tried to snag German scientists of the Reich for its own programs, several acts of subterfuge and moral laxity were committed. One of the chief beneficiaries of this breaking of American law was NASA, which acquired the services of Wehrner Von Braun, a force behind the dreaded V-2 rocket, to work on its space program.

THE UNUSUAL SUSPECTS

The New World Order

The Nazi Regime may have been the forerunner of the New World Order, with Hitler set to conquer the world with the aid of several corporations. But as Hitler proved too unstable, he was removed from his position of power through an inglorious suicide and the Reich was dramatically dismantled. As the dark forces behind the NWO settle down to wait for another opportunity to realize their dream, they took steps to ensure that their more loyal servants would still be available to continue the work.

MOST CONVINCING EVIDENCE

After being caught by American forces, Gehlen bargained for his freedom by offering microfilm copies of everything that his Nazi intelligence service had gleaned about Russia. The US made a deal with Gehlen for the microfilm and removed his name from the lists of Nazi POWs in American hands.

MOST MYSTERIOUS FACT

Allen Dulles' older brother, John Foster Dulles, besides being Secretary of State in the Eisenhower Administration, also acted as American liaison to IG Farben, a chemical company that not only supported the Nazi Party, but even had a plant in Auschwitz itself. Farben made the Zyklon-B crystals that were used in Auschwitz's gas chambers.

SCEPTICALLY SPEAKING

War is a lot like organized sports today – if your team is losing far too often, you just get out of your contract and become free agents. New boss . . . same as the old boss. Given how much is known about what became of certain Nazis it seems unlikely that any organized conspiracy was in operation. The power of The Odessa has been exaggerated.

SATANISTS

According to many, Satanists are a dark force that's out to snare the youth of the world. Satanists are seen as agents of the Devil, the ultimate enemy of God so Satanism is the direct antithesis to Christianity. By luring the disaffected, the lonely, and the angry into their coven of evil with promises of sexual gratification and power, by enticing impressionable young people with the appeal of the forbidden, by disguising their corrupting message in various forms of pop culture, Satanists are perceived as being on the front-lines in the eternal battle between Good and Evil.

Satanism can manifest itself in many ways, from a black-clad and alienated teenager fancying himself to be a Satanist because he listens to Marilyn Manson, to the more organized Church of Satan. Its precepts can be found in the works of Anton LaVey, whose Satanic Bible lays out what it means to be a Satanist.

Satanists make a clear distinction between their faith and that of devil worship. In Satanism, the image of Satan is seen merely as an archetype, while that of devil worship focuses on an actual god-like figure. While

Satanists may distance themselves from devil worshippers by insisting that their faith is more philosophical, they cannot escape the suspicion and wrath of the world around them, being blamed for everything from the moral decay of society to the ritualistic murder of babies. With so many fingers being pointed at them, it's difficult not to wonder what Satanists are really up to.

THE STRANGE PART

Satanists are often blamed for the abuse of children and accused of conducting human sacrifice in their occult ceremonies. These charges gained world-wide attention in several reported cases of Satanic abuse of children, most notably in the McMartin Infant School Case in the US, in 1983, and in the Broxtowe Case in England, in 1987. In these and many other similar cases, children complained of being forced to undergo Satanic rituals and endure attendant abuse which includes being drugged, being forced to eat faeces and insects, and witnessing babies being cut out alive from their mothers' bodies.

THE USUAL SUSPECTS

Satan

As the world moves closer to the final battle of Armageddon, the powers of evil are quietly gathering their forces among those outcast by society. What better way to combat Christianity than by forming its antithesis and giving your followers cool black T-shirts?

Rock Musicans

Fundamentalist Christians have long regarded rock music as the Devil's work. From Elvis gyrating in the Fifties to the latest ear-splitting Slayer album, rock is thought to be nothing more than the Devil luring innocents from the way of righteousness. The methods of doing this can be through a call to licentiousness such as. Kiss' *Rock And Roll All Night*, Chuck Berry's *My Ding A Ling*) to the more direct messages of black metal music, which doesn't hide its Satanic influences. The suspected spreading of messages was thought to be even more sinister during the backward masking craze of the mid-Eighties, when Satanic messages were reportedly found in records played backwards. The most notorious of these was Led Zeppelin's *Stairway To Heaven* which, when played backwards, allegedly proclaims "I worship Satan". Needless to say, the release of Marilyn Manson's *AntiChrist Superstar* sent many into apoplexy.

THE UNUSUAL SUSPECTS

Comic Book Writers

Characters such as *Hot Stuff* (an impish devil published by Harvey Comics) Marvel Comics' Daredevil, and more occult-laced books such as DC Comics' *Sandman* and *Hellblazer*, encourage the view that comic books are a prime breeding ground for Satanic messages. In the warped reasoning of certain fundamentalist Christian conspiracy theorists, comic book writers must therefore be the secret force behind Satanism.

Bill Clinton

Because he openly enjoys rock music and has committed adultery with Monica Lewinksy (among others), Bill Clinton has been accused of operating under Satanic influences and of being the chief representative of Satan on Earth.

MOST CONVINCING EVIDENCE

The public acceptance of what many fundamentalists consider to be Satanic influences in popular culture would suggest that there must be a well-organized plan for domination. The use of Ozzy Osbourne's *Crazy Train* to sell a popular automobile is noteworthy. Osbourne is lead singer of heavy metal band Black Sabbath – a band suspected of Satanism – and is notorious for an incident where he bit the head off a bat during a stage performance. This inroad, by suspected Satanists, into corporate culture, and, through advertising, to world-wide acceptance, could be the beginning of the end.

MOST MYSTERIOUS FACT

The FBI investigated Satanic crimes, but found little hard evidence to support claims of murder and abuse. Kenneth Lanning, head of the investigating unit, cautioned in 1989 against hysteria, pointing out the damage such allegations could have on innocent people.

SCEPTICALLY SPEAKING

There is little evidence for a Satanic conspiracy – not, in itself, too surprising. Let's see: believe in a God who promises eternal happiness in a rather nice-sounding place called Heaven, or in one who rules a fiery pit of agony and torture. Wow – tough choice.

THE ORDER OF THE SOLAR TEMPLE

For most of us, this world isn't enough. We need to believe that there must be an extra layer of the fantastic, some golden thread of hope running through our day-to-day existence that connects us to something larger, something more majestic, more magical. Many of us turn to organized religion for this hope, or to friends, books, or whatever it is that opens the door to a wider world. Sometimes, though, the need to believe in this golden thread leads people down dark paths, making them vulnerable to the monsters that live there, all too ready to prey on their weaknesses and needs for their own ends.

The Order of the Solar Temple gave its followers a dream that was as fantastic as they come – it offered its dedicated adherents the chance to "transit" themselves to the planet Sirius, moving through the "illusion of death" to a better life off-world.

The Order has the official name of the International Chivalric Order Solar Tradition but is also known as the Cross and the Rose. Luc Jouret founded it, in 1977. Jouret convinced his followers that he was Jesus Christ, and had also been a member of the Christian Order of the Knights Templar in the Fourteenth Century. Along with Joseph Di Mambro (who had led the group Foundation Golden Way before it was assimilated into the Order), Jouret transfixed believers with a sword, ceremonies and robes said to have been given to Jouret 1,000 years ago.

The two leaders spoke often of how their followers' sins would be forgiven if they died through fire, a process that would send them across the galaxy to a new life on Sirius. They laced the cult's belief system with bits of Rosicrucian and Templar thought, survivalism, and heavy dollops from the *Book of Revelations*.

Their believers tended to be among the wealthy, and the Order gleaned millions from its adherents. This dedication extended even to suicide and murder. In 1994, 53 members of the Order perished in a rash of murder/suicides in Switzerland and Quebec, reportedly including among them Jouret and Di Mambro. In 1997, another five members died in Quebec, with three teenagers fortunately being able to talk their way out of accompanying their parents on the "journey" to Sirius.

The Order still exists today, and has around 500 members across the globe.

THE STRANGE PART

Members of the Order held many high-powered positions within industry, banking and government. When Mambro believed the child of a fellow cult member to be the Antichrist, he ordered its death and the infant had a wooden stake driven through its heart. The power and influence of cult members was such that no prosecution was brought.

THE USUAL SUSPECTS

The French Government

One possible reason for the mass suicides/murders in 1994 may be because Di Mambro felt the French government was out to get them. A letter sent to the Quebec daily Le Monde, apparently by Di Mambro, stated that the French embassy in Canada would not renew Di Mambro's wife's passport – ostensibly on orders of the French government. This harassment, as Di Mambro saw it, was reason enough to kill 53 people for a trip to Sirius. The question remains, why were the French government so interested in the order.

THE UNUSUAL SUSPECTS

THE PLANET SIRIUS

Sirius keeps popping up in the examination of conspiracy theories. Whether it's the home planet of the Men In Black or the better world envisioned by the Order of the Solar Temple, it plays a disturbing role wherever it surfaces.

Also suspected: black ops mind-control experiments; and Knights Templar.

MOST CONVINCING EVIDENCE

The methodical approach to detail in Solar Temple deaths is unsettling. In 1994, several victims' bodies were discovered in a secret underground chapel, its walls lined with mirrors. The bodies were dressed in ceremonial robes, arranged in a circle, with the heads facing outwards and the feet inwards. The majority had plastic bags tied over their heads, with bullet holes through the bags, showing that many were shot to death. One victim was found with eight bullet wounds in the head, and another with a broken jaw, which neatly discounts all deaths as suicide. The fires, designed to purify their bodies for their interplanetary trip, were set to ignite by remote control, usually triggered by a telephone call.

MOST MYSTERIOUS FACT

Jouret was drawn to Ayers Rock, reportedly by its mystic energy. When he asked the Aborigines, who maintain control over the Rock, if he could perform a religious service there, they refused.

SCEPTICALLY SPEAKING

It is a tragedy that people are so credulous, but when you have such a high level of gullibility you do not need a conspiracy to explain away the Order of Solar Temple. Anyway, why is Shambhala/Nirvana/Oz always supposed to be on another world? If Sirius was as depressing as Manchester on a rainy Sunday it would cut down on the religious fanaticism.

THE TEMPLARS

The First Crusade of the forces of Western Christendom to reclaim the holy sites of Palestine from Muslim forces took place between 1095 and 1099 AD. By the end of the war, the Holy City of Jerusalem had been captured, and the Kingdom of Jerusalem had been created. The Knights Templar was a monastic order that came into being some time around 1120 in Jerusalem in order to provide protection to the pilgrims from Europe visiting the Holy Land. Founded by a group of nine French knights, the order's full title was The Poor Knights of Christ and of the Temple of Solomon. Within a few decades, the group grew substantially and became an officially-sanctioned Christian order backed by the Pope and by the combined Monarchs of Europe.

The order's sponsor, and the man who drew up the codes of conduct and oaths of poverty that the members followed, was Cistercian Abbott St Bernard of Clairveux, the chief spokesman of united Christendom, often called "The Second Pope". Because of their members' vows of poverty and the donations they took from the wealthy pilgrims they escorted, the Templars quickly became rich. With wealth came power, and back in Europe after the Crusades, the influence of the Knights Templar grew. Pope Innocent II had exempted the Templars from all authority other than that of the Papacy, so they were exempt from law. This same immunity allowed them to practise usury – lending of money for interest – and they became major financiers to European kings. In the process, they created a structure that would later become the banking and finance industry.

Perhaps making use of their legal immunities, the Templars held secret meetings and rituals at which the business of the Order was conducted. The truth of what went on at these meetings has long been debated, but whether it was Satanic worship or financial strategic discussions, the end was the same. By the start of the Fourteenth Century, King Philip "The Fair" of France was deeply in debt to the Templars. Rather than repay them, he chose to conspire with the Pope, Clement V, who resented Templar influence. On October 13, 1307, Philip had the Templars arrested for Heresy, which allowed him to seize all their funds and torture the knights into confessing to a variety of bad deeds, including demon-worship, possession of occult powers, trampling the Cross, and sodomy. On

March 22, 1312, the Order was formally dissolved by Clement V's Papal Bull entitled "Vox In Excelso".

THE STRANGE PART

It has long been held that Freemasonry was formed from the dying embers of the Knights Templar. Many Templars fled from Europe to Scotland, where the Order was not suppressed. It is suspected that the Order survives to the present day, both within Freemasonry and separate to it as an individual organization. Long used to manipulating governments and finance, the Templars have kept light hold on the reins of power, and still sit in the background of Western society, waiting for the right moment to reveal themselves again.

THE USUAL SUSPECTS

The Freemasons

There is a fair amount of evidence to link the Templars to the Freemasons. Several Masonic degrees and rites draw explicitly on Templar imagery, and even use Templar titles. Given that the Order fled to Scotland and that there is a Scottish Rite (or branch; the three Rites are theoretically separate organizations) of Freemasonry, the Templars could well have become the Freemasons, which would leave them still in power at the beginning of the Twenty-first Century.

THE UNUSUAL SUSPECTS

The Assassins

The famed Assassins of the Middle East were the fighting force of the Ismaeli Sect of Islam – ruled today by the Aga Khan. Known to work via infiltration, the Assassins may have compromized the Knights Templar during the Crusades as a way of gaining a foothold in the Western world – a foothold on which they have been building ever since.

MOST CONVINCING EVIDENCE

One of the most compelling pieces of evidence for the continued existence of the Templars is the existence of the Templar Research Institute, part of a mysterious group known as CIRCES International Inc, a non-profit-based fraternal charity. According to its charter, the Templar Research Institute is dedicated to chivalry, but conspiracy theorists – as usual – have their doubts.

MOST MYSTERIOUS FACT

On March 19, 1314, the last Grand Master of the Knights Templar, Jacques de Molay, was burnt at the stake. As he died, he cursed King Philip and Pope Clement, telling them that they would join him within the year. The Pope died within five weeks of the prediction, and Philip died within eight months.

SCEPTICALLY SPEAKING

There is no need to look any deeper into the mystery of the Templars than the obvious facts. A greedy King and an unscrupulous Pope wanted to get rid of their enemies, so they trumped up a load of charges and tortured the Templars for confessions, then shut the order down.

THE TRIADS

Trading on the images of blood oaths, mysterious rituals and the Death Of A Thousand Knives, the Triads – Chinese criminal organizations – have a rather exotic reputation. Like several other criminal organizations, they arose as rebellious conspiracies to overthrow unpopular, restrictive or invading governments. Triads have one of the longest pedigrees of all the crime organizations. Triads have their roots in a precursor, imaginatively named "The Red Eyebrows", that was founded during the First Century BC to overthrow the Han Dynasty.

The first proper Triad organization – that is, the first one that can be traced directly through to the current day – was the Hung League, which arose during the Seventeenth Century. Also called The Heaven and Earth Society, it was supposedly founded by five monks for the purpose of rebelling against the Chi'ing dynasty and returning power to the Ming dynasty. Many other rebellious criminal secret societies arose during the Eighteenth and Nineteenth Centuries, but most of their energies went towards organizing criminal activities against the common citizens, rather than encouraging anti-governmental terrorism.

In modern China and Hong Kong, the Triads are extremely active, but are more often visible as small-scale gangs rather than large entities run by criminal masterminds. They provide muscle and expertise at street level, running small extortion rings, prostitution, forgery, fencing stolen goods and distributing drugs on a day-to-day basis. Before a major government clampdown in 1956, the Triads had been much more organized, with a comparatively rigid control structure, treaties and some degree of co-operation.

Emigration from Hong Kong and Taiwan allowed the Triads to set up in the United Kingdom and in America. Government reports have assessed that, although much of the crime in the Asian communities in both countries is linked to the Triads, they are not controlled from Hong Kong or China. However, such findings might well be prompted by vested interests – neither the British nor the American governments want to admit to yet another powerful, organized crime body operating on their territory, and it is also in the interests of the Triads that they should be severely underestimated.

THE STRANGE PART

Despite protestations that there is little central organization, there is a serious Triad-related problem across the UK and US with forged credit cards. It appears that Triad members terrorize vulnerable waiters in Chinese restaurants into copying credit card details from customers paying for a meal. These card details are then shipped to a central source and passed back to the Far East, where forged credit cards are manufactured in bulk using the stolen details and then passed for world-wide distribution. This sort of co-ordination would be tricky to achieve if the Triads were as fragmented and as preoccupied with in-fighting as government reports suggest they are.

THE USUAL SUSPECTS

The Network

It is feared that following the hand-over of Hong Kong to China, the Triads have moved out into the world at large. It is thought that from their new operational HQs in Australia, the Triads have joined with the Yakuza, the Tongs, the Mafia and the IRA to extort money on a grand scale from governments and major corporations, partly through electronic terrorism such as viruses and hacker scares.

THE UNUSUAL SUSPECTS

Japan

When the Japanese invaded China in the Thirties, they paid the Triads to work for them. Even though the Communists under Mao Tse Tung eventually won, the Japanese government paid the Triads in Hong Kong (through an organization called the Lee Yuen Company) to police the residents and suppress any anti-Japanese activity. The Japanese government may still be the force behind Triad activity today.

MOST CONVINCING EVIDENCE

Although the theft and re-distribution of fake credit cards is well-documented in England, the extent can be quite shocking. One restaurant in Birmingham was found to be the source of 19 incidents of credit card duplication (with subsequent fraudulent transactions) in the Far East in just 14 days, which suggests a very well-polished organizational structure.

MOST MYSTERIOUS FACT

In one well-publicized interview of a notorious Triad enforcer, known as BC, by the journalist Terry Gould, several allegations were made about the scope of gang activities. BC revealed that there is a large Triad organization called The Big Circle, and said that it consisted of several sections. There were so many members of The Big Circle, in fact, that many of them did not know that they were part of the same organization. There is a degree of debate as to whether The Big Circle was just a large Triad, like the 14K, which is known to have several subsidiary groups, or whether it was an over-arching unificatory power, dictating policy and action.

SCEPTICALLY SPEAKING

Although the case for central organization is quite persuasive, given the endemic violence between rival Triad groups, it seems more likely that the apparent co-operation is merely one small skein of mutual interest. In most matters, on a day-to-day basis, the Triads remain a collection of petty gangs, operating under a common name purely because of the fear the Triad name can cause.

T

THE WINTEL CONSPIRACY

Morris' Law states that every 18 months, the power of the "heart" of the computer – its Central Processing Unit, the bit that actually does all the calculations required to run programs, crunch data and show things on your screen – doubles, while its price remains constant. What Morris' Law doesn't tell us, is that this growth rate is wholly artificial; it is man-managed, because the current computer hardware market is led and dominated by just one company – Intel.

When blue-chip computing firm IBM was designing the PC, they needed a CPU chip. They purchased Intel's 8086 processor, and Intel has been at the top of the CPU design industry ever since. IBM was also looking for an operating system, so users could control their computers. Microsoft, a small company run by Bill Gates, sold IBM the rights to MS-DOS, which seemed to fit their requirements.

The triumvirate of IBM, Intel and Microsoft developed a standard for a product that rapidly became part of every office and can now be found in the majority of homes in the Western world. Increasingly, any small to medium company that wanted to be competitive in its marketplace rapidly came to rely on machines built around Intel parts, and driven by Microsoft software.

In late 1988, Intel and Microsoft realized that they didn't need IBM, and Intel licensed its processors for use by anyone who wanted to build a machine. True, competition drove the price of individual machines down, but as every machine made returned money to Intel and Microsoft, they didn't lose out – unlike IBM, who lost out big-time. Indeed, in early 1999 IBM announced that it was, effectively, ceasing to make PCs.

Cheaper prices increased the potential market for the product, bringing more money into the partnership that was becoming known as "Wintel", a term coined to describe the alliance between Microsoft and its operating system, Windows, and chip-maker Intel. Cheaper prices also meant more machines, more people and more businesses relying on Intel and Microsoft to survive.

In 1996, when the Internet began to be recognized as a potentially major business tool, Microsoft and Intel claimed it would never take off. Microsoft began to develop The Microsoft Network. But so rapid was the uptake of the 'Net that by 1997, Microsoft had been forced to embrace the technology fully, and, with Windows 98, integrated Internet access tools into its operating system.

Today, over 95 per cent of businesses in the West have at least one Intel-powered machine, running Microsoft software. Almost two-thirds of homes have a similar machine.

THE STRANGE PART

Microsoft Windows 98 has long been able to check your computer and tell Microsoft what files your computer has on it, and what software you use. In fact, it does this every time you tell it to perform a "Windows Update" by modem or, if you've installed the "Microsoft Critical Update Notifier", every time you switch the machine on and it connects to Microsoft to look for updates. Since the introduction of the Pentium III (from Intel, of course), every Intel computer released has had an individual identification number, traceable from sales records. This ESN or Electronic Serial Number is readable across the Internet by any Web Site you visit, and that information can be stored and collated without you even knowing.

THE USUAL SUSPECTS

Bill Gates

Gates is a social outcast, a geek made good who is pilloried by the press, his colleagues and his customers. His massive anti-trust lawsuits with the US Department of Justice and his other legal wrangles with competitors have honed his paranoia to increasingly high and unstable levels. It's not unfeasible that he really, genuinely wants to keep an eye on all of us.

THE UNUSUAL SUSPECTS

The CIA

It has been rumoured that the CIA infiltrated the Wintel alliance in the early stages, after realizing the possibilities. Information gathered by the

Pentium III will be channelled straight to CIA databanks. Other rumours have implicated the NSA and/or Mossad, who have apparently offered Wintel a cross-development deal in order to buy into the program.

THE FREEMASONS

Gates is often believed to be a high-ranking Master Mason. It is not beyond credibility that the intrusive nature of Windows 98, coupled with the Pentium III, is a project implemented to further extend the reach of the organization that helped him "get where he is today".

MOST CONVINCING EVIDENCE

It is no secret that Intel has Pentium processors capable of achieving calculation speeds of 2 gigahertz – more than four times as fast as the currently available CPUs. The company has admitted that it is holding back the release of these super-chips while the performance of computers is ramped up towards that speed. Meanwhile, Microsoft is holding a new Windows release in hand, Windows 2000, which is based on the successful NT operating system, and requires more processor power than previous versions.

MOST MYSTERIOUS FACT

Intel has been the force behind the introduction of every new CPU development since 1982. This was the point where the 8086 CPU chip was selected by IBM to be the heart of a new product – the Personal Computer. Similarly, Microsoft, under the direction of Bill Gates, provided the MS-DOS operating system for IBM to use, at a very nice profit per machine. Gates bought all rights to MS-DOS, from another company which created it, just a short while before doing the deal with IBM.

SCEPTICALLY SPEAKING

The amount of information that such a trawl would bring in would require an amazing amount of processing power to sift through, and what would anyone do with it when they had it? Why should the CIA, the Masons, Mossad or Bill Gates care if you have some dirty photos on your computer anyway?

CLONES IN POWER

For a long time now, the KGB has allegedly been using sophisticated human cloning techniques to create and manage doubles of important world leaders. The KGB is not operating in isolation, but with the help of the CIA, MI6 and Mossad. By co-operating in this way, the intelligence community has created for itself a powerful set of clone operatives that can be used to keep world leaders under control, and prevent them from getting carried away with their imagined independent power.

The ultimate sanction, of course, is to kill the original and replace him or her with the clone. Intelligence agencies decided that is more useful to keep both active, because it provides the opportunity to heighten the confusion surrounding the issue, and allows for a reserve should anything untoward happen to one or other version of any given leader.

Western politicians become aware of this practice once they get into power, but there is little they can do to stop it – the technology itself is guarded as carefully as the Roswell crash. Indeed, many don't even particularly object, as the intelligence agencies are prepared to do serious favours for obedient politicians, and the clone will sometimes undertake more hazardous assignments.

Now that the Union of Soviet Socialist Republics has broken up and the KGB is stuck in a disintegrating situation, certain enterprising officers are making serious money by selling copies of documents and reports classified as "Above Top Secret". One such file, long talked about in the intelligence community but only recently uncovered, documents the history of the clone who calls himself William Jefferson Clinton. The clone – Clinton 2 – is an exact double of the current US President, apart from a few minor details like a facial mole (removed since Clinton 1, the original Clinton, came to power), and a more-than-generous set of genitalia. The file reveals that the Russians have been cloning people for more than 75 years.

Recent splashes in the West's media about advances in cloning technology serve a dual purpose. Not only do they allow for the idea of human cloning to slowly gain acceptability in the populace, but they also allow governments to dismiss allegations of human clones by pointing to the scientific "impossibility" of such a feat. President Clinton himself (or, more properly, themselves) has condemned the idea of cloning people, part of the elaborate smokescreen around this issue.

Certain political commentators and journalists are aware of this duplication – indeed, they have to be, in order to comment realistically on presidential schedules and workloads without giving the game away. They're aware of the penalties for talking about it. For anyone else, even senior White House staff, getting proof of this deception usually proves lethal. There is huge potential for blackmail and destruction implicit in the cloning conspiracy, and the intelligence agencies ruthlessly suppress knowledge of it, less the scandal ruin them.

THE STRANGE PART

The son of the chief of the Czechoslovakian Communist Party was a friend of Clinton's in Prague and at Oxford. He was killed mysteriously when he was thrown to his death – allegedly the file describes this unpleasant operation in full, explaining that as a result of his friendship, he had stumbled across details of the Clinton clone. Additionally, prior to his death in a "boating accident", former CIA Director of Intelligence William Colby was going to market a computer game based on espionage, in partnership with a former, long-standing KGB chief – an odd enough event in itself. Rumour however suggests that, in fact, they had teamed up to extort money from the government through the use of the file, and the computer game was a cover for explaining the sudden influx of cash.

THE USUAL SUSPECTS

THE KGB

Given that it is Soviet science that is being used here, the KGB has to be the prime suspect for being the ringleaders in the cloning conspiracy. By keeping a tight control on world leaders, the KGB was able to manufacture (rather than merely manipulate) circumstances. In the so-called Cold War, which gave the KGB true power over the people, most of the hostilities were stage-managed. Only when things got truly dangerous, as when JFK came close to starting a nuclear war, did they take more direct action.

The CIA

Often seen as the KGB's partners in crime on this issue, the CIA could easily have been the real masterminds behind the whole operation. In this model, the Russians developed the technology, but it was the CIA that showed them how to make use of it. Rather than cloning soldiers and scientists, which had been the original Russian intention, the CIA suggested techniques should be developed for cloning prominent politicians – and for deploying those clones to best effect.

THE UNUSUAL SUSPECTS

MI6 and Mossad

As junior partners in the affair, the British and Israeli intelligence services may not do much of the actual work involved, but they could be the "power behind the throne". It has been suggested that the heads of both the KGB and CIA have been cloned and those clones work for a joint operation run in London and Tel Aviv. This might also explain why the British royal family is allowed to get away with embarrassing behaviour.

The American Medical Association

Just where did the technology and know-how to clone humans come from anyway? The AMA could be manipulating events to fit their own long-term goals.

MOST CONVINCING EVIDENCE

The US Secret Service's top physical surveillance expert, who could have found out about the program through observing the President, was killed along with other personnel when his plane crashed near Jackson Hole, Wyoming in August 1996. Witnesses claim to have seen a missile hit the plane. The President, who would ordinarily have been on the flight, left separately by helicopter to attend his own birthday party.

MOST MYSTERIOUS FACT

Bill Clinton impressively obtained KGB transcripts of Krushchev condemning Stalinists. How did he manage this without grooming from the KGB?

SCEPTICALLY SPEAKING

There is no hint of super-fast ageing techniques for clones, so Clinton 2 must have been cloned around the time of Clinton 1's birth. How did the Russians know to clone William Jefferson while he was still so young? Even if they had picked him at random and groomed him, could the CIA and KGB possibly have got him into power without anyone knowing? It seems unlikely at best.

THE USENET CABAL

With the exponential growth of the Internet over the last few years, the number of people now regularly on-line is massive, and continues to grow rapidly. One of the primary tools of communication across the 'Net is the World Wide Web, but in the late Eighties and early Nineties, before the Web arrived, a discussion board conferencing system known as Usenet stood in its place. The system is still very much in use today.

Usenet conferences are each themed around a specific topic. A user can post a message to a conference – called a "news group" – and that message (or "posting") is then visible to anyone reading (or "subscribing" to) that news group. Anyone reading a posting can reply with a posting of their own which, in turn, can be read by anyone subscribing to that newsgroup.

Usenet News is still active, and there are now of thousands of groups, but its importance to the Internet community as a whole has decreased sharply as the Web has gained prominence. At its peak, Usenet was the primary Internet tool for communicating with people outside your sphere of acquaintance, and through the Usenet system the Cabal was born.

The Usenet Cabal was a secret society of Internet users, led by an anonymous figure referred to as Aleph Null at Node-1. Each member recruited three others, and no more. When you recruited your three members, you did not inform the person above you in the chain of who they were or how they could be contacted. That way, the Cabal's membership list remained entirely secret, even from Aleph Null.

The Cabal described itself in its own documentation as being: "... like the Freemasons, or the Shriners", and declared "We will never know how many members we have. As far as each of us is concerned there are only four members of the Cabal". This meant that the leaders of the Cabal were guaranteed anonymity.

Each member knew the people he or she recruited, and the person who recruited him or her, and so messages could be passed down – and up – the chain. Cabal documentation declared "Once we are part of the network we can send requests up and down the chain, using the organization to achieve our ends. The Cabal does have a purpose. We are a way of harnessing the forces of chaos without getting our arms torn off in the process."

In practice, Aleph Null sent instructions down through the ranks, instructing members in certain areas to undertake specific actions, for unknown purposes. Because no-one could say how many different branches of the Cabal branched off from Aleph Null at Node-1, it would be very easy to send part of an action plan to one branch, another part to a second branch, and so on. Even if one of these branches worked out what it was being asked to do, it would not be able to gather the overall picture.

College kids, out for a laugh, cheerfully obeyed their seemingly-innocent instructions. The result was a loyal army of dupes, in place to wreak all sorts of havoc, if that was what Aleph Null had in mind ... but the chances are, Aleph Null was a college kid out for a laugh too.

THE STRANGE PART

The Cabal seemingly disintegrated in the early Nineties under the weight of pressure from the Web, but it appears to have recently reformed as The Internet Cabal. Membership applications have been sighted, along with bulletins from Aleph Null. This time however, members are encouraged to anonymously e-mail requests and comments to Aleph Null directly, at the e-mail account aleph0@hotmail.com. The Internet Cabal instructs members to keep it completely secret, claims to be the successor of the Usenet Cabal, and declares that its interests are "To save the planet, to promote the advancement and enrichment of all Cabal members in society, and to make the world a cooler place."

THE USUAL SUSPECTS

Kibo

One of Usenet's "gods", James "Kibo" Parry was omnipresent on Usenet for a while in the late Eighties and early Nineties. Whenever his name was mentioned in a Usenet conference, he would find it and reply to that group, making himself legendary in the process. A cheerful freethinker, he has often been tipped as the benevolent and mischievous founder of the wholly-innocent Cabal.

The Freemasons

In sharp contrast, the other top theory is that the Cabal was controlled by a circle of leading Masons, out to manipulate the Internet community. These patriarchs carefully couched the Cabal in anarchic terms so as to appeal to the primarily student-based Usenet community.

THE UNUSUAL SUSPECTS

The Democratic Party

One theory suggests that the Usenet Cabal was set up by a techno-savvy member of the Democrats, who wanted to undermine Republican government dogma and influence the next election. When Clinton came to power, its work was done, and the group was disbanded.

Temple Of Spooky Electric

A mystical order with roots both in chaos magic and in voodoo, The Temple's instructs its members to worship Legba – the Master of Crossroads and Communication and, it seems, of the Internet. Some theorists suggest that the Cabal was part of one of the Temple's mysterious rituals, which blend technology with traditional Caribbean magic.

MOST CONVINCING EVIDENCE

Perhaps the best evidence for the Cabal being a simple student prank is its own constitution. The Cabal insisted that people should not believe in it, and that no member should ever heed any call for money that apparently emanated from within the Cabal – a fairly unusual set of instructions for any secret society.

MOST MYSTERIOUS FACT

One of the Internet Cabal's dictates to new members required them to write the message "The Hour is come, but not The Man" on a piece of cardboard and tack it to any convenient telegraph pole or street lamp. What does this signal mean, and who is it for?

SCEPTICALLY SPEAKING

The chances of getting clear information down a chain of people as scattered as the Cabal is small. Individuals will modify messages, and the overall effect will be like Chinese Whispers – perhaps only the first five or six tiers of the Cabal would ever actually be getting clear instructions from Aleph Null.

BARCODES

The barcode was first conceived in 1948. A graduate student at the Drexel Institute of Technology in Philadelphia, Bernard Silver, overheard the president of a local chain of grocery shops talking to a Dean. The businessman wanted the Institute to develop a system that would automatically read product information at supermarket checkouts. The idea interested Silver, and he enrolled a friend of his, Norman Woodland, to help him develop the project.

Together, the two worked on a device for classifying objects. Their first attempt used ink that glowed in ultraviolet light, but it was expensive and tests proved its unreliability. Undeterred, they looked for more stable options, and late in 1949 Silver and Woodland filed a patent, granted in 1952, on "the art of article classification . . . through the medium of identifying patterns".

In 1969, an American retail organisation, the National Association of Food Chains, called for systems to speed checkout times, and a barcode trial in Cincinnati revealed that there would need to be an industry-wide standard for coding. This was developed in 1970, and in 1973 the US government defined the Universal Product Code (UPC) symbol set that is still used across the world today. Although the first supermarkets were using UPC readers by 1974, barcodes themselves did not become widespread until 1981, when the Defense Department adopted the UPC, insisting that all products sold to the military should include clear UPC bar-coding. From this basis, the barcode has spread out to cover most product areas.

THE STRANGE PART

Why was the US military so keen to see barcodes win universal acceptance? Adoption of the Universal Product Code was not particularly crucial, as other coding systems could have proved far more convenient for military purposes. For whatever reason, it was the military's adoption of the barcode that has pushed it to the point where it is now on 95 per cent of products that are sold in the Western world. Recent developments in laser technology have allowed barcodes to be written by computer on to fragile, soft or living matter, such as eggs, meat and, potentially, the human skin.

THE USUAL SUSPECTS

Satan

The big bug-bear of the more paranoid members of the Right-wing religious community is that barcodes are a work of evil. *The Book of Revelations* 13:16-18 reads: "And he causes all, both small and great, rich and poor, free and slave, to receive a Mark on their right hand or on their foreheads, and that no one may buy or sell except one who has the Mark or the name of the Beast, or the number of his name. Here is wisdom. Let him who has understanding calculate the number of the Beast, for it is the number of man; and his number is six hundred three-score and six." To fundamentalist Christian conspiriologists the barcode is the Mark of the Beast, and its prevalence is a sign that the end-times are coming.

THE UNUSUAL SUSPECTS

ALIENS

Government plans to introduce bar-coded smart-cards are actually being forced through by the Greys, who want a ready way to identify us. The system will enable the aliens to keep track of us through locator signals from the chips. The barcodes to be issued will be based on a genetic code worked out by the aliens, so that they can tell certain vital biochemical facts about us without having to go through the usual time-consuming abductions and tests.

MOST CONVINCING EVIDENCE

UPC barcodes consist of 12 numbers, and are broken into two sections by terminator lines at the beginning, middle and end. These terminator lines are called the guard bars. Although guard bars do not have a value as such within the UPC, in print they appear exactly the same as the UPC symbol for 6 if it were to be enlarged very slightly. This means that every barcode contains three large sixes, beginning, middle and end – 666, the Mark of the Beast. More worryingly, some government agencies are already describing schemes for identification of welfare claimants that would involve scanning fingerprints of two fingers, reading information from the microchips embedded in the hairline, or by barcoding at the base of the hand.

MOST MYSTERIOUS FACT

There appears to be an updated UPC barcode that includes the letters F and H within itself. It has been speculated that following on from the messages of the Book of Revelations, these letters stand for the Forehead and the Hand respectively – the locations where the Mark of the Beast is to be engraved.

SCEPTICALLY SPEAKING

The barcode is an immensely useful tool for the retail trade. It greatly speeds checkout times, allows for instant computerized stock control and purchase pattern analysis, and makes classification of goods easy and simple. That it is useful in tracking information about us – what we buy and where we buy it from – is undeniable, but that's business. To assume that this is the work of the Devil or of little Grey men is to complicate matters unnecessarily.

BLACK HELICOPTERS

The phenomenon of "black helicopters" is a relatively new entry into the world of conspiracy, but it is no less ominous for that. Making their first appearance in the early years of the Seventies, in the US, the black helicopters have been theorized to be many things, none of them terribly comforting.

The description of the machines by eyewitnesses is nearly universal: they appear to be sleek, state-of-the-art flying craft, painted a deep black – reportedly to throw off radar tracking – and are usually devoid of markings or insignia. They are equipped with high-intensity searchlights, and move through the skies with a silence thought impossible by today's level of technology. Their activities are equally inscrutable – while they tend to be spotted in remote areas, small fleets have been seen flying low across cities. The black helicopters routinely break FAA regulations by failing to display an identifying green light and by flying below minimum height limits.

There have been instances of the helicopters pursuing citizens. For instance, a teenager was chased for 45 minutes by a black helicopter in Louisiana, in 1994, and in a similar case a car was followed down US Highway 395 in Washington State. Sometimes the black helicopters open fire on people on the ground. When the crew of the helicopters are seen, they are dressed in black uniforms, appearing as forbidding as the craft they travel in.

Sightings of the black helicopters occur throughout the US, with a curious focus in Texas and Colorado. When asked about the origin of the airships, local authorities routinely claim they are Federal government or military craft, but the military – unsurprisingly – claims to have no knowledge of them.

THE STRANGE PART

Some reports claim the black helicopters are also capable of shapeshifting, occasionally taking on the form of a flying saucer.

THE USUAL SUSPECTS

Underground Government Bunkers

The helicopters have been thought to be associated with massive underground bunkers, constructed for the top echelons of the US government and military for use should there be an obliterating global catastrophe. These safe holes for the powerful fall under the aegis of several secretive US organizations, including the NSA, the Pentagon and the CIA. FEMA (the Federal Emergency Management Agency), long-suspected to be a front for the New World Order, also controls these bunkers. The helicopters could be based there, maintaining security and keeping out curious taxpayers.

Also suspected: the Drug Enforcement Agency; the CIA; Wackenhut Security (used extensively for US government programs); and civilian helicopters painted black.

THE UNUSUAL SUSPECTS

The New World Order

The black choppers are feared to be the first wave of assault in the implementation of the New World Order. Trained in covert activities, they could merely be waiting for the word to strike.

Aliens

Black helicopters were often reported in areas of cattle mutilation and UFO sightings, which suggests a link between the two type of incident. The choppers could be working in tandem with the aliens, ensuring their experiments on cattle proceed unhindered, or could themselves be procuring the unfortunate animals for their other-worldly allies.

MEN IN BLACK

Since sightings of the Men In Black have dropped off in the past few years, perhaps they've simply traded in their black Cadillacs for the more refined ride of a matte black helicopter. The appearance of men in black uniforms aboard the choppers supports this theory.

Also suspected: military biological black ops; mass hallucination.

MOST CONVINCING EVIDENCE

In some instances, low-flying helicopters have been reported to disperse a mysterious material that is lethal to small animals and makes humans terribly ill. In one instance in Nevada in 1995, a farmer lost 13 of his livestock to a black helicopter spraying. Half a year later, vegetation still had not grown back in the area where the spray had fallen.

MOST MYSTERIOUS FACT

Since 1933, the United States of America has been in a state of emergency. It has never been revoked since that time, not even following the end of World War II. And why should it be? A state of emergency allows the President more power than he would usually have, as outlined in the Constitution of the United States. At any time, a state of martial law can be declared, suspending the rights of American citizens – those rights that they believe are inviolable. The black helicopters, apparently answerable to no one, could be simply lying in wait for the day when the President tires of democracy.

SCEPTICALLY SPEAKING

What's most depressing about these all-powerful machines of death is their complete lack of fashion sense. Black is so 1988. A nice two-tone blue shade, with perhaps a fashionably ironic smiley face sticker on the windscreen, could do absolutely loads for their public image.

A CURE FOR CANCER

Although at one point cancer was relatively rare, but it is now the second most common cause of death in Western society after heart disease. In 1992, it was estimated to account for some 25 per cent of deaths in the West. While some scientists have claimed that the ascendancy of cancer is a natural result of reducing the impact of other life-threatening conditions that tended to kill people earlier in life, the incidence of cancer is increasing the younger age groups. Cancer is not a disease of the old. Billions of dollars have been spent on cancer research over several decades. The industry is forever claiming that a cure is almost ready, just a few years away, and that many more forms of cancer are being successfully dealt with. Yet the death toll from the disease continues to rise.

THE STRANGE PART

The International Agency for Research in Cancer has announced that almost 90 per cent of human cancer is determined through environmental factors, and is theoretically avoidable. These factors include most of the well-known carcinogenic threats, including smoking, eating lots of animal fats and little fruit and vegetables, exposure to excessive sunlight, several food additives, consumption of alcohol, pollution, electromagnetic radiation, working environment and certain medical drugs and procedures. Despite this, as Hans Ruesch (a medical historian) indicates, less than 10 per cent of the US National Cancer Institute's budget investigates environmental factors, and less than 1 per cent is devoted to research into nutrition.

In fact, many substances known to be carcinogenic – such as the low-calorie sweetener Aspartame – are sold as safe largely on the basis of animal testing. According to German cancer scientist Dr Werner Hartinger: "Their constant consumption is legalized on the basis of misleading animal experiments which seduce the consumer into a false sense of security."

THE USUAL SUSPECTS

The Medical Industrial Complex

Cancer research is big business. Although the causes of most cancers are well-known, prevention would be bad for a number of very important tax-generating companies, including tobacco and alcohol producers, meat and dairy farmers, and companies that make chemical additives. Rather than risk the wrath of such a large and powerful group, the government allows drug companies and big business to dictate the policies of cancer research. The optimum result for the Medical Industrial complex would be an expensive pill that suppresses tumour growth while leaving incidence levels of cancer unchecked. That way, there would always be a big pool of clients, all of whom will need it for life and will continue smoking and drinking, therefore providing vast profits for all concerned. This emphasis is carried through in cancer research because of the funding that comes from drugs companies. Nutrition is ignored because no one wants to fund that work; it is less profitable in the long term.

THE UNUSUAL SUSPECTS

The New World Order

As part of their plan to panic the public into accepting a unified single world government, the NWO is letting panic about cancer grow among the public. When the threat seems great enough, it will announce that only a united world front can help solve the problem. If a cure is found before that time, it will be extremely inconvenient for the NWO.

MOST CONVINCING EVIDENCE

Double Nobel-prize-winning scientist Dr Linus Pauling has announced that: "Everyone should know that most cancer research is largely a fraud and that the major cancer research organizations are derelict in their duties to the people who support them." Similarly, according to Dr John Bailer, editor of the journal of the US National Cancer Institute and staff-member of the institute for 20 years: "My overall assessment is that the national cancer programme must be judged a qualified failure . . . The five year survival statistics of the American Cancer Society are very misleading. They now count things that are not cancer, and, because we are able to diagnose at an earlier stage of the disease, patients falsely appear to live longer. Our whole cancer research in the past 20 years has been a total failure. More people over 30 are dying from cancer than ever before . . . More women with mild or benign diseases are being included in statistics and reported as being 'cured'. When government officials point to survival figures and say they are winning the war against cancer they are using those survival rates improperly."

MOST MYSTERIOUS FACT

In *The Healing of Cancer, The Cures, The Cover-ups and the Solution Now!* Barry Lynes writes: "In 1953, a United States Senate Investigation reported that a conspiracy existed to suppress effective cancer treatments. The Senator in charge of the investigation conveniently died. The investigation was halted. It was neither the first nor the last of a number of strange deaths involving people in positions to do damage to those running the nation's cancer program."

SCEPTICALLY SPEAKING

The people in charge of cancer research, and their friends and families, die of cancer too. They're patently not suppressing a genuine cure.

FREE ENERGY

The term free energy has two potential meanings. One involves extracting extra energy from a mechanical or electrical process for little or no extra effort or energy input, so that, in effect, the extra energy you obtain is free of charge. This is largely a matter of increasing efficiency, and can lead to savings, but is not necessarily revolutionary. The other use of the term is to refer to a system that either outputs more energy than it takes in, or appears to do so. More energy is returned than is used leading to a net gain in energy. Devices that yield this sort of free energy – so far theoretical – are known as "over unity" devices.

This latter definition is fairly contentious. The laws of thermodynamics state that energy cannot be created or destroyed but merely transferred, so in a universal sense there is no free energy to be had. However, the laws of thermodynamics apply to the universe as a whole. There is a type of energy known as ZPE, or Zero-Point Energy that permeates the universe and resulting from an electric flux that flows throughout reality, perhaps linked to some sort of parallel dimension. The famed inventor and electrical innovator Nikola Tesla, along with colleagues Henry Moray and Walter Russell, described ZPE and built electrical devices to demonstrate its properties. It may be possible to tap into this energy. If this could be done, it would yield a source of free, unlimited, pollution-free power.

Another potential source of free energy is the apparent correlation between rotational spin and gravitational pull. Although the bulk of mainstream science refuses to get involved or even look at experimental results, there is evidence to suggest that if a disc (or similar object) is spun very rapidly, its apparent weight decreases. A static disc dropping a fixed distance will take a certain amount of time to hit the ground, as predicted by standard gravity equations. If it is spinning very rapidly, and is dropped through a vacuum to eliminate the distortions that might be introduced by air resistance, it can take up to 40 per cent longer to hit the ground. The spinning disc is apparently negating a significant part of the force exerted by gravity. If correct, this phenomenon allows for the possibility of anti-gravity devices. More importantly, certain electromagnetic field theories suggest that it could be harnessed to yield significant amounts of energy over unity.

THE STRANGE PART

In addition to over unity devices, it is rumoured that several inventions that yield considerably more energy for no extra cost have been suppressed. Before going strangely silent, several motor researchers have, over the years, announced modifications to cars that would yield up to 300 miles driving range per gallon of fuel at 60mph. A British amateur scientist developed a substance that reflected heat; a house treated with the substance, called Starlight, would have perfect insulation, and heating bills would be almost entirely eliminated. NASA purchased the rights to Starlight for several million pounds and nothing has been heard of it since.

THE USUAL SUSPECTS

VESTED INTERESTS

It is commonly assumed that industrial concerns are responsible for the suppression of any device that promises significant energy savings. The oil industry is held to be particularly concerned over the prospect of reduced fuel sales, and is quite aggressive in making sure – by hook or by crook – that no such invention gets to the open market.

THE UNUSUAL SUSPECTS

THE MILITARY

The American government has classified more than 3,000 patented devices and patent applications relating to free energy under a secrecy order over the last 40 years, effectively suppressing them. Some people think that the US military is stealing workable technology to maintain a sizeable advantage as the world's sole military super-power.

MOST CONVINCING EVIDENCE

US inventor Tom Ogle demonstrated a test run, in 1977, of a device he had designed that allowed him to get more than 100mpg from a five-ton Ford truck. A Shell representative asked him what he would do if offered $25 million for the device, and Ogle said he would turn it down, as he didn't want the system bought and put on the shelf. Ogle died mysteriously in 1981.

MOST MYSTERIOUS FACT

Inventor Dennis Lee (often attacked by certain sectors of the free energy community for being unreliable) has often accused the establishment of suppressing certain technologies that would greatly reduce the cost of the average person's energy bills. He was arrested for a civil code registration violation, and spent two years in prison. He was eventually released, without ever having had a trial or having been convicted for the offence of which he was accused.

SCEPTICALLY SPEAKING

There is undoubtedly a lot of money to be made from being able to convincingly claim access to free energy technology. From multi-million dollar payoffs to financial investments and sales of gizmos, would-be inventors can get a lot of cash. Some commentators suspect that the whole field is just a con trick.

MICROWAVE MIND-CONTROL

There is plenty of research published into the usage and effects of microwave radiation in a military environment, particularly with respect to psychological and physiological effects on people. The US government has often claimed that the Soviet Union and, in particular, the KGB spearheads this type of research. However, there is evidence to suggest that the CIA have also been looking into exactly the same area since Project Pandora in the Fifties. Results obtained by the CIA have also been shared with the NSA and the Department of Energy.

Part of this research has always been carried out at WRAIR, the Walter Reed Army Institute of Research. In 1973, researchers made a stunning breakthrough – microwave signals could be pulsed in such as way as to stimulate the inner ear into receiving mock audio signals that duplicated the sound of spoken words (or anything else, for that matter). By making the cells of the cochlea vibrate in the correct pattern, the microwave audiograms could be transmitted directly to the parts of the nerve system that deals with hearing. The effect was the frightening sensation of hearing unreal voices.

In *The Body Electric*, Dr Robert Becker and Gary Seldon pointed out the potential utility of such a weapon: "This device has obvious applications in covert operations . . . [it can be] designed to drive a target insane with 'voices', or to deliver undetectable instructions to a programmed assassin." This research has continued, and there are several scientific papers that detail the work, such as those of Professor James Lin of the University of Illinois' Bioengineering faculty. Meanwhile, WRAIR has been turning its attention to the effects of high-powered microwave radiation on living targets, and has delivered papers on microwave weapons (known as MWs) to military symposia. More disturbingly, a military psychiatrist attached to WRAIR's medical centre has suggested that the institute may be conducting experiments with MW audiogram induction (making a target hear voices) without permission, upon certain of his long-term mental patients.

THE STRANGE PART

Former Deputy Director of the CIA, Ray Cline, still active in the intelligence community, is the chair of the Global Strategy Council, an American organization for discussing military strategy. In 1991, the GSC published a white paper describing suggested domestic and foreign uses for a wide range of microwave mind-control devices. The Army officially classifies such weapons as "non-conventional". Vernon Shisler, US Army delegate to NATO for non-conventional weapons, acknowledged that the various forms of directed energy weapons were available to the Department of Defense. Several people consider themselves to be on the receiving end of such non-lethal attacks. Often noted as subversive or generally unsympathetic to the government, they believe that they have been selected as guinea pigs because the state is suspicious of their motives in general. By choosing such people on which to experiment, the government is effectively killing two birds with one stone.

THE USUAL SUSPECTS

CIA

Many of the harassment campaigns and other actions attributed to the MW research systems are remarkably close to those laid at the CIA's door during MKULTRA and MHCHAOS. With the collapse of Russia, the KGB is no threat, so the CIA is turning its attention to dealing with the "menaces" of civil rights and civil liberties advocates.

THE UNUSUAL SUSPECTS

Microsoft

Perhaps the least credible of all theories is that Microsoft is sponsoring the intelligence community in its mind-control experiments. Exactly why the software giant should be doing so remains unclear.

MOST CONVINCING EVIDENCE

Because of documented CIA operations experimenting on the US public, regulations have been put in place that restrict CIA and military experiments. Surveillance of, and compiling personal information on the US public and experiments upon any involuntary subject have all been prohibited. In 1992, a Senate subcommittee complained about the Department of Defense's tendency to hide its activities behind a screen of contractors. Such contractors are not accountable to Congress. Worse still, they are tacitly licensed to act with the authority of the intelligence community, yet are not bound by the same regulations, which is why contractors are used.

MOST MYSTERIOUS FACT

It has been suggested that MWs are being tested in conjunction with campaigns of harassment designed to destabilize the mental state of targets. It may be that microwave influence exerts a greater hold over a target when he or she is under pressure as a result of harassment. The Electronic Surveillance Project Association, privately founded to monitor and, where possible, to counteract harassment of civilians, claims to be in touch with a number of individuals being harassed in this manner. The victims report a wide range of disturbances, including sudden, unexplained hostility on the part of formerly friendly neighbours, unprovoked hostility and mockery from total strangers, petty burglaries, deteriorating health, sleep deprivation, vandalism of property, and hostility from the authorities such as police, doctors and lawyers.

SCEPTICALLY SPEAKING

Sometimes, paranoia really is just paranoia. The media often maintain that the wearing of tinfoil hats helps defeat microwave mind-control weapons.

STRATEGIC DEFENSE INITIATIVE (STAR WARS)

In his undying battle against the Soviets, Ronald Reagan had a vision. It was a vision he put forth in March, 1983, a plan he felt sure would protect the US from any treacherous nuclear attack from the "evil empire". Once his futuristic Strategic Defense Initiative had been set in place, Reagan felt, America would be impregnable.

Dubbed "Star Wars" by the media, the SDI was a military research operation with a single goal: to create an defence system against ballistic missiles by creating layer upon layer of defensive capabilities, composed of futuristic weaponry usually found in science fiction novels. Defences, situated in space an on Earth, would include sub-atomic particle beams, nuclear X-ray lasers, and electromagnetic rail guns.

Reagan fully believed in SDI, pressuring both NATO and a dubious America to accept the idea. However far-flung it may have sounded, it still worried Soviet leader Mikhail Gorbachev. In 1986, Gorbachev put forth a proposal to rid the world of all nuclear weapons in 15 years, but only if the US was prepared to mothball SDI. Even with such a prize before him – the threat of nuclear war almost completely erased – Reagan would not abandon his beloved "Star Wars", pursuing it with a rather curious tenacity.

With an estimated initial budget falling somewhere between $100 billion to $1 trillion, the "Star Wars" program was given high priority. But as the years passed, its dreams were not fully realized. Dissent set in between government forces that saw SDI as the perfect civilian defence system and the military, which was more concerned with using the laser beams to protect its own nuclear weapons. Scientists walked off the project, with many pointing out the sheer impossibility of managing all its components successfully – as well as how easy it would be for enemies to circumvent the systems.

Was Reagan really so concerned about the threat of a Soviet attack, or was he actually defending against something else? Something that would require weaponry in space?

THE STRANGE PART

In a speech to the UN General Assembly on September 21, 1987, Reagan puzzled his diplomatic audience by stating how the world would forget its differences if faced by an alien threat. He reportedly made more references to this alien attack theme in other speeches, including one made to a graduating class.

THE USUAL SUSPECTS

Alien Attack

With US Intelligence fully aware of the impending dissolution of the USSR, the true purpose of SDI was to protect Earth from imminent alien attack. The satellites put into Earth orbit bristling with particle beam weapons and chemical lasers would be our first lines of defence against a fleet of invading spacecraft. Suspected aliens are the Draconians, the purported masters of the Greys, the creatures who are hiding on Earth and working in tandem with world governments. The Hubble telescope is also theorized to be designed not to photograph nebula and black holes, but to keep an eye out for the advancing Draconian armada. This theory ties in neatly with the Roswell crash in 1947, which may have been the beginning of a possible alliance between the Greys and the US government. In a deal with the Greys, the government gained the technology – using reverse engineering – that lies behind weapons such as particle beams. The Greys, who are not happy to be subjects of the Draconians, also helped to provide the computing power that was required to run SDI.

THE UNUSUAL SUSPECTS

The New World Order

The installation of SDI could have been simply the beginnings of a space-based weapons system designed to enslave the population of the Earth under the yoke of the New World Order. George Bush, Reagan's successor as President, and also a Republican, suspiciously made several references to the NWO in speeches.

NANCY REAGAN
Long-suspected to be pulling the strings of government as her husband's faculties declined, Nancy might be the originator of the "Star Wars" – especially given that she employed the services of an astrologer.

MOST CONVINCING EVIDENCE

Perhaps the money used to fund the reverse engineering of downed spacecraft in such facilities as S-4 and Area 51 came directly from the Strategic Defense Initiative budgets. This makes sense, since many of the weapons systems used in SDI were classified as "highly experimental".

MOST MYSTERIOUS FACT

Billions were spent on SDI during the Reagan and Bush Administrations, but Clinton mysteriously abandoned the project in 1993. It's interesting to note that during Clinton's tenure aliens have been in the news more than ever, with a renewed promise to photograph Cydonia, and Clinton himself addressing the nation about the possibility of life on Mars. All of this suggests a more alien-friendly US.

SCEPTICALLY SPEAKING

With a space track-record including the Hubble and several failed Mars missions, the US-funded SDI would undoubtedly have had all the deterrent effect of a fly on a windscreen for any invading alien force.

SUBLIMINAL MESSAGES

One of the most sinister tools available to media and entertainment companies and to unscrupulous government departments is the insidious form of mind control known as subliminal messaging. The principle is simple. Our conscious minds take a certain amount of time to register a visual image, approximately a tenth of a second. Film and television works by displaying considerably more that one image every tenth of a second. It is this increased frame rate – as much as 60 frames a second for films – that provides the illusion of continuous movement from what is, in fact, a selection of static images. The unconscious human mind, however, is understood to be aware of each individual frame, which is processed in a pre-rational manner that keys directly into your brain, bypassing all your normal conscious filters.

In 1958, shortly after the Korean War and its attendant discussions of mind control, a cinema at Fort Lee in New Jersey installed a device that flashed advertising messages reading "Eat Popcorn" and "Drink Coke" on to the screen. Each message appeared for just a tiny fraction of a second, far too short a period for the words to be noticed by members of the audience. The advertising executive concerned, James Vicary, was widely reported in magazines and newspapers as saying that he had carried out a six-week study to test the effects of these subliminal (the literal meaning is "below the threshold") messages on thousands of movie-goers. He arranged for the advertising messages to flash up approximately once every five seconds throughout movies. He claimed that as a result of his messages, sales of Coke had increased by almost 20 per cent, and sales of Popcorn had gone up by nearly 60 per cent.

Understandably, the public was outraged and frightened by an advertising technique that could directly affect people's minds. The US government swiftly responded by saying that subliminal advertising would result in loss of broadcast licences, but this was overturned as a violation of the First Amendment that guarantees freedom of speech. Subliminal advertising remains legal in the US to this day.

THE STRANGE PART

Scientific studies into subliminal effects consistently fail to turn up any evidence that it actually works. However, some conspiracy theorists believe that this only proves a powerful conspiracy is at work that has the power to keep its existence shielded from the public.

THE USUAL SUSPECTS

The Devil and His Minions

Subliminal messages can allegedly be implanted in audio recordings – the technique is called back-masking. To hear implanted messages clearly, you have to play the recording backwards, but in theory the subconscious mind might be able to back-play such hidden messages and allow the listener to be influenced by the message content. Given that the majority of subliminal messages seem to be back-masked in rock songs telling teenagers to "just do it" and to "make love" the inescapable conclusion is that they are the work of Satan trying to undermine the Christian values of society.

The Military-Industrial Complex

Government and business concerns are the main source of all subliminal influence according to this theory. They use the adverts to keep us all docile, obedient and buying products, so the financial system stays healthy.

THE UNUSUAL SUSPECTS

Microsoft

It has been suggested that a range of subliminal images can be found in the Microsoft Windows 95 start-up screen. These include a dark, rearing horse to the left side of the screen, a large black bird with outstretched wings to the top right of the image, a rock star just to the right of the Windows logo, and across the centre and left of the logo, a couple are making love. What these images mean, though, is anyone's guess.

The Betty Ford Clinic

Rehab clinics need addicts. Could the most famous clinic of all be using subliminals to drive people to drink, in order to cure them later?

MOST CONVINCING EVIDENCE

In the Seventies, former ad executive, Wilson Key, hit the limelight with his claims that subliminals were being used all around us. He said that secret messages, used for the purposes of inducing a state of sexual arousal in the public, were to be found everywhere. These made people more receptive to the advertising messages they supported. Key famously discovered the word "Sex" on hotel menus, on cigarette packs, in gin adverts and almost everywhere else he looked. Key maintained that business concerns and government forces were joining forces in order to control our minds.

MOST MYSTERIOUS FACT

Wilson Key is still more or less the only expert to denounce subliminal advertising. While the Christian Right-wing often latches on to the dangers the technique poses to teenagers through evil rock music, many well-known public champions and political commentators stoically avoid the issue. Businesses and political institutions consistently deny having anything to do with them. Why? What do they have to hide?

SCEPTICALLY SPEAKING

Subliminal advertising does not work. Concern about subliminals is nothing is generally whipped up by radical Christian interest groups desperate for someone to blame for rebellious teenagers. Anyway, why should just seeing the word "Sex" make you want to drink gin or buy a book on conspiracy theories?

T

AIDS

It has been called the Black Plague of the Twentieth Century, a disease so virulent and widespread that its victims are counted in the millions. AIDS has become one of the great fears of our time, terrifying not only because of its lethal and incurable nature, but also because of the moral stigma that is attached to the disease. To be diagnosed with AIDS is not only to be faced with a life-destroying ailment but to be tarred with questions about your most private behaviour. Many members of society tacitly (and not so tacitly) regard AIDS as a punishment sent from above for "immorality".

The first appearance of AIDS is disputed, but most authorities point towards its rise in the late Seventies. At first, it was thought only to be a viral disease limited to homosexuals, with much media attention focusing on the "bathhouse" lifestyles of urban gays. But as time passed, AIDS began to show that it infected anyone, regardless of sexual inclination. Researchers discovered that it was transmitted during the sharing of bodily fluids, (unprotected sex), through the sharing of needles, and through infected blood transfusions. It could also be passed from mother to unborn child in the womb, and through breast feeding. No more was it a disease specific to the gay community – AIDS threatened the world.

However, is it possible that AIDS is more than just another disease Nature has thrown our way? Could AIDS be something darker than that, something that man himself created? As the disease continues to baffle researchers, questions are raised that this calamitous virus, which could potentially wipe out the entire human species, may have slipped out of a man-made Pandora's Box.

THE STRANGE PART

The AIDS virus seems to infect some races more than others, with a markedly higher infection rate among Latinos, Native Americans, and Blacks. Death also comes more quickly to members of those races once they are infected with AIDS, which prompts some theorists to pose the question of why a naturally-occurring virus would evolve so it could differentiate between different human races.

THE USUAL SUSPECTS

The US Government and Military

There are strong indications that AIDS may have been a government chemical weapon that ran off the tracks of its original course – which was to deal with the problem of overpopulation. In 1969, at a House Appropriations hearing, the US Defense Department, through its Biological Warfare division, pleaded for tax dollars to develop a disease with the capability of attacking its victim's immune system while being resistant to the human immune system's attacks. The money was granted.

In the early Seventies, Henry Kissinger wrote a National Security Memorandum in which he discussed the problem of overpopulation in the Third World and stated that the problem should be a priority in the foreign policy of the US. Indeed, the overpopulation problem was considered a threat to the national security of the US. It's also interesting to note that following World War II, several ex-Nazis and Japanese germ warfare specialists were engaged by the US military.

The new disease, it is rumoured, was targeted at homosexuals first, because it was felt that the majority of people wouldn't take it seriously in the early stages, seeing it more as a marginalized gay problem than a general medical problem facing everyone. How the disease was actually introduced into the population is disputed, although a Hepatitis B vaccine, issued to several thousand gay men in San Francisco and New York, in 1978, seems the likely launch mechanism.

The CIA

In an attempt to destabilize Cuba, the CIA may have tried to introduce African Swine Fever into the population. The plan, while successful, backfired, with ASF returning to the States, mutating to the disease we call AIDS today.

Also suspected: a black ops genocide program aimed at blacks and homosexuals; the World Health Organization.

THE UNUSUAL SUSPECTS

Pharmaceutical/Research Companies

In an effort to keep much-needed grant income rolling in, pharmaceutical and research facilities have created the myth of the AIDS crisis, lumping together several diseases under one umbrella in order to instill a sense of panic. The use of drugs such as AZT and Interferon in the treatment of AIDS is also suspicious. The drugs are expensive, and there's a body of opinion that reckons the drugs do more damage than good. Yet the sales of such drugs help keep profit margins high, and stockholders happy.

Pesticides

The Third World has always been a dumping ground for chemicals the rest of the world doesn't want, including extremely toxic pesticides. One group of pesticides, organophosphates, is remarkably lethal. The symptoms this group of pesticides cause in humans include those associated with influenza – such as headache, sweating and diarrhoea – are disturbingly similar to those attributed to AIDS.

Worldwide Pollution

Another theory states that AIDS is simply a mutated virus, the progress of which has been aided by modern technology. For a start, the highest levels of chemical pollution the planet has ever seen favour mutations, then jet travel helps viruses to move around the globe more rapidly than ever before. A virus in Durban, Africa can easily meet with one in Chicago, Illinois in the space of a day, which means that the rate at which new virus strains develop has been accelerated dramatically.

Also suspected: improper handling of infected test monkeys in laboratories; a natural cleansing plague created by Nature to handle overpopulation.

MOST CONVINCING EVIDENCE

In its proposal to the House Appropriations hearing in 1969, the Defense Department said it could have the new disease up and running within five to ten years. The first incidents of AIDS were reported in the late Seventies, showing that, if nothing else, the Defense Department is punctual.

MOST MYSTERIOUS FACT

Of those who received the Hepatitis B vaccination in New York in 1978, more than half were diagnosed with AIDS by 1984.

SCEPTICALLY SPEAKING

As anyone involved in cancer research will tell you, there is more money to be made in treating a disease than in actually curing it, even diseases manufactured in a government lab. If AIDS is ever cured, rest assured a more lethal disease will suddenly appear on the horizon. Perhaps it already has – we call it Ebola.

THE CHALLENGER EXPLOSION

It was January 28, 1986, when the Challenger blasted off on a voyage that was the centre of media attention. On board was a civilian teacher, Christa McAuliffe, who was destined to become the first teacher in outer space. McAuliffe had been specially chosen by NASA officials for the honour, and with her good looks and upbeat spirit, she quickly became a darling of the media.

But 73 seconds after takeoff, America watched in horror as McAuliffe's dream ended in a massive explosion. As the smoke from the destroyed shuttle craft billowed across the sky, throwing debris down into the Atlantic Ocean, a stunned shock fell across the nation. Something had gone terribly, terribly wrong. Seven crew members had met horrible deaths in the destruction of Challenger.

This was not the first time NASA had lost crew members. Three astronauts had died on what would have been the Apollo One mission. But that was in the early days, and by the time of the Challenger disaster, NASA had hoped that such tragedies – and public relations disasters – were things of the past. The optimism that had surrounded the space program, enveloping it almost like a protective shield, was rent asunder by the Challenger explosion. NASA's dreams of further space exploration ground to a virtual halt for almost two years.

THE STRANGE PART

In the investigations that followed, blame for the explosion was placed on an O-Ring, a simple rubber seal, positioned between the Solid Rocket Boosters, which gave the shuttle the power to escape Earth's gravity. The reason for the O-Ring's failure? The weather on the day of the Challenger launch was uncharacteristically cold for Florida at that time of year, around 28.5 degrees Fahrenheit. The O-Rings were not designed to operate under such chilly conditions, and as a result, were unable to restrain hot gases from igniting the main liquid fuel tank. This glaringly obvious mechanical problem, obvious to the technicians of NASA, led to the explosion.

THE USUAL SUSPECTS

NASA

NASA's apparent laziness and arrogance is the root cause of the disaster, according to some theorists. Riding high on public approval over the success of the shuttle missions, NASA had become proud and complacent. In the excitement of the Challenger launch, with the attendant swirl of cameras and television coverage, the problem of the O-rings may have been overlooked as inconsequential. Engineers at the Agency knew full well that the O-rings were not designed to function in the unusually-cold weather, but decided to go ahead with the launch anyway, even though the launch manual expressly forbade such action. Even more disturbingly, this wasn't the first time NASA had experienced performance faults with O-Rings – erosion of the rings had been discovered after flights five years previously, but nothing had been done to correct the problem.

Parts Manufacturer

In 1977, the parts manufacturer and engineering company that designed the O-Ring apparently became aware of the defect the equipment experienced in cold weather. The company went as far as reporting its findings to the commission that had appointed the company to design a new rocket. Again, nothing was done. In the case of Challenger, NASA had allegedly put pressure on the company to provide a waiver concerning the functionality of the O-rings in cold weather, a waiver which would allow the launch to proceed. Faced with the prospect of angering one of its most lucrative contracts, the company agreed.

THE UNUSUAL SUSPECTS

THE GREYS

The Greys may have destroyed Challenger in an effort to slow down human exploration of space. Thwarting NASA's dreams and crushing public interest in the space program would suit the Greys, because they fear it might attract the attention of another alien race – the reptilian Masters – which they are trying to avoid.

THE NSA

The NSA may have played a part in destroying the shuttle for reasons similar to those that might have prompted the involvement of the mysterious Greys – to control mankind's contact with extra-terrestrial life. Worries about the chances of the Challenger mission coming across evidence of alien life, combined with the fiasco over the release of photos of the Face on Mars, may have prompted the NSA into drastic, direct action.

THE GREAT GALACTIC GHOUL

Several attempts to explore space, American and Soviet, have met with mysterious problems and setbacks that baffle technicians. Missions to Mars have been affected particularly badly, but relatively simple trips into Earth's orbit have also had problems. The rash of problems has been nervously blamed on the Ghoul, a mysterious force that could be the Greys or something as yet unidentified, which is apparently determined to maintain a glass ceiling around the Earth.

Also suspected: Fundamentalist Christians; secret factions of NASA controlled by MJ-12.

MOST CONVINCING EVIDENCE

Huge sums of money (reportedly running into the millions) were granted to the bereaved families of the Challenger explosion by the US government and the Morton Thiokol company. The speed with which the money was handed over might imply a guilty conscience as well as a need to brush the entire incident under the carpet as quickly as possible. In many government legal cases, civilian plaintiffs are subjected to ridicule and forced to navigate a costly path through a jungle populated by lawyers determined to break them down, emotionally and financially. Not this time.

MOST MYSTERIOUS FACT

Despite a clear indication of negligence and disregard for human life, NASA is still sending people up into space. Its cynicism appeared even worse when news filtered out that the Challenger crew may not have died instantly, as was promptly reported in the media, but may have remained alive for the entire fall to the ocean – if not longer.

SCEPTICALLY SPEAKING

Want to get away with murder? Call your victims heroes and have the President of the United States read a nice poem about them. There is little evidence of conspiracy but sure signs that our governments are often indifferent to the cost of human life.

GLOBAL WARMING

One of the greatest menaces facing modern civilization is global warming, the unstoppable upwards shift in the world's overall temperature. The results of even a very few degrees increase in average global temperature can be profound and devastating.

While deserts start to spread rapidly outwards from the hottest regions, polar ice caps melt, raising the sea level which leads to flooding in low-lying countries. The weather becomes more violent and less predictable, with a significant increase in storms, and a greater seasonal shift – hotter summers and colder winters.

With a continued rise in global temperature, much of the world's arable land will be rendered unproductive. Comfortably habitable regions of the planet will be compressed between severe winter blizzards on one side and severe summer droughts on the other, areas close to sea level, including many islands, will have to be totally abandoned. The result of all this is a collapse in society – but don't be fooled. Global warming it is not a natural phenomenon.

Weather modification technology, in the form of weapons that affect the weather, has been in use for decades. In 1975, a senior US Senator announced, in the *Providence Journal* newspaper, that "the US did, in fact, use rainmaking techniques as a weapon of war in Southeast Asia", by which he meant Vietnam. The title of his article was "Unites States and Other World Powers Should Outlaw Tampering With Weather for Use as War Weapon", a heartfelt but rather worrying sentiment.

The Senator went on to say "We need a treaty now to prevent such actions – before the military leaders of the world start directing storms, manipulating climates, and inducing earthquakes against their enemies. The basic idea of environmental warfare is simple." His sentiment was that action should be taken at that time, so that in the future, no country has to worry about an enemy directing a storm at them.

Unfortunately, the Senator rather missed the point. Working in collaboration, the US and Russia have been modifying the world's weather systems to push towards environmental collapse. Much of the technology they are using is based on the Orgone work of Wilhelm Reich. He was the inventor of the Cloudbuster device, which can indeed make rain or disperse cloud as required.

By making the environment deteriorate, the world powers hope to panic the people of Earth – the whole Earth – into accepting a single, unified government and abandoning most of their industrialization. This move will also require severe depopulation, which weather upsets will be able to achieve through droughts, floods, hurricanes, ozone depletion, volcanic eruptions, fires and earthquakes. The pro-industry scientists claiming that global warming is not the result of industrial process are right. It isn't business or cars, but governments.

THE STRANGE PART

Pentagon researcher Dr L Ponte claimed, in July, 1982, that Soviet advances in manipulating the flow of the global jet stream with small explosions could be used to set up standing waves that could permanently re-shape weather patterns. The technique could be used, for example, to make Siberia temperate rather than arctic, to turn the American mid-West into a desert, or to thaw the Arctic ice cap. In 1968, Professor Gordon MacDonald, who went on to be a member of Nixon's Presidential Council on Environmental Quality, wrote a chapter in a book called *Unless Peace Comes*. In it, he detailed how science would shortly be able to create floods and drought, steer hurricanes and warm or cool the Earth.

THE USUAL SUSPECTS

The New World Order

Firmly set on fulfilling a vision of a single global government, with one over-arching religion, in a lower-technology society based around country-side living for a reduced global population, the NWO wants to panic the world into accepting its leadership. The NWO, in its role of caring shepherd to the peoples of the world, doesn't declare the underlying purpose of its unifying mission – to prepare for the coming of the Antichrist.

The United Nations

To some people, the UN is the NWO, but its goals are in fact much more mundane. The United Nations wants proper power, not just rubber-stamp notes of disapproval. Fears raised by the global warming issue will help the UN take its first step to providing a genuine, unified, governmental dictatorship of the planet.

THE UNUSUAL SUSPECTS

The Sub-Arctic Nations

Irritated by having to rely on the US and other major agricultural suppliers for grain, the Arctic belt of states – Canada, Norway and Sweden,

Siberian separatists, and certain Chinese factions – have decided to move the world's concentration of arable land within their borders. Global warming will achieve this nicely, giving them real influence in world affairs.

MOST CONVINCING EVIDENCE

On 10 December, 1976, the United Nations General Assembly approved a treaty called "Convention on the prohibition of military or any other hostile use of environmental modification techniques." This treaty specifically states that "Each State Party to this Convention undertakes not to engage in military or any other hostile use of environmental modification techniques having widespread, long-lasting or severe effects as the means of destruction, damage, or injury to any other State Party." Similarly, an American law drafted in the Sixties (USC Title 15, Section 33 [Commerce and Trade], Chapter 9A) forbids the commercial or trade use of weather modification activities or attempts. Why would laws and treaties be necessary if the matter was all science fiction?

MOST MYSTERIOUS FACT

In many instances of severe geological or meteorological disturbance, scientific observers have noted odd optical effects. *The New York Times* on 5 July, 1977, commenting on a vast earthquake in China (on 26 July, 1976) which killed 650,000 people, reported that "Just before the first tremor at 3.42am, the sky lit up like daylight. The multi-hued lights, mainly white and red, were seen up to 200 miles away. Leaves on many trees were burned to a crisp and growing vegetables were scorched on one side, as if by a fireball." This type of effect, both visual and radioactive, is closely linked to the forces used in the machines Reich invented.

SCEPTICALLY SPEAKING

Surely, if science were capable of modifying the world's weather patterns to such an extent, it would be used to ensure the greatest possible profit for major corporations by minimizing the impact of pollution on the biosphere, rather than maximizing it? After all, governments desperately want tax money.

THE JONESTOWN MASSACRE

The images coming from Jonestown in 1978 were ghastly. Bloating in the sweltering heat of the South American sun lay the bodies of hundreds of people, the result of an apparent mass suicide. Some of the bodies had their arms linked around friends, as if they had gone to face the afterlife together. All were members of a religious cult called "The People's Temple". Allegedly, they had been convinced to drink cyanide-laced Kool-Aid by their charismatic leader, an American religious leader and sometime-faith-healer called Jim Jones. His body was also found among the dead, but Jones had opted out of taking cyanide like his followers, dying instead of an apparent self-inflicted gunshot wound.

The events leading up to this massive loss of life (later estimated at over 900 fatalities) were equally strange. Jones, the son of a member of the racially-intolerant Ku Klux Klan, surprisingly preached a doctrine that called for a better world where there was harmony between the races. He dreamt of building a version of Utopia. Considering himself the reincarnation of not only Jesus Christ but also Vladimir Lenin, Jones founded his People's Temple in Ukiah, California. His followers, who were mostly black, were kept in line by Jones' own security force, who relieved the cult members of all the money they had, which generally arrived in the form of government assistance cheques.

Reports that followers who tried to leave his Temple were abused and sometimes died, prompted Jones to move to the more anonymous San Francisco, where he was able to expand his Temple. As the media continued to hound him, in 1977, Jones decided on a spot deep in the jungles of South America as the location for his "Utopia". Without question, his followers moved with him, and he was able set up the infamous "Jonestown", a community in which he was the only law.

But still the reports of abuse continued. By 1978, the furore was so loud that it prompted US Congressman Leo Ryan to fly down to Guyana to look into the problem for himself. On 18 November, 1978, Ryan entered Jonestown, along with a few curious reporters and the deputy chief of the US mission to Guyana, Richard Dwyer. As they were preparing to return to the US from a nearby airfield, the entire investigative party, with the mysterious exception of Dwyer, was shot dead.

Shortly after the killings took place on the airfield – or perhaps as he gave the order that lead to the deaths of the investigators – Jones issued his suicide order. Within hours, the People's Temple turned into a charnel house. Jonestown, as an example of the lethal power of religious cult leaders, was disturbing enough. But as time passed, it became clear that there was more to Jonestown than simple religious mania. Soon, the highest levels of the US Government were implicated, adding a new dimension of horror to an already sickening tragedy.

THE STRANGE PART

Even though Jones' body was found in Jonestown, dead from a self-inflicted gunshot wound, the apparent suicide weapon was found 200 feet from the body. This would indicate that either Jones was murdered himself, or it wasn't Jones at all. Close examination of the corpse revealed that it lacked Jones' tattoos . . .

THE USUAL SUSPECTS

Jim Jones

Jones' history reveals he was more than a simple faith healer. He was a fund raiser for politicians, including the impeached President Richard Nixon. While he professed grandiose ideals of Utopia, he was a strong supporter of the Republican Party. In 1961, he worked for a year in Brazil, rumoured to be doing work for the CIA. It was this work, or rather the $10,000 he earned from it, that allowed him to set up his first Temple in Ukiah. While in Jonestown, his followers were numbed with drugs, fed next to nothing, worked as slave labour and were forced to run through practice "suicide drills". Jones may have been running a massive mind-control experiment in Jonestown, with the help of the CIA. When it became apparent that the news would be released after Ryan's visit. Jones simply erased the evidence.

The CIA

There are several links with the CIA and Jones. Aside from his work in Brazil, Jones' associates included a member of UNITA, the CIA-sponsored

Angolan army, and Dan Mitrione, who worked for another CIA-bankrolled outfit, the International Police Academy. Jones' mind-control experiments in Guyana could easily have been an extension of the CIA's MK-Ultra work, undertaken in a location far from the prying media. In fact, drugs used in Mk-Ultra were also found in Jonestown. It's also interesting to note that Dwyer, the sole survivor of Ryan's party, was listed in the book *Who's Who In The CIA*.

The US Government

The US Embassy helped Jones move his temple into Guyana, and when its was reported that cult members had been shot, not poisoned, it was discovered that a group of American Green Berets had been in the area. Green Berets are valued for their skill in covert killing, and were a favourite tool of the military in Vietnam. A cover up was suspected, especially with the US government's reluctance to return bodies of the dead to their families. Many bodies were "accidentally" cremated.

UNUSUAL SUSPECTS

Worldvision

A world-wide evangelical order, Worldvision has been long suspected of working with the CIA. After the Jonestown deaths, Worldvision repopulated the village with ex-CIA Laotian mercenaries. Ex-Worldvision employees include John Hinckley Jr (would-be assassin of Reagan) and Mark David Chapman (assassin of John Lennon). Both assassins, according to some theorists, were under the influence of mind-control when they acted.

Black Genocide Plan

Jonestown could have been the start of a genocide plan, akin to the Nazi "Final Solution", but aimed at black people.

MOST CONVINCING EVIDENCE

When coroner C Leslie Mootoo suggested that the Jonestown deaths were murder, not suicide, thus warranting investigation, the US Army disagreed. The bodies were left to rot in the sun.

MOST MYSTERIOUS FACT

Several people who could explain the truth about Jonestown, including ex-Jones aide Michael Prokes, and authors Jeanie and Al Mills, have been found murdered.

SCEPTICALLY SPEAKING

Jones had money and chose to victimize members from minorities, so who was going to kick up a fuss? The mass suicide of the cult is tragic, but not surprising – it had happened before with other groups and will continue to happen as long as cult leaders such as Jones are allowed to emerge.

THE OKLAHOMA BOMBING

On April 19, 1995, a massive explosion in Oklahoma City, Oklahoma destroyed a huge part of a Federal office building, killing many of the people inside. Until that moment, America considered itself immune to terrorist attack, lulling itself into a false sense of security by glossing over terrorist attacks such as the bombing of the World Trade Center. The Oklahoma bombing was high-profile however, and, as well as killing and injuring a lot of people, it also inflicted some nasty wounds on the US national psyche.

Timothy McVeigh, a Gulf War veteran, was convicted of the bombing. Certainly, there is plenty of evidence that he was peculiar enough to have carried it out. He sent a series of letters to his sister some considerable time before the bombing took place, in which he wrote about his "anger and alienation". These letters included comments about committing suicide, about dropping out of society and into hiding, and about the government of the "Evil King". The letters were so disturbing that McVeigh's family suspected him of being the Oklahoma bomber almost immediately. His sister believes that McVeigh's mania against the government stemmed from the army's insistence that he repay them $1,000 that he had been overpaid.

McVeigh had applied for Special Forces training, and had failed the assessment course. He claimed in one of his letters that his assessment at Fort Bragg had revealed that he would be in line for performaing several unsavoury duties should he make the grade. Special Forces operatives, he alleged, could be required to work with civilian police, silencing – killing – people who were considered a security risk. They would also be expected to help "the CIA fly drugs into the USA to fund covert operations." It was the evil nature of these assignments that turned McVeigh against the US government.

But is McVeigh actually guilty? It has been suggested that the Oklahoma bombing was conducted by US Secret Service agents to distract attention from a far more critical action – the attempted rebellion of a cabal of top military officers against the US government. Sickened by the Clintons' excesses – not the sexual ones, but Hillary's supposed theft of 50 million dollars from the US reserve, and Bill's treasonously-illegal alleged sale of nuclear missiles and launch codes to Israel – a group of morally-upstanding army and navy officers planned to arrest Clinton and expose him.

The cabal was killed. Oklahoma was then bombed shortly afterwards, to monopolize media attention and thereby cover the deaths of the cabal members. It also served to draw the minds of more junior officers away from potential presidential scandals, and concentrate them on the humanitarian emergency. McVeigh was a soft target to frame because he was so insanely paranoid about the government.

THE STRANGE PART

Media Bypass magazine is a small publication dedicated to exposing intelligence agency action, and to presenting the truth to the public. On the morning of the bombing, Lawrence Myers, a writer of bomb manuals and other survivalist literature, with connections to the US military, was in the offices of *Media Bypass*, attending an interview for a job that would involve writing about serial bombers. While he was being interviewed, the Oklahoma bomb went off, and the story broke. He was hired on the spot, and quickly became the editorial controller of the magazine.

THE USUAL SUSPECTS

The CIA

Acting to preserve the Clinton administration and avoid a scandal that would weaken America, the CIA killed the anti-Clinton conspirators. They set up the Oklahoma bombing as a smoke-screen. To arrange this, the CIA must have been planning the multiple assassination and subsequent bombing for at least a week.

THE UNUSUAL SUSPECTS

Christian Identity

This is the American version of the British Israelite movement. It claims that white Americans are the true descendants of Moses. Certainly, the Identity is very popular with right-wing maniacs and it may have been involved in the bombing. There have been suggestions that McVeigh was acting on the instructions of a powerful Christian Identity leader to help fulfil the prophecies leading to the return of Christ.

MOST CONVINCING EVIDENCE

On Monday 17 April, 1995, Special Prosecutor Kenneth Starr reportedly handed a sealed indictment charging Hillary and Bill with embezzling $47 million, and receiving moneys in payment for conveying missile launch codes and tracking codes to Israel. That same evening, a plane carrying top members of the military and intelligence communities crashed in Alabama, killing everyone on board. Witnesses said that they heard two explosions in the air before one on the ground, suggesting sabotage or a missile strike. One army officer on the supervisory boards of the NSA and the ASA – the Army Security Agency – was among the dead. Some 36 hours later, Oklahoma was bombed, just before the sealed indictments were due to be made public. Instead, the special circumstances of the bombing delayed the indictments, and swung public support back to the President.

MOST MYSTERIOUS FACT

Media Bypass resolved to fire Myers, but they re-hired him the same day when he suddenly conducted an interview with McVeigh (in a maximum security prison at the time, and inaccessible to normal journalists) and offered it to the magazine in return for his continued employment.

SCEPTICALLY SPEAKING

Killing scores of innocent government workers seems rather like overkill, whether the plan is to move attention away from a minor rebellion and or to get a spook into a job. Surely the former goal could have been better achieved by declaring the whole incident a matter of national security, and the latter by giving Myers a stronger curriculum vitae?

WACO

On Sunday, February 28, 1993, at around 9:30am, the US Bureau of Alcohol, Tobacco and Firearms (BATF) attempted to enforce a search warrant at premises occupied by a religious cult – the Mount Carmel stronghold in Waco, Texas. Besides wanting to search the compound occupied by the apocalyptic Branch Davidians for a suspected illegal stockpile of explosives and firearms, the agents also carried an arrest warrant for the charismatic leader of the cult, David Koresh.

Something went terribly wrong. A gun battle erupted between the agents and members of the Branch Davidians, leaving four agents dead and 16 wounded. Several Branch Davidians were also killed or wounded. Pulling back, the BATF initiated a siege of the Mount Carmel compound that lasted 51 days. It involved the FBI, the Attorney General, Janet Reno, and President Bill Clinton. It ended in a mysterious fire, with Mount Carmel burning to the ground – an event that was broadcast live on CNN. In the ashes, investigators found the bodies of 17 children and over 60 adults, among them the body of Koresh himself.

Questions quickly surfaced as to how the stand-off could spin out of control so rapidly after 50 days of relatively peaceful negotiations. As the FBI propelled tear gas into the compound from combat engineering vehicles (CEVs), they also knocked down walls with the machines, possibly killing children inside the compound – children that the government repeatedly told the media it was trying to protect. The sudden fire later that day is also questioned, with both sides blaming the other for starting it.

Since that fateful day in 1993, Waco has become a symbol of many things – from the cost of fervent religious belief, to the ruthlessness of a government trying to cover up its own mistakes.

THE STRANGE PART

As a justification for sending tear gas into Mount Carmel, Janet Reno, the newly-appointed Attorney General, stated that the Branch Davidians were beating babies inside the compound. Janet Reno relied upon the FBI for her information, and the FBI later admitted that there was no proof to confirm the truth of the assertion she had been led to make.

THE USUAL SUSPECTS

The BATF and FBI

There is still some question as to who actually fired first at the start of the siege, and there are rumours that the BATF may have been either a little gun-happy or ill-prepared for the raid on the compound. In Congressional hearings that followed the grisly end to the siege, BATF agents, not surprisingly, claimed that the Branch Davidians fired first. Directly after the raid, however, one agent claimed to have fired first – killing a dog. He later retracted that story. The Branch Davidians stand by their claim that they only fired when fired upon. The BATF also claimed that Koresh's people were manufacturing methamphetamines – another assertion, later shown to be a lie.

The FBI also did its part to inflame the situation. One team of agents deliberately harassed the Davidians by playing loud music (such as Tibetan chants and Christmas tunes) through the night, directing blinding spotlights into the compound, and shutting off their electricity. The team of negotiators felt these activities weakened their attempts to end the siege peacefully. The FBI wasn't entirely truthful in its reports to Janet Reno. Reportedly, Reno was apprehensive about an attack on the compound, but quickly changed her mind when a FBI agent remarked about the possibility of child abuse – a possibility that was never substantiated. A simple desire by the BATF for revenge could also have played a significant part.

David Koresh

Koresh believed himself to be the reincarnation of Jesus Christ, and the siege of his compound would have given reality to his apocalyptic visions. He was fascinated by the Book of Revelations, and throughout the siege, talked about writing a manuscript to explain the meaning of the Seven Seals. He claimed to be in contact with God, who reportedly gave him advice throughout the ordeal. The FBI also endured several rambling sermons over the phone from Koresh. The burning of the compound would be a fitting end in Koresh's messianic eyes, since his beloved Revelations spoke of the World itself ending in fire. This may explain why the Davidians displayed signs that read "Flames Await".

Bill Clinton

While Clinton professed concern about the children inside the compound, he also made it clear that the decision to gas the compound was Janet Reno's alone. Having washed his hands of blame, Clinton could have been using the Waco tragedy as a way of improving his political image – as a no-nonsense President.

THE UNUSUAL SUSPECTS

The New World Order

A favourite theory of the Far Right is that Waco was evidence of a United Nations plot to disarm everyday Americans in preparation for the imminent implementation of a One World Government, the dreaded New World Order. Why else raid a compound for guns in a state like Texas, where everyone owns at least one gun?

Neo-Nazi Conspiracy

David Koresh and the Branch Davidians may have been agents of a global Nazi conspiracy, dedicated to resurrecting the Third Reich and giving Hitler's public image a more positive spin. Other members of this conspiracy include right-wing conservatives like Pat Buchanan, and racist skinheads everywhere. "Remember Waco" has become a battle cry for neo Nazis in the States, apparently.

GUN CONTROL ADVOCATES

Waco may have been orchestrated by gun control advocates, possibly working in conjunction with Clinton's Democratic Party, as a way of demonstrating the dangers of allowing just about anyone to own a gun.

MOST CONVINCING EVIDENCE

Gunfire was heard within the compound as the fire consumed the building. Whether this was Koresh killing his followers in accordance with his apocalyptic visions, or whether it was BATF/FBI agents exacting revenge is not known, and probably never will be. What is undisputed, is that whoever was firing inside had something to hide.

MOST MYSTERIOUS FACT

Bodies were difficult to identify after the Waco fire, leading many to believe that Koresh managed to escape the inferno.

SCEPTICALLY SPEAKING

If Koresh had had his own television show and dressed in a bad suit, he'd not only have been left alone, but called a pillar of the community.

COMET IMPACTS

Throughout the history of the Earth, comets have been slamming into our planet and changing the course of history. It is well known that asteroid and comet impacts occur regularly to all the planets in the solar system. Just a few years ago, Jupiter was hit by the comet Shoemaker-Levy, which inflicted a million-megaton blast on the gas giant. Sooner or later, a gigantic comet is going to smack into us, and plunge our planet into a nuclear-style winter.

Internationally-renowned geologist Professor Alexander Tollmann of the University ofVienna has suggested that the flood experienced by Noah was in fact caused by a comet that hit the Earth 12,000 years ago. The flood is recorded in several of the world's religions, and although religious texts are notably poor as a source of historical information, the stories they tell about the flood are backed up by the myths and legends of almost every prehistoric society. While firm information is understandably sketchy over such huge periods of time, linguistic and anthropological research dates these legends to around 10,000BC.

There is scientific evidence in the form of greatly-increased levels of Carbon-14 radioactive material found in fossilized trees that were alive at the time of the flood. The impact would have devastated ozone layers, causing greater production of the Carbob-14 radioactive isotope. By referring to myths that tell of seven burning suns and other great disasters, Tollmann believes he can date the impact to precisely 9,600BC.

The scientific community accepts other comet impacts. In 1905, a comet is known to have exploded over Tunguska in Siberia with the force of 30 megatons, devastating more than 50 square miles (well, assuming it wasn't an alien craft . . .). Similarly, the extinction of the dinosaurs 65 million years ago is thought to have been the result of climatic changes that ran their course over several thousand years that were started by the impact of a giant comet.

THE STRANGE PART

On March 11, 1998, the Smithsonian Astrophysical Observatory announced that Asteroid 1997XF11, discovered in December 1997 by Jim Scotti of the University of Arizona, would pass extremely close to the Earth in the year 2028. It was estimated that the huge rock, some 2km across, could get as close to the Earth as 48,000 miles. The asteroid 1997XF11 was immediately placed on the Potentially Hazardous Asteroid (PHA) list because the Earth could end up directly in the path of the asteroid with only slight variations in some of the factors that were used to calculate its path. A NASA team quickly disagreed, saying that there was no chance that 1997XF11 would hit. The next day, the Smithsonian team retracted their suggestion, agreeing with NASA.

THE USUAL SUSPECTS

NASA

It has been alleged that NASA may want to cover up the impending impact of a major asteroid such as 1997XF11. By keeping the disaster secret, NASA would have time to prepare for the impact, spending 30 orderly years during which it could build shelters and stockpile food. Once the asteroid had hit, NASA would be perfectly placed to take over what was left of the world and remake it according to its own plans. Going public now with details of the major disaster due to happen in 2028 would only cause panic and lead to 30 years of anarchy.

THE UNUSUAL SUSPECTS

THE ELDER RACE

Some conspiriologists believe there was an advanced civilization on the Earth before ours – the Elder Race. Most of the Elder Race was wiped out by a global catastrophe – possibly a comet impact – but hidden remnant of survivors have been controlling the destiny of mankind for thousands of years via a selection of secret societies. The aim of the remaining members of the Elder Race is to help mankind make technological progress until we possess a technology advanced enough to deal with the next big comet impact.

MOST CONVINCING EVIDENCE

Victor Clube, Professor of Astrophysics at Oxford University, agrees that Tollmann's theory about the origins of Noah's flood is entirely plausible. Clube himself suggests that a large comet impact 1,500 years ago was behind the fall of civilization and the ensuing Dark Ages in Europe.

MOST MYSTERIOUS FACT

In the *Austin Chronicle*, a Texan newspaper man, Michael Ventura, mentioned a presidential scientific advisor who was denouncing stories of 1997XF11 within hours of the Smithsonian announcement – surely he hadn't left himself enough time to study the information properly. Ventura suggested that the asteroid presented more of a threat to White House authority than anything else did. It seems that 1997XF11 will pass fairly close to Earth in 2002 and 2008 (it orbits the sun every 1.75 years), but Ventura alleges that we'll hear nothing about the asteroid in those years, because information is being suppressed.

SCEPTICALLY SPEAKING

When the Smithsonian and NASA teams first evaluated the data on 1997XF11, they were using a fairly small amount of information, so the margin of error was high. As soon as the media started getting panicky, other researchers provided more extensive data. Within 24 hours, all involved had calculated the asteroid's path based on studying around eight years' worth of orbital data, and in doing so reduced the margin of error considerably. The asteroid should miss us by hundreds of thousands of miles.

GULF WAR SYNDROME

The 1991 Gulf War was considered a success by the media and the US government: the Iraqi forces, led by Saddam Hussein, were driven out of Kuwait by the superior military strength of the United States and the coalition forces. But while George Bush and Colin Powell still bask in the glow from that military victory, a more malignant reminder plagues thousands of soldiers involved in the War. It is an insidious disease that has puzzled doctors and destroys the lives of those it affects – it is called GWS, or more commonly, Gulf War Syndrome.

A list of the symptoms of Gulf War Syndrome illustrates how debilitating it can be: night sweats, disturbances of the nervous system, tumors, drastic weight loss, diarrhoea, insomnia, chronic fatigue, intense joint discomfort, bizarre rashes, disturbing personality changes, and loss of mental faculties. There have also been reports of extensive blood loss. GWS is a vicious and virulent affliction, which unsurprisingly leads many sufferers into severe depressions, and even suicide.

Despite seemingly inarguable evidence that soldiers contracted the disease while fighting for their countries, the existence of Gulf War

Syndrome is denied by many governments, including the US. Having risked their lives in what many consider to be a war more about oil prices than about human freedom, these soldiers now find themselves abandoned by their governments.

THE STRANGE PART

The symptoms of Gulf War Syndrome bear many similarities to those of HIV – unexplained rashes, insomnia, and weight loss, among others. In some cases, sufferers have tested positive for HIV, but mysteriously, there's no sign of the HIV virus.

THE USUAL SUSPECTS

Saddam Hussein

Hussein has tested and used biological weapons against his enemies for some time now, most notably before the Gulf War on his own Kurdish people, wiping out entire villages. It is believed that he also used biological weapons against the coalition forces, arming some of his Scud missiles with lethal doses of toxins. The deadly material could also have come from the smoking ruins of chemical factories and Iraqi weapons bunkers destroyed by the coalition forces, drifting across the desert wind to infect soldiers. Hussein may have infected his own soldiers, hoping their dead bodies would transfer the disease to those burying the bodies.

Forced Inoculations

In preparation for a biological attack – that according to the US never happened – soldiers were forced to take pills and undergo inoculations. The pills, thought to be Pyridostigmine Bromide, and the vaccinations (including shots for anthrax), were extremely experimental. If they were not the direct cause of Gulf War Syndrome, these inoculations are thought to have aided in its spread.

THE UNUSUAL SUSPECTS

The Soviets

Hussein is thought to have obtained some of most virulent bio-weapons from the Soviet arsenal. The dreaded "Novichok" series is believed to be one of the most feared toxins known to man, and may be in Iraqi hands.

MOST CONVINCING EVIDENCE

The numbers of infected soldiers speak for themselves. Estimates place the number of sick soldiers at well over 150,000, with some 10,000 already dead from GWS. (These numbers may be optimistic.) An examination of GWS points clearly to a virus that is not natural, but shows all the earmarks of having been produced in a laboratory. One of the chief suspects for GWS is a manufactured agent called Mycoplasma fermentans (incognitus). It contains the majority of the (HIV) envelope gene, which is suspected to have been added in its laboratory modification. Of all the countries involved in the Gulf War coalition, only France refused to undergo inoculations. So far, there have been no reports of GWS among French soldiers.

MOST MYSTERIOUS FACT

Gulf War Syndrome is highly contagious, with wives and partners of infected servicemen coming down with symptoms that may emulate those of cervical cancer or sexually-transmitted diseases. It has been shown to be capable of spreading through simple casual contact, sex, and may even be capable of airborne contagion. It has been blamed for the disfigurement of babies, with infants being born without an eye or limb. Perhaps the most disturbing components of the Syndrome are reports that it can be passed to animals, with victims' pets dying of the disease. If GWS can pass from one species to another, then it is a threat to all life, and not just humanity.

SCEPTICALLY SPEAKING

It all comes down to money. Governments continue to deny that any biological agents were used in the Gulf and refuse to admit that forced inoculations might be to blame for GWS. If they admit that there was, the question of legal liability comes up. That is not going to happen.

THE HINDENBURG

The Hindenburg was one of the finest airships ever constructed, representing the apex of dirigible design technology of the time. The pride of the Zeppelin Company of Germany, with a length of 804 feet and an diameter of 135 feet; the Hindenburg set a record for the largest aircraft ever to fly. When it first took to the air for tests on March 4, 1936, the Hindenburg looked set to usher in a new golden age in air travel.

Several new designs were incorporated into Hindenburg, including the placement of passengers inside the hull instead of the usual practice of carrying them in a gondola suspended below. And so it was with great media excitement that Hindenburg flew across the Atlantic for a trip to the US, scheduled to land in Lakehurst, New Jersey on May 6, 1937. Captained by Ernst Lehmann, with a crew of 61 and carrying 36 passengers, the Hindenburg majestically sailed across the world, a veritable palace in the air. While hundreds lined the ground to watch the beautiful ship drift across the evening skies, radio broadcasters relayed the event to listeners across the country.

But then, things went horribly wrong. As the airship was descending, its mooring lines were dropped to the 200 men waiting below, ready to help winch the ship down to the earth. Suddenly, flames could be seen at Hindenburg's stern. Before anything could be done, the flames raced across the zeppelin. In a matter of seconds, the palatial airship had exploded. All in all, less than a minute had passed since the sighting of the first flame.

The horrific conflagration claimed 36 lives. The deaths, coupled with the newspaper pictures and film of the Hindenburg exploding, brought the golden age of the airship to a tragic close. But was the tragedy of the Hindenburg more than an accident?

THE STRANGE PART

Even though the Hindenburg was filled with hydrogen gas to give it its lifting power – hydrogen is extremely flammable – the dirigible was considered so safe it had a smoking room.

THE USUAL SUSPECTS

ANTI-NAZI FORCES

By 1937, the world was becoming aware of the atrocities being committed by Hitler's National Socialist Party. Since the Hindenburg proudly displayed the sign of the Nazi Party – a giant swastika – on its vertical fins, and had been used to drop propaganda pamphlets across Germany, it was seen as a symbol of Hitler's power. As such, its destruction would have been a blow to the Nazi Party, and thus irresistible to Hitler's enemies.

INSURANCE SCAM

The money to be made by the loss of the Hindenburg, let alone the claims for loss of loved ones, would have been astounding. The destruction of the ship, considering the flammability of its hydrogen, would have been easy enough to engineer considering the possible financial rewards.

THE US GOVERNMENT

Many in Roosevelt's administration were not comfortable with a swastika-covered Nazi airship flying over American shores, and may have taken steps to remove the blot to their patriotic vision, rationalizing the unavoidable deaths by telling themselves only Germans would die.

THE UNUSUAL SUSPECTS

THE NAZI PARTY

The Hindenburg may have been set to explode in New Jersey while surrounded by Americans, as a blow to the Roosevelt Administration for refusing to sell helium – a much safer gas for dirigibles – to Germany.

CORPORATE REVENGE

Other dirigible companies were not as successful as the Germans, in particular the British. Out of revenge, corporate forces could have sabotaged the Hindenburg to hit their enemies where it hurt the most – in the wallet.

MOST CONVINCING EVIDENCE

As he was being led away from the burning remains of his ship, a baffled Captain Lehmann continuously repeated: "I don't know what happened, I don't know what happened". He died in hospital the next day from his injuries, still repeating that confused statement.

MOST MYSTERIOUS FACT

The chairman of the Zeppelin Company, Dr Hugo Eckener wanted to avoid the dangers of hydrogen for the Hindenburg, opting instead for the much safer helium. Unfortunately, the US was the only country with natural helium resources. Fearing that Germany would use the helium for war craft, the US passed the Helium Control Act to stop businesses from exporting the gas to the Third Reich so Eckener had to use hydrogen.

SCEPTICALLY SPEAKING

Apart from the possibility of a static charge building up and discharging with sparks, the engineers of the Hindenburg thought it safe to smoke while they were surrounded by 7,063,000 cubic feet of hydrogen. Smart guys – real smart.

TWA FLIGHT 800

It is perhaps the greatest unspoken fear of every air – that the craft in which they are passengers will crash. While many pretend to be blasé about air travel, few escape a momentary fear at some point during a flight. This horrible fear was realized for the passengers and crew of TWA Flight 800 on July 17, 1996. Eleven minutes into the journey from New York's Kennedy Airport, destined for Paris, France, the Boeing 747 suddenly exploded about ten miles from Long Island, killing everyone on board.

An investigation into the disaster was quickly launched, with boats out collecting the wreckage from the plane, searching for some clue as to what may have caused the explosion – an explosion that gave no warning, according to evidence later found on the craft's black box recorders. Finally, the National Transportation Safety Board, after investigating with the FBI and the CIA, determined that Flight 800 crashed because its centre-wing fuel tank had exploded. Arcing between two wires, with a spark igniting the jet's volatile fuel might have caused this. The investigation was then closed down.

Many people dispute those findings. Eyewitnesses claim to have seen something arcing into the sky after Flight 800, with much speculation that what they saw was a surface-to-air missile. Was Flight 800 hit by a terrorist attack, or was it something far darker – such as a missile fired by the US Military? In the eyes of the US government, the case is closed, but in the eyes of conspiracy theorists, including members of the military and the airlines themselves, there was no investigation – only a cover up.

THE STRANGE PART

Dr Vernon Grose, who had served as a board member of the National Transportation Safety Board, had defended the board's official explanation for the crash of Flight 800. He changed his mind and began to feel that there was, indeed, a cover up. He pointed his finger at the FBI and its suspicious suppression of eyewitness testimony that what appeared to be a missile had hit Flight 800.

THE USUAL SUSPECTS

The US Military

The US military may have been practising manoeuvres, including the firing of missiles, in an area designated as W-105, located off the southeast coast of Long Island. A Navy "hot area", W-105 is about 30 miles away from where TWA Flight 800 mysteriously exploded. In a potentially lethal gaffe, the first report of the accident is thought to have come from the Pentagon, which is again highly suspicious, particularly as the snippet of news was quickly covered up. The airspace surrounding TWA Flight 800 was heavy with military aircraft that night, once again indicating possible military involvement.

A photograph taken by Linda Kabot, reproduced in *Paris Match*, clearly shows a missile in the sky at the time Flight 800 exploded – there's a clear view of a cylindrical object with the bright light of an exhaust at one end. Her photograph was discounted by authorities on the basis that she was facing away from the actual explosion when she took the picture. This poses the disturbing question of just how many missiles are flying around American airspace at any given time. It's interesting to note that the FBI paid little heed to such eyewitness reports in its investigation.

Terrorists

The popular image was of terrorists firing a rocket while balancing in a dinghy. The fact that the suspected missile that was launched could not have been fired that way (too big) didn't stop the media from embracing it and does not mean there was not a terrorist plot.

THE UNUSUAL SUSPECTS

UFO Attack

Flight 800 could have run across a UFO, which was monitoring the military activity below. The UFO destroyed the plane as a reaction to being discovered.

Military Black Ops

A secret base is rumoured to be in the area near where Flight 800 went down. "Project Phoenix" is thought to be an underground, top-secret facility located at Montauk Air Force Base, which is itself thought to be abandoned. A possibility exists that Flight 800 was destroyed by a secret weapon from this base, which would explain the cover up, undertaken in the name of American national security.

MOST CONVINCING EVIDENCE

Data taken from nearby air traffic control towers clearly show a blip appearing on radar screens. This blip then rises, and begins to follow Flight 800. It is later seen to move to the front of the plane before merging with the plane's flight path.

MOST MYSTERIOUS FACT

The Navy didn't find the black box recorders for a week, claiming the locator beacons had broken. Subsequent investigation showed this not to be so, suggesting the boxes were found earlier than reported and were tampered with so the data fitted with the military's story.

SCEPTICALLY SPEAKING

Two words: lawsuit; avoidance.

A-Z OF COMMONLY SUSPECTED CONSPIRATORS

American Medical Association Some of the most paranoid conspiracy theories currently in circulation portray the American Medical Association as an organization dedicated to suppressing alternative, cheaper cures to a range of diseases from cancer to AIDS. The bizarre rational behind many of these alleged conspiracies is that the American Medical Association has no interest in promoting health, because healthy people do not require their expensive services. Of course, the American Medical Association is not in these fiendish schemes alone and its members are to be found conspiring with the giant pharmaceutical corporations and the American Academy of Science. Some also allege they are in league with the grey aliens who pay them to cover-up any evidence of implants in abductees.

Black Magicians With so many of the traditional good guys of our culture getting blamed for plotting hideous conspiracies against the rest of us, it is reassuring to know that at least one traditional bane of humanity gets some of the blame from time to time. Involved in phenomena ranging from cattle mutilations to Big Foot, Black Magicians are said to be working their dread powers to harm society at large. If certain researchers are to be believed, being a Black Magician is a good career path, as it can take you as far as the White House or even to starring roles in hit Hollywood movies.

Cathars A heretical Christian sect, the Cathars were ruthlessly suppressed and seemingly eradicated from Europe in a Papally-sanctioned crusade. Some conspiracy theorists feel that the Cathars are still active behind several significant conspiracies. Whether their former fortress in the Montsegur area of France contained a hidden treasure that fuelled the rise of the Knights Templar, or whether the sect held special knowledge about Jesus Christ that could have blown the medieval church asunder, is hard to determine today. Modern conspiracy theories point to the Cathars' main aims as being revenge on France and the Papacy, as well as the more usual global domination.

Defence Intelligence Agency A super-secret branch of the United States intelligence community, the DIA has been accused of being the controller of the MIB and of master-minding the UFO cover-up, fulfilling the same role as SI8 in the UK. In one of the most bizarre court actions of all time, a plaintiff in California named the DIA as one of the many guilty parties when she tried to sue the US government for $5.6 billion. She claimed she had been turned into a cyborg as part of a secret holocaust program against black women in America. The case was dismissed – whether or not the decision was influenced by the power of the DIA and the conspiracy she was trying to expose is anyone's guess.

Elder Race Some orthodox archaeologists are willing to admit that evidence of water erosion on the Sphinx could mean that it was built in 9,000 BC. No surprise, then, that conspiracy theories revolving around the idea that our current civilization may have been pre-dated by an even more advanced one thousands of years ago, have been gaining credibility. Plots to suppress this knowledge while the military exploit the remains of this Elder Race's technology may be hard to prove, but seem less outlandish when you turn a conspiracy buff's eye on the links between NASA, the Giza plateau in Egypt, and sections of the military-industrial complex. Suggestions that surviving remnants of the Elder Race themselves are behind the cover-up are definitely in TBTB territory.

Food and Drug Administration The FDA, as it is commonly known, is the body responsible for licensing medicines in the USA. As such, it is cited in a whole host of medical conspiracies that are designed to keep the public ill and ensure that drug companies, doctors and hospitals can make very healthy profits. Alleged to be run by everyone from communists to a secret order of German mystics, the FDA was also responsible for the downfall of orgasm guru Wilhelm Reich who claimed his orgone generators could cure all disease.

Grand Order of The Fiery Wheel Often referred to simply as The Wheel, this organization is held responsible for the conspiracies behind the conspiracies. It is an occult group, said to be the hidden controller of such notable conspirator groups as the Masons and the Templars. Aside from a few mentions in obscure tracts dating from 1754, produced by one of the many secret societies they control (the Elect Cohens), The Wheel has managed to remain almost invisible. This feat alone is surely testament to the legendary power its members wield over all aspects of our world.

House of Windsor The British royal family is believed by many – especially in those countries that have felt the extensive reach of the former British Empire – to be the prime force behind a myriad of conspiracies. In Iran, conspiracy buffs believe that the House of Windsor still not only has the United Kingdom firmly within its grip, but, by using various secret organizations, also controls the United States of America and Germany. The current lack of anything resembling an Empire and the inability of the house of Windsor to even prevent press intrusion into their personal lives is dismissed as merely an effective cover-story. Given the Windsors' massive demonstrable wealth and well-established links to Freemasonry, it can be harder to argue against the evidence of an Iranian conspiracy theorist than you might expect.

IBM Big corporations have become natural targets for paranoid believers in some of the more extreme conspiracies of our time. Corporations do not come much bigger than the Big Blue itself: IBM. Rumoured to have had a hand in reverse-engineering modern computing technology from crashed alien spacecraft, IBM has also been dragged into the wild schemes of those who believe silicon chips are the work of the Devil. More plausible conspiracies concerning the computer industry seem set to continue to be overlooked in favour of spectacular tales of computer chips able to control people's thoughts.

Jesuits Any religious organization whose founder uttered the line: "Give me the child and I will give you the man," are bound to find itself slap bang in the middle of a whole host of conspiracy theories. Accusations ranging from practicing mind control, organizing child pornography rings, being the shock troops in Papal plans for world domination to being the suppressers of the truth about Christ have been laid at the hands of the Jesuits. Whether these conspiracies involving the original men in black are based on hard evidence or on religious prejudice is open to argument.

Kremlin Once the first place to be blamed if there was even a slight hint of conspiracy in the air, current public perception has it that those now in the Kremlin couldn't even organize a bout of drunkenness at Vodka Factory Number 12. Don't be fooled. Some seasoned conspiracy and Kremlin watchers believe that the break-up of the former Soviet Empire is a ploy designed to decoy the West into a false sense of security. Now no longer considered a serious threat, the way is left open for the Kremlin to get on with the serious business of running the world away from the glare of publicity.

Leary, Timothy Given the outrageous nature of his life (he helped start the drug revolution in America and escaped from prison in the US to live in exile with the Black Panthers in Algeria) it is not surprising that Timothy Leary heads the lists of suspected conspirators. Opinion is divided whether he was working on the side of the angels or as a member of the team led by the Devil, but there are good reasons for believing that his championship of LSD may have resulted from links with the CIA. It may well have been Leary who gave the American military the idea of the Internet.

Meonia Meonia is a secret mystical order charged with protecting the fate of the British Isles, with creating the British Empire and with trying to herald the dawning of a new golden age. Past members may have included Mary Queen of Scots, Sir Isaac Newton and the poet W B Yeats – a noted occultist. It is open to conjecture if the organization retains any power in the wake of its wartime confrontations with *Thule Society*, but some researchers feel Princess Diana's ancestral links to Meonia may have played a part in her untimely death.

New Agers New Agers are a favourite target of Christian fundamentalist conspiracy theorists. These theorists give credence to the idea that New Age beliefs and practices are part of a concerted plot to undermine the Christian faith and promote the worship of Satan. Tarot cards, crystals and attempting to commune with dolphins, are all seen as part of an insidious scheme to lead people into contact with dangerous supernatural forces. The mass suicides by such groups as the Heaven's Gate cult are seen as carefully constructed ritual sacrifices to Old Nick himself, as part of a grand, audacious conspiracy to bring about the apocalypse rather than as tragic isolated incidents.

Office of Naval Research Yet another branch of the US military that has been implicated in many of the conspiracies surrounding the UFO phenomena, the Office of Naval Research is also at the centre of two intriguing wartime tales. Researchers into the Philadelphia experiment (which may, or may not, have succeeded in breaking the known laws of physics and, in 1943, making a ship become invisible) cite ONR as the agency behind its cover-up. ONR is also alleged to have hushed up the accidental explosion of an experimental nuclear device in 1944, responsible for the Port Chicago disaster in which over 300 US sailors were killed.

Project Phoenix No one knows exactly what Project Phoenix is or even if it definitely exists – two probable reasons why it has attracted so much attention in conspiracy circles. The name may suggest that the project is designed to exploit alien technology or technology recovered from the remains of a civilization populated by the *Elder Race*. The US Congress cancelled it in 1958, but it seems to have continued right through to the present, thanks to generous funding from the US military's infamous black budget. The people behind Project Phoenix could be among the globe's key conspirators as Phoenix is said to have plotted the UFO cover-up, the assassination of JFK and the rise of the US military-industrial complex.

Queen Elizabeth I Leaving aside the rumours circulating over the true identity and even sex of Britain's 'Virgin Queen', Elizabeth 1 appears to have been at the centre of a web of intrigue and machination that set a pattern for British monarchs throughout the following centuries. Doctor John Dee, possibly the most important occultist in British history, is recorded as acting as her personal physician, foreign agent and mystical advisor. Many conspiracy theories cite this powerful partnership as the origin of the numerous secret societies and magical orders dedicated to expanding the British Empire and defending the monarchy.

Roosevelt, Franklin D US President Franklin D Roosevelt features in many conspiracies, but one of the most diabolic has to be the creation of the trailer park. The trailer park conspiracy currently doing the rounds is that FDR did not instruct his advisors to come up with the idea of trailer homes as a response to the Depression's housing crisis, but to locate people in flimsy dwellings in areas prone to hurricanes. The reasoning behind this was that it was an effective way of ridding the county of its poorest people. Little did FDR know that by creating trailer parks, he was setting up the perfect breeding ground for generations of conspiracy believers.

Sufis An Islamic mystical sect, the Sufis are said to be connected to such conspiracy notables as the Knights Templar, Whirling Dervishes, Chinese Tongs, the Cult of the Assassins, Masons, pirates and a host of black power groups with a belief in some non-traditional aspects of Islam. Added to this is their belief in the concept of "rendi" – adopting the appearance of something else, so you may carry out your desire in secret. Consequently, the sect have the perfect credentials to be suspected of conducting high-level conspiracies. Almost absolute secrecy and general inscrutability has ensured that the aim of Sufi-inspired conspiracies tends to remain unknown, but they must have a sense of humour – the supposedly English tradition of Morris dancing is said to be their invention.

Thule Gesellschaft The *Thule Gesellschaft* is known to have played a significant role in the early formation of the Nazi party and its spurious Ayran ideology and the power wielded by its occultist members may have grown even further when the Nazis came to power. Whether or not they were the power behind Hitler's abominable throne, the Thulists certainly had an influence on certain sections of the fearsome SS. Many people believe that the defeat of Germany in Word War II did not put an end to the TG's conspiracies to seize global power. Working from hidden underground headquarters located in Antarctica, the reach of the *Thule Gesellschaft* is said to extend to controlling NASA, which they infiltrated via Nazi rocket scientists recruited by the US at the end of the war. A variety of secret neo-Nazi and occult organizations are also controlled by the Thules . . .

United Nations Given that it already functions in many ways as a form of world government – albeit with very limited power – we cannot be too surprised that the United Nations is at the heart of many conspiracy theorists' accusations of dark machinations, schemes and secret projects. While some see the blue helmets of UN peace-keeping troops as a boon to the world's war-torn states, many researchers in the conspiracy field see them as an embryonic global army designed to bring about One World government by force. Some theorists point to the fact that the United

Nations was set up in 1947 – the same year as a UFO is reported to have crashed at Roswell, New Mexico – and suggest that the UN may be conspiring to bring about One World government on behalf of an alien power. Of course, those involved with the UN may just be dupes of a cabal of high-degree Masons.

Vril Society Yet another mystical order, the Vril Society can be proved to have had an influence on the formation of the ideology of many important members of the Nazi Party. It is mentioned heavily in connection with secret Nazi flying-saucer technology. While members of the *Thule Society* are rumoured to have escaped at the end of the war by literally going underground, members of the Vril Society are said to have flown the coop in the experimental Nazi spacecraft that today we know as UFOs. Of course, this knowledge is kept secret from the public to disguise the fact that World War II is not finished yet.

Westphalian Brotherhood Often cited as the ultimate bosses of everyone including the top-degree Masons, the Mafia, the Knights Templar and many modern occult orders, the Westphalian Brotherhood is an umbrella name given to a multi-tentacled Illuminati group that has been in existence since at least the early 1600s. Its *modus operandi* is to infiltrate an existing secret society and take it over. Given the ultra-secret nature of the organization, it is not surprising that little is known of its aims other than that conspiracy buff favourite: world domination. The Brotherhood seems to have a special fondness for the region of Germany from which it derive its name and was closely linked to Heinrich Himmler, who chose Westphalia to build his mock-medieval fortress. The Westphalians can be added to the long list of those who may have been responsible for creating the Nazi menace.

Xists According to the conspiracy-fuelled cult The Church of SubGenius, Xists are aliens on the side of humanity who will eventually save the Earth from The Con – a massive, age-old intrigue designed to rob humanity of all freedom and fun. The more fanatical followers of the Church's mysterious founder and icon, the pipe-smoking Bob Dobbs, claim the Xists have been behind many secret societies and counter-conspiracies designed to tackle the machinations of the bad aliens who are the real power behind the all-encompassing The Con. To a believer of the

Church, everything from the hollow Earth to the practice of having to wear ties to work is explainable in terms of the on-going war between the Xists and their intergalactic foes.

Yellow Hats A mysterious order of Tibetan mystics, the Yellow Hats, or "Dugphas" in their own tongue, may be the true controllers of the fate of the world. Many conspiracy theorists have spotted their hand on the tiller throughout the course of history. The Yellow Hats are followers of the Bon religion that was introduced to Tibet in the Fifth Century and they believe in the mysterious underworld realm of Shambhala, where their orders originate. In the Twentieth Century the Yellow Hats are known to have been involved with many mystical factions of the Nazi party and with the time-travel experiments that allegedly took place at Camp Hero, the US air force base at the centre of the infamous Montauk Project. Hard to spot directly, despite the attention-attracting headgear that has given them their nickname, the Yellow Hats seem to be a conspiracy force to be reckoned with.

Zionist Occupational Government Conspiracy theorists in the US militia movement, the Klu Klux Klan and in other anti-Semitic organizations, are keen to point to the Zionist Occupational Government as the true controller of the American government – hence the organization's name. The ZOG is perceived as being the force behind a host of diabolical schemes. Armed with racist propaganda, as much as anything resembling evidence, believers in ZOG hold that the world is under threat by a global Jewish cabal and that the United States has already fallen to their machinations. The banking system, black helicopters and the use of fluoride in water are all cited as conspiracies originating from ZOG.

GLOSSARY

Black Budget Money is power, and every conspiracy needs substantial finances if it is to stand a chance of being successful in today's world. Allegedly, a favourite source of funding for many conspiratorial groups and projects is a black budget – into which government-approved money is channelled by creative accounting and outright fraud so that it can be used to fund secret projects and operations. Black budgets are often boosted by illegal involvement in areas such as drug-running, money-laundering and arms-dealing. The famous Iran-Contra scandal is one instance of an American black budget deal that became public knowledge.

Black Ops Covert action undertaken by an intelligence agency that is not known or authorized by its government can be referred to as a Black Operation or Black Op for short. As such activities are not officially known about – let alone approved or run by – the appointed authorities, Black Ops are the favourite tools of conspiracy organizations that have infiltrated or control such agencies as MI6, the CIA, and the KGB.

Cabal The word means "an intrigue or secret power elite", and some conspiracy theorists argue that the english word is derived from "cabbala" – the name of an ancient Jewish mystical system. However, it is more commonly believed that "cabal" originates from a secret group of policy-makers to Charles II whose names were Clifford, Arlington, Buckingham, Ashley and Lauderdale. Those who believe that this book is itself part of a conspiracy should note that the secretary to the original cabal was one Robert Southwell.

The Con A term first used by the most conspiracy-astute cult of the late Twentieth Century, The Church of SubGenius, it has been widely taken up and misinterpreted by many conspiracy theorists. The Con is short for The Conspiracy, and refers to the group that controls every other conspiracy you have heard of, and all of those so successful that you never even imagined they existed. It is a Unified Conspiracy Theory that includes everybody but does not blame any known group.

Conspiriologists The term many conspiracy theorists like to use to describe themselves or anyone else who has taken an interest in researching the truth behind various dark plots. It is used in preference to phrases such as conspiracy buff or the one often quoted by sceptics – delusional, paranoid fantasist.

Counter-Conspiracy Many conspiracies seem to evolve as an attempt to counter the actions of another conspiracy. This type of counter-conspiracy is best illustrated by rumours that the Royal Family created a vast organization of inter-connected secret societies in order to mount an attack on a conspiracy by the Roman Catholic Church which was, in turn, conspiring to achieve world domination. Without a conspiracy to attack, the counter-conspiracy would never have existed. This kind of logic is sometimes used by people who want to prove that the original conspiracy must exist.

Cover-up A large amount of conspiracies revolve around attempts to cover up the truth about events such as assassinations, UFO landings, murders, the origin of religion, business cartels and why it is so hard to buy a cheeseburger for breakfast from the major fast-food chains. Essential elements for a successful cover-up include bare-faced lying, discrediting witnesses, destroying evidence, dreaming up a good cover-story and an ability to control the media.

Cover-story A plausible cover-story is an essential part of any plot to successfully cover up a conspiracy. The cover story needs to be good enough to persuade most people that the official version of events is the only one you can believe without being accused of being a paranoid nut. Conspiracy researchers spend most of their time proving you have to be a paranoid nut in order to ignore the facts and believe cover stories.

Doing An Elvis Many conspiracy buffs believe that Elvis is not dead – he has merely successfully faked his own death. As a result, the phrase "Doing An Elvis" is applied to simulating your own demise in order to escape a life of fame, the taxman or Mafia plots to have you wiped out.

Dupes In conspiracy circles, the vast majority of people are regarded as dupes. Dupes believe what they are told by the authorities and by the media and never question that things might not be as they seem – in short, they are the people who never believe in conspiracy theories. It's not exactly a term of abuse, but there is an implication that the most heinous plots of our time are only able to exist because dupes are too trusting, are not paranoid enough and never question the way the world works.

Greys Apparently the most common variety of all the extra-terrestrials visiting Earth, the Greys – small creatures with off-white skin and big, dark insect-like eyes – are also the most commonly mentioned in conspiracy theories. Accused of being involved in everything from Roswell to cattle mutilations and the attempted assassination of Ronald Reagan, the Greys seem to specialize in dark doings, often entering into secret government treaties and hatching plots designed to cause harm to the human race.

HIGS Acronym standing for Hoodlums In Governments, HIGS was coined by the conspiracy world's favourite unorthodox scientist, Dr Wilhelm Reich when he was being harassed by the US Food and Drug Administration and the FBI. He used HIGS to describe those who use extreme bully-boy tactics. HIGS has since been widely used by conspiracy buffs as a term for government agents involved in any form of intimidation or persecution undertaken in an attempt to suppress the truth.

Illuminati Strictly speaking, "Illuminati" should only refer to the organization founded in Bavaria in 1776, but the Illuminati's reputation is so strong that you can find the name used in many dictionaries to describe any "underground intellectual movement or secret society" or anyone claiming to possess special enlightenment. The original Bavarian Illuminati are strong contenders for the title "father of all conspiracy groups" and the title is often used by conspiriologists to describe any hidden elite aiming for world domination and possessing enlightenment.

Mystical Order Distinguished by a belief that all of their members' plotting and machinations serves some form of higher spiritual purpose, Mystical Orders are alleged to be behind many major conspiracies. While they may not claim paranormal powers like the members of some Occult Orders, conspirators of a mystical bent are often notable for their interest in dressing up in robes, performing weird initiation rites and pledging their lives to an assortment of ancient deities.

Media Control For any plot to be effective or for any cabal to achieve real power, it needs to remain secret and have the ability to prevent any negative information about it surfacing in the public domain. Given the widespread reach and influence of the media today, this means that the ability to censor and control the media is an essential pre-requisite for successful conspiracy. Probably the favourite way of ensuring such control is ownership – which, in the eyes of some conspiriologists, immediately puts Rupert Murdoch and Ted Turner under some suspicion.

Military Industrial Complex In an odd speech at the end of his term of office, President Eisenhower warned of the growing power of the Military Industrial Complex which, he implied, threatened America's political institutions and the personal liberty of its citizens. Quite what inspired the former General to speak out about this cabal is unknown, but his fears seem to have been realized within a few years when the Military Industrial Complex railroaded the US into the costly Vietnam War, which led to a period of very healthy profits for the major arms manufacturers.

Mind Control Among conspiracy groups, exercizing control over the minds of the population of a country or the world is second only in popularity to achieving world domination. Mind control is a favourite tool for enforcing power – often involving the creation of assassins whose minds are controlled. Routes to successful mind control are as diverse as subliminal audio messages in records and fluoridation of drinking water.

Misinformation As much as it is the job of intelligence agencies to gather information, it is also their role to provide a constant stream of misinformation to confuse the public and divert attention away from anything they feel needs to be covered up. Planted misinformation may be behind a multitude of conspiracy theories. For instance, if you want to test fly experimental aircraft without revealing what you are up to, it can be useful to have rumours in circulation concerning alien spacecraft. It is well known that conspirators will create misinformation about totally bizarre schemes to deflect the focus away from themselves. what better way to do this than through a book packed to the gills with conspiracies?

NINP Acronym standing for Not Impossible, Not Provable. In conspiracy circles, the NINP tag is applied to a theory that sounds eminently believable, but for which it is impossible to provide hard evidence. Fortunately for most conspirators, NINP is a tag that can be applied to nearly all conspiracies apart from those which are TBTB.

Occult Order Similar in nature to "Mystical Order". People who conspire through the machinations of an Occult Order are often attributed with using the supernatural powers they hold, to aid them in achieving their aims. Prone to conducting arcane rituals and doing battle with other Occult Orders that have opposing aims, Occult Orders – despite their supernatural powers – seem unlikely to end up controlling the word in the near future.

One World Government The establishment of One World Government is seen in the conspiracy genre as the imposition of world-wide rule by some form of international organization, broadly similar to the United Nations. While not everyone views the death of the nation state and the birth of global peace as a particularly bad thing, no one is keen to be controlled by an un-elected elite. As a result, people with One World Government plans usually have to resort to using diabolic conspiracies to achieve their objective.

Patsy Someone set up by conspirators to take the blame for their misdeeds. The most well-known example of a patsy set up for a major conspiracy is Lee Harvey Oswald – the man chosen by whoever assassinated JFK to take the rap and persuade the public that the killing was just the work of a lone gunmen. No surprises, then, that when Oswald decided he did not like this role and muttered the immortal words "I'm just a patsy" to the press, a bullet with his name on it was only minutes away.

Paranoia The state of mind that many conspiracy buffs find themselves experiencing when they begin to delve into the dark machinations of the cabals behind the surface of apparent, commonly-accepted realities. Given that many conspiracies may have been designed to make anyone who stumbles upon them appear as if they are completely paranoid, this mental condition can be seen as an occupational hazard for conspiracy investigators. Remember: just because you are paranoid, it does not mean that they are not plotting against you.

Sceptic To conspiriologists, a sceptic is someone who has yet to acknowledge the truth about a conspiracy and spends unnecessary time trying to poke holes in their most cherished theories. Some sceptics, who invest a great deal of energy trying to make those who believe in conspiracies acknowledge common-sense explanations, are labelled "professional sceptics" and accused of being in the pay of those running the conspiracies. All part of the cover-up, you see.

Secret Society Whether people suspect the Masons, The Shriners or the Grand Order of the Fiery Wheel, behind most conspiracies there is often said to be some form of secret society. What is a secret society – an organization that keeps its membership, aims and influence cloaked from outsiders; desire to take over the world as a basic aim is merely an optional extra.

TBTB Acronym specific to the conspiracy genre, standing for Too Bizarre To Believe. TBTB conspiracies are those that succeed by being so implausible that no one will take them seriously enough to invest any time investigating them. Another advantage of TBTB conspiracies for those behind them, is that evidence can be left in full view, safe in the knowledge that it will be overlooked because of the extreme nature of the conspiracy. It has been argued that the abduction of Elvis by Rock-'n'-Roll-loving aliens is the perfect TBTB conspiracy.

Unified Conspiracy Theories Also known as Jumbo Conspiracy Theories. A Unified Conspiracy Theory is any hypothesis that ties up absolutely everything into one big plot whereby everything is interconnected and explained by a single Unified Conspiracy Theory. It is not uncommon to find a Unified Conspiracy Theory that manages to link the pyramids, Jesus, George Washington, the Bank of England, Roswell, JFK's assassination and the films of George Lucas into one seamless machination created by a joint Freemason/Zeta Reticulan alien organization.